A TREASURY OF
XXth CENTURY MURDER
COMPENDIUM I

Rick Geary was born in 1946 in Kansas City, Missouri and grew up in Wichita, Kansas. He graduated from the University of Kansas in Lawrence, where his first cartoons were published in the University Daily Kansan.

He worked as staff artist for two weekly papers in Wichita before moving to San Diego in 1975.

He began work in comics in 1977 and was for thirteen years a contributor to the Funny Pages of National Lampoon. His comic stories have also been published in Heavy Metal, Dark Horse Comics and the DC Comics/Paradox Press Big Books.

During a four-year stay in New York, his illustrations appeared regularly in The New York Times Book Review. His illustration work has also been seen in MAD, Spy, Rolling Stone, The Los Angeles Times, and American Libraries.

He has written and illustrated three children's books based on The Mask for Dark Horse and two Spider-Man children's books for Marvel and 2 Gumby collections. His children's comic Society of Horrors ran in Disney Adventures magazine from 1999 to 2006.

In 2007, after more than thirty years in San Diego, he and his wife Deborah moved to the town of Carrizozo, New Mexico.

A TREASURY OF XXth CENTURY MURDER
COMPENDIUM I

Including:
The Lindbergh Child
The Terrible Axe-Man of New Orleans
Madison Square Tragedy

Compiled and Illustrated by
RICK GEARY

nbm GRAPHIC NOVELS
Nantier • Beall • Minoustchine
NEW YORK

Also available by Geary:

A Treasury of Victorian Murder:

Vol. I, pb.: $9.95, e-book: $6.99

Jack The Ripper pb.: $9.95, e-book: $6.99

The Borden Tragedy, pb.: $9.99, e-book: $6.99

The Fatal Bullet, pb.: $9.95, e-book: $6.99

The Mystery of Mary Rogers, pb.: $9.99

The Beast of Chicago, pb.: $9.95, e-book: $6.99

The Murder of Abraham Lincoln
pb.: $9.95, hc.: $15.95

The Bloody Benders, hc.: $15.95, pb.: $9.95

The Case of Madeleine Smith
pb.: $8.95, hc.: $15.95

A Treasury of Victorian Murder Compendium II
hc.: $29.99

A Treasury of XXth Century Murder:

The Lindbergh Child
pb.: $9.95, e-book: $6.99

Famous Players
hc.: $15.95, pb.: $9.95

The Axe-Man of New Orleans
hc.: $15.99, e-book: $6.99

The Lives of Sacco & Vanzetti
pb.: $9.99, e-book: $6.99

Lovers Lane
hc.: $15.99, e-book: $6.99

Madison Square Tragedy
hc.: $15.99, e-book: $6.99

Black Dahlia
hc.: $15.99, e-book: $6.99

Fiction:

Louise Brooks, Detective
hc.:$15.99, e-book: $6.99

**see more on these and order at our website:
nbmpub.com**

We have over 200 titles
Catalog available upon request
NBM
160 Broadway, Suite 700, East Wing,
New York, NY 10038

(To order by mail add
P&H: $4 1st item, $1 each addt'l.)

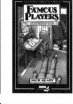

Table of Contents

ISBN 978-1-68112-063-8
© Rick Geary 2008-2013
Library of Congress Control Number 2016961507
1st printing March 2017
Printed in China

Also available wherever ebooks are sold.

nbm GRAPHIC
NOVELS
Nantier • Beall • Minoustchine
N E W   Y O R K

THE LINDBERGH CHILD

THE SENSATIONAL CASE THAT TRANSFIXED THE NATION.

THE QUESTIONS THAT REMAIN TO THIS DAY.

THE ATROCIOUS KIDNAPPING AND MURDER OF THE INFANT SON OF AMERICA'S HERO Col. CHARLES A. LINDBERGH

THE HOUSE AT HOPEWELL, NEW JERSEY

WRITTEN AND ILLUSTRATED by RICK GEARY

THE LINDBERGH CHILD

BIBLIOGRAPHY

Behn, Noel, *Lindbergh: The Crime*. (New York, Atlantic Monthly Press, 1994)

Douglas, John and Mark Olshaker, *The Cases That Haunt Us*. (New York, Scribner, 2000)

Fisher, Jim, *The Ghosts of Hopewell, Setting the Record Straight in the Lindbergh Case*. (Carbondale IL, Southern Illinois University Press, 1999)

Linbergh, Anne Morrow, *Hour of Gold, Hour of Lead*. (New York, Signet Books, 1974)

Mappen, Marc, *Murder and Spies, Lovers and Lies: Settling the Great Controversies of American History*. (New York, Avon Books, 1996)

Waller, George, *Kidnap: The Story of the Linbergh Case*. (New York, The Dial Press, 1961)

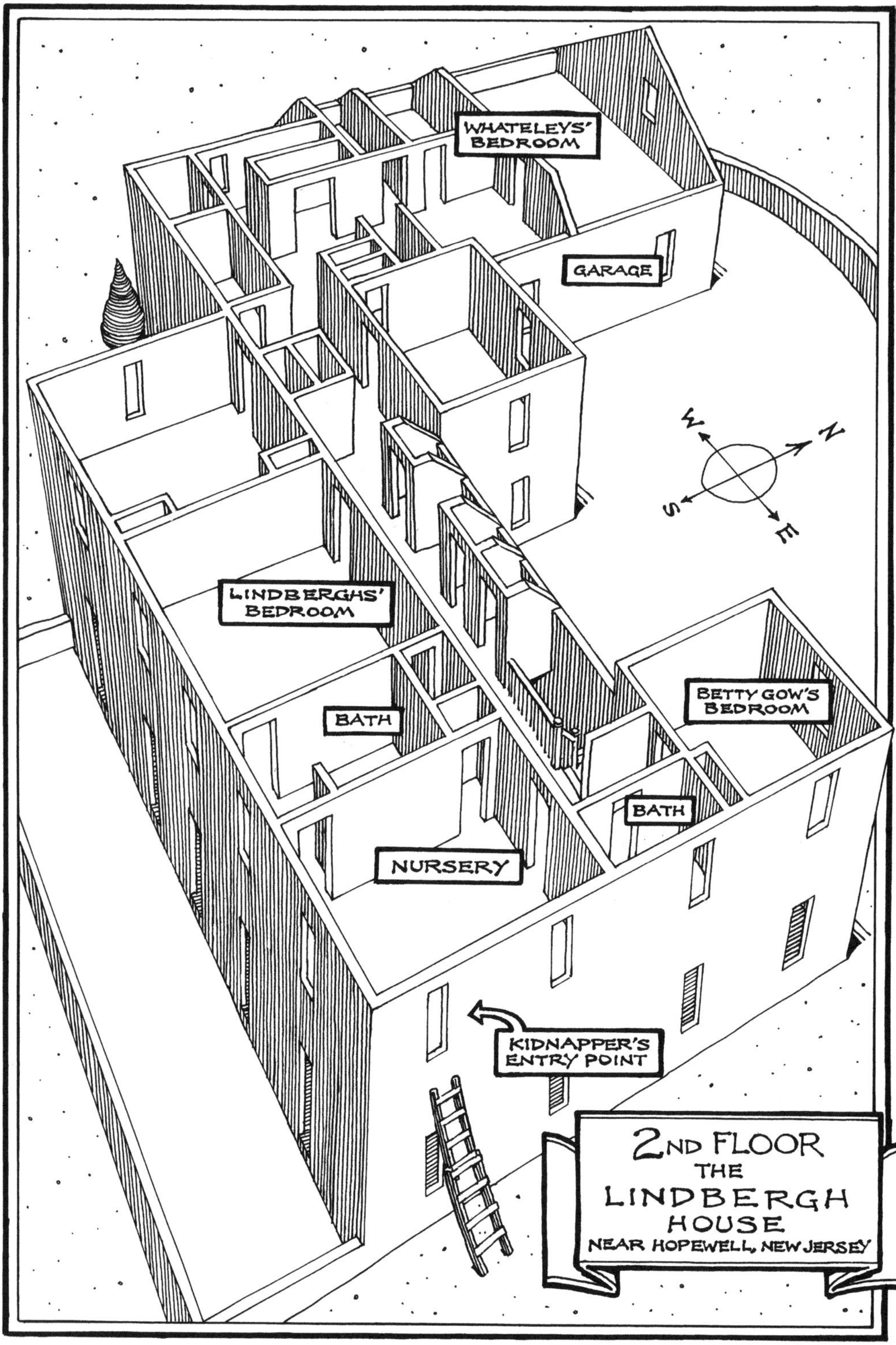
WHATELEYS' BEDROOM
GARAGE
W
N
S
E
LINDBERGHS' BEDROOM
BATH
BETTY GOW'S BEDROOM
BATH
NURSERY
KIDNAPPER'S ENTRY POINT
2ND FLOOR
THE
LINDBERGH
HOUSE
NEAR HOPEWELL, NEW JERSEY

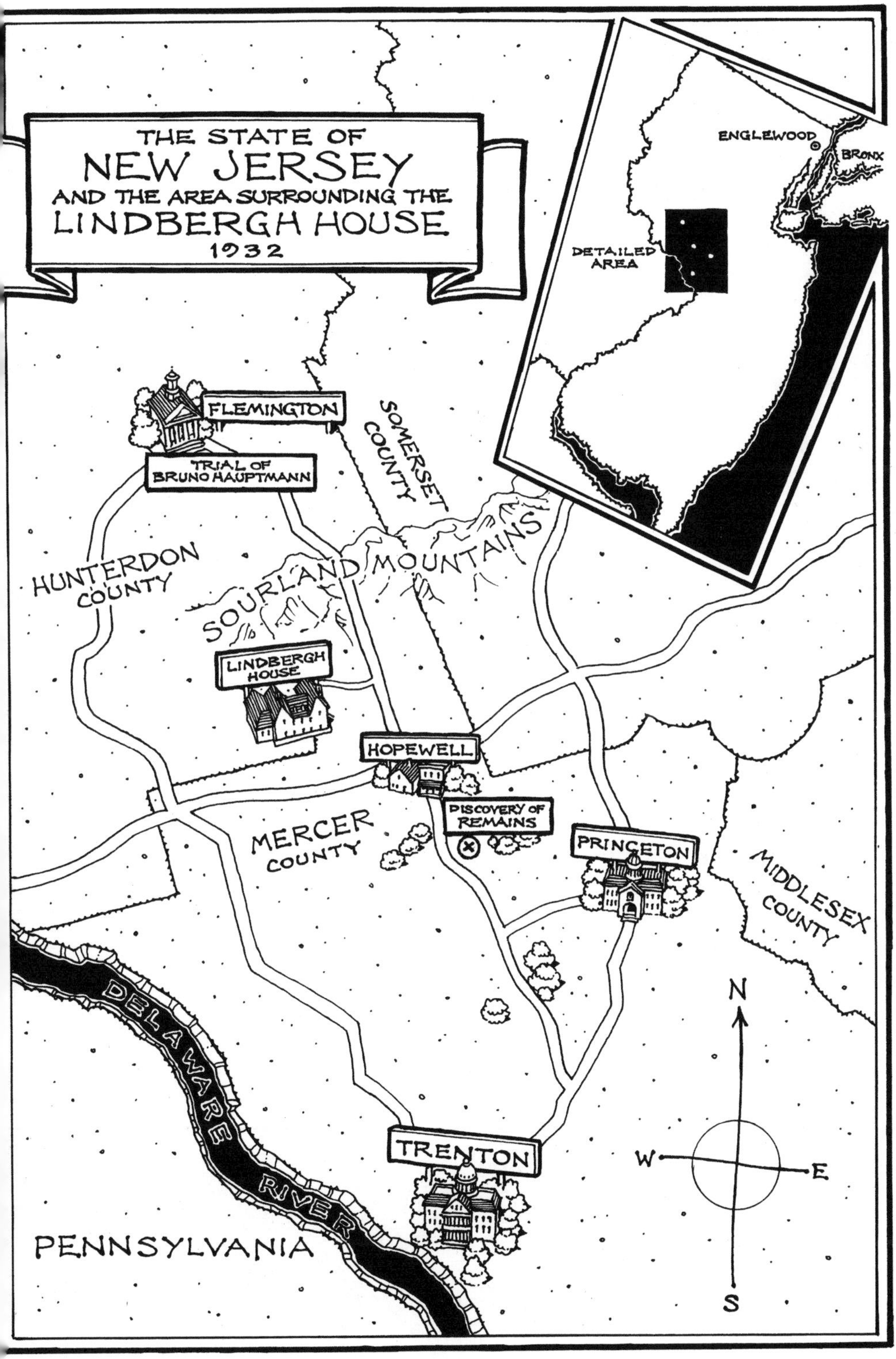

THE STATE OF
NEW JERSEY
AND THE AREA SURROUNDING THE
LINDBERGH HOUSE
1932
ENGLEWOOD
BRONX
DETAILED AREA
FLEMINGTON
TRIAL OF BRUNO HAUPTMANN
SOMERSET COUNTY
HUNTERDON COUNTY
SOURLAND MOUNTAINS
LINDBERGH HOUSE
HOPEWELL
DISCOVERY OF REMAINS
MERCER COUNTY
PRINCETON
MIDDLESEX COUNTY
DELAWARE RIVER
TRENTON
PENNSYLVANIA
N
W
E
S

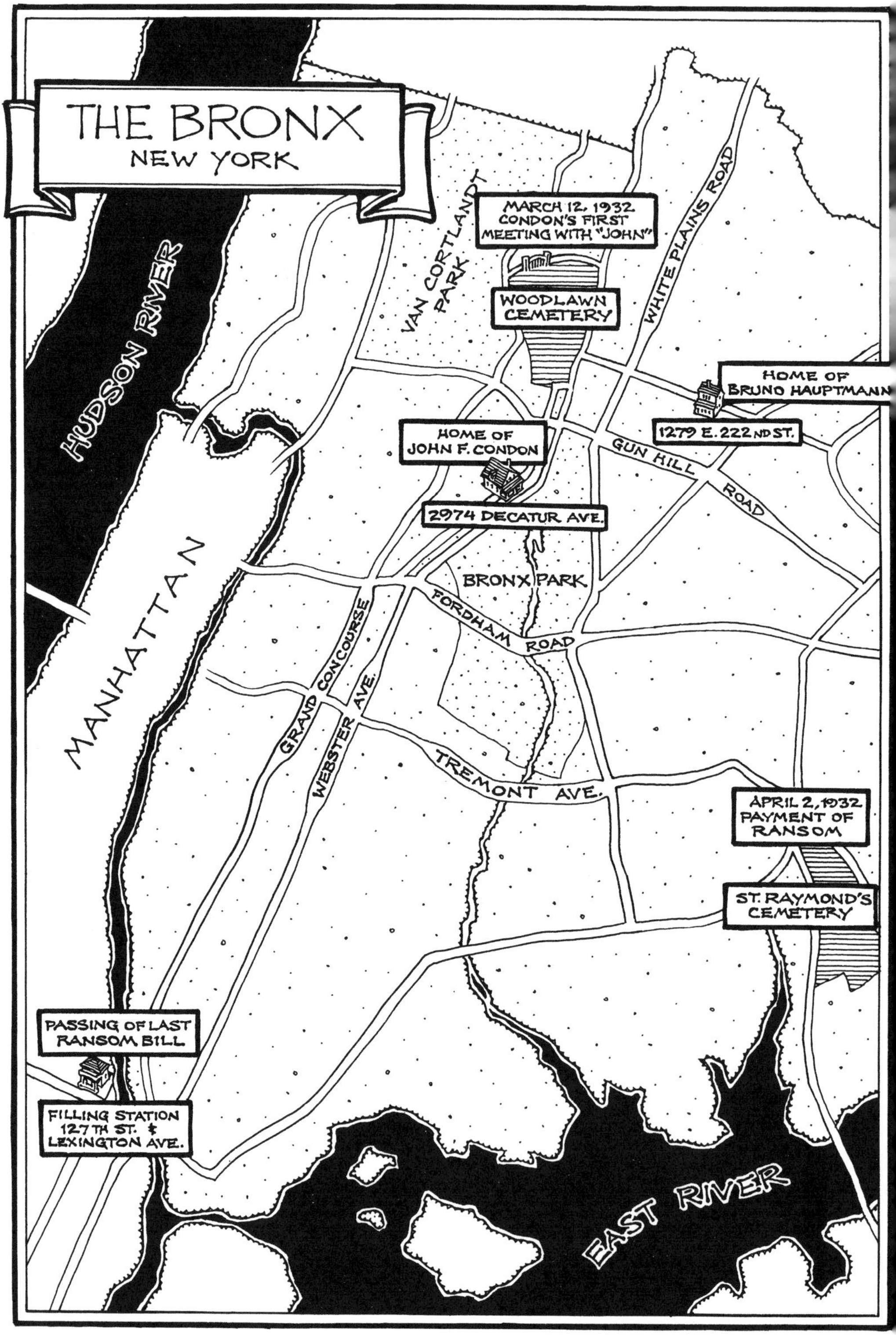
THE BRONX
NEW YORK
HUDSON RIVER
VAN CORTLANDT PARK
MARCH 12, 1932
CONDON'S FIRST
MEETING WITH "JOHN"
WOODLAWN CEMETERY
WHITE PLAINS ROAD
HOME OF
BRUNO HAUPTMANN
1279 E. 222ND ST.
HOME OF
JOHN F. CONDON
2974 DECATUR AVE.
GUN HILL ROAD
BRONX PARK
FORDHAM ROAD
MANHATTAN
GRAND CONCOURSE
WEBSTER AVE.
TREMONT AVE.
APRIL 2, 1932
PAYMENT OF
RANSOM
ST. RAYMOND'S
CEMETERY
PASSING OF LAST
RANSOM BILL
FILLING STATION
127TH ST. &
LEXINGTON AVE.
EAST RIVER

PART ONE
THE LONE EAGLE

SATURDAY, MAY 21, 1927
CHARLES A. LINDBERGH BECOMES THE HERO
OF THE AGE WITH HIS COURAGEOUS SOLO FLIGHT
ACROSS THE ATLANTIC.

AFTER 33½ HOURS IN THE AIR, HE LANDS HIS TINY PLANE AT LE BOURGET FIELD IN PARIS.

Spirit of St. Louis

TUMULT! ECSTASY! INTERNATIONAL ADULATION!

FOUR MILLION PACK THE STREETS OF NEW YORK CITY JUST TO CATCH A GLIMPSE OF HIM.

THE SHY, HANDSOME 25-YEAR-OLD WEARS HIS FAME WITH GRACE AND MODESTY. INCIDENTALLY, HE IS A BACHELOR.

BUT NOT FOR LONG! WHILE ON A GOOD-WILL MISSION TO MEXICO CITY IN DECEMBER OF 1927, HE STAYS AT THE HOME OF DWIGHT MORROW, THE AMERICAN AMBASSADOR.

HERE HE MEETS AND FALLS IN LOVE WITH ANNE, AGE 21, SECOND-OLDEST OF THE MORROWS' FOUR OFFSPRING.

ELISABETH

ANNE

DWIGHT, JR.

CONSTANCE

14

ON MAY 27, 1929, THEY MARRY.

THE NEW MRS. LINDBERGH PROVES AS INTREPID AS HER HUSBAND, AS SHE ACCOMPANIES HIM ON HIS AVIATION EXPLOITS.

TOGETHER, THEY SET A TRANSCONTINENTAL SPEED RECORD AND MAP AIR ROUTES TO THE FAR EAST.

ALL THE WHILE, THEY MUST ENDURE THE SCRUTINY OF THE CURIOUS PUBLIC AND THE EVER-INTRUSIVE PRESS.

THE AVIATOR'S CELEBRITY, HOWEVER, IS CRUCIAL TO THE FLEDGELING AIRLINE INDUSTRY, IN WHOSE FUTURE HE BELIEVES FERVENTLY.

THE COUPLE'S DESIRE FOR SECLUSION ONLY INTENSIFIES WHEN, ON JUNE 22, 1930, ANNE GIVES BIRTH TO A SON — CHARLES AUGUSTUS LINDBERGH, JR.

THE PUBLIC HUNGERS FOR THE SMALLEST TIDBIT OF NEWS CONCERNING THE INFANT.

LATER IN THE YEAR, THE LINDBERGHS PURCHASE A TRACT OF 360 ACRES NEAR THE VILLAGE OF HOPEWELL, NEW JERSEY — BELOW THE SOURLAND MOUNTAINS, ABOUT 15 MILES FROM PRINCETON.

HERE, THEY BEGIN CONSTRUCTION ON A LARGE HOUSE — THEIR SANCTUARY.

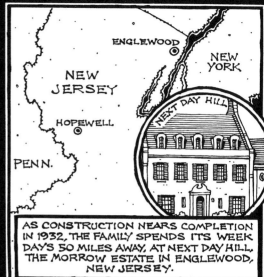

AS CONSTRUCTION NEARS COMPLETION IN 1932, THE FAMILY SPENDS ITS WEEK DAY'S 50 MILES AWAY, AT NEXT DAY HILL, THE MORROW ESTATE IN ENGLEWOOD, NEW JERSEY.

ANNE IS AT WORK ON A BOOK OF HER ASIAN TRAVELS, WHILE CHARLES TRAVELS DAILY TO HIS OFFICE IN NEW YORK CITY.

WEEKENDS FIND THEM IN RESIDENCE AT THEIR NEW HOME, THOUGH MUCH OF THE INTERIOR REMAINS UNFINISHED.

THE SOLITUDE OF THEIR LOCATION, THE BLEAK BEAUTY OF THE COUNTRYSIDE, PROVIDE THE PEACE AND RESPITE THEY LONG FOR.

THEIR PERSONAL STAFF CONSISTS OF THREE INDIVIDUALS.

THE ENGLISH BUTLER, ALOYSIUS "OLLY" WHATELEY AND HIS WIFE, ELSIE, WHO SERVES AS COOK AND HOUSEKEEPER.

AND THE BABY'S NURSEMAID, BETTY GOW, AGE 25, A RECENT IMMIGRANT FROM SCOTLAND.

PART TWO
THE CRIME

THE WEEKEND OF FEBRUARY 27-28, 1932,
FINDS THE LINDBERGHS, ACCORDING TO RECENT
CUSTOM, AT THEIR NEW HOME.

DURING THIS TIME, CHARLES, JR. DEVELOPS A
SERIOUS COLD, AND ON MONDAY, FEBRUARY 29,
MRS. LINDBERGH DECIDES NOT TO RETURN TO
ENGLEWOOD.

17

TUESDAY, MARCH 1, 1932
THE EVENTS OF THIS DAY ARE ATTESTED TO BY COLONEL AND MRS. LINDBERGH AND THEIR SERVANTS.

IN THE MORNING, THE BABY'S COLD NOT HAVING ABATED, ANNE LINDBERGH SUMMONS BETTY GOW, WHO HAS BEEN WAITING AT NEXT DAY HILL.

THE NURSEMAID ARRIVES AT ABOUT 2:00 PM.

BY AFTERNOON, THE CHILD SEEMS SOMEWHAT IMPROVED...

AND AT 6:15 PM, THE TWO WOMEN BEGIN TO PREPARE HIM FOR BED.

THEY DRESS HIM IN HIS WOOLEN DR. DENTON SLEEPING SUIT,...

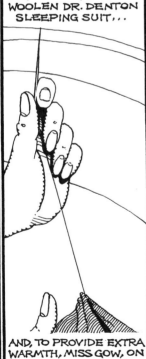

AND, TO PROVIDE EXTRA WARMTH, MISS GOW, ON THE SPOT, SEWS A FLANNEL NIGHT-SHIRT FOR HIM.

TWO WIRE THUMB-GUARDS ARE SECURED TO THE INFANT'S HANDS.

(AT COL. LINDBERGH'S INSISTANCE, AS PREVENTATIVE OF THUMB-SUCKING.)

MRS. LINDBERGH CLOSES THE SHUTTERS OF TWO OF THE ROOM'S THREE WINDOWS.

SHE HAS TROUBLE WITH THE PAIR IN THE SOUTHEAST CORNER. THEY ARE WARPED AND WILL NOT QUITE COME TOGETHER.

SHE LEAVES THE ROOM AT 7:30, AS MISS GOW SECURES THE BABY IN HIS CRIB BY MEANS OF TWO LARGE SAFETY PINS.

THE NURSEMAID REMAINS IN THE ROOM UNTIL SHE IS CERTAIN HER CHARGE IS ASLEEP...

LEAVING AT ABOUT 8:00 PM TO JOIN ELSIE WHATELEY IN THE SERVANT'S SITTING ROOM.

THE EVENING HAS TURNED COLD AND BLUSTERY AS COL. LINDBERGH ARRIVES HOME AT ABOUT 8:30 PM.

AFTER A FULL DAY OF APPOINTMENTS, HE HAS FORGOTTEN AN IMPORTANT ENGAGEMENT THIS EVENING. HE WAS TO BE GUEST OF HONOR AT NEW YORK UNIVERSITY'S ALL-ALUMNI CENTENNIAL DINNER.

TWO THOUSAND ATTENDEES AWAIT HIM AT THE WALDORF-ASTORIA HOTEL.

AS THE LINDBERGHS SIT DOWN TO DINNER, BETTY GOW TALKS ON THE TELEPHONE TO HER BOYFRIEND, HENRY "RED" JOHNSEN.

REGRETABLY, SHE HAS TO BREAK THEIR DATE FOR THIS EVENING.

AFTER DINNER, HUSBAND AND WIFE RELAX IN THE IN THE LIVING ROOM.

AT ONE POINT, THE COLONEL HEARS A NOISE FROM OUTSIDE — A SHARP SOUND LIKE BREAKING WOOD.

NOTHING IS THOUGHT OF THIS, SINCE THE NIGHT IS UNUSUALLY WINDY.

AT 9:30 PM, THE LINDBERGHS CLIMB THE STAIRS TO THEIR BEDROOM.

SHORTLY THEREAFTER, CHARLES RETURNS DOWNSTAIRS TO WORK IN THE LIBRARY...

WHICH IS SITUATED DIRECTLY BELOW THE NURSERY.

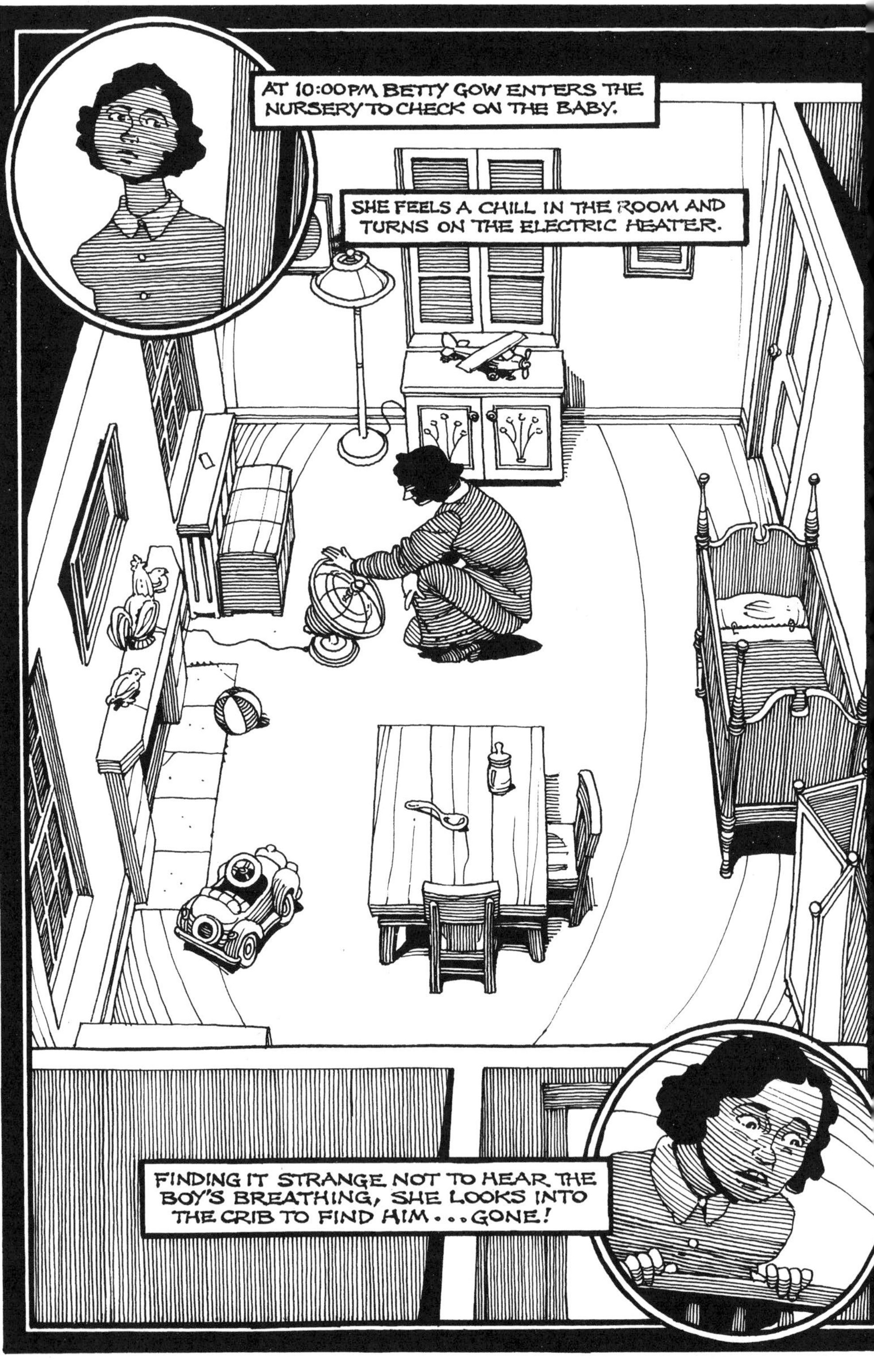
AT 10:00PM BETTY GOW ENTERS THE NURSERY TO CHECK ON THE BABY.
SHE FEELS A CHILL IN THE ROOM AND TURNS ON THE ELECTRIC HEATER.
FINDING IT STRANGE NOT TO HEAR THE BOY'S BREATHING, SHE LOOKS INTO THE CRIB TO FIND HIM . . . GONE!

MISS GOW'S FIRST THOUGHT IS THAT THE BOY IS WITH HIS MOTHER. BUT ANNE LINDBERGH WONDERS IF CHARLES TOOK HIM AS A PRACTICAL JOKE, FOR WHICH THE AVIATOR IS NOTORIOUS.

THIS IS QUICKLY FOUND NOT TO BE THE CASE.

COL. LINDBERGH EXAMINES THE NURSERY.

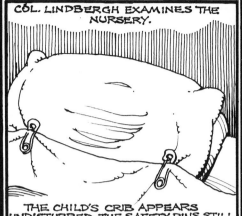

THE CHILD'S CRIB APPEARS UNDISTURBED, THE SAFETY PINS STILL IN PLACE ON THE BLANKET, THE IMPRINT OF HIS TINY HEAD STILL ON THE PILLOW.

THE SOUTHEAST WINDOW IS CLOSED, BUT NEXT TO IT, ON THE RADIATOR COVER, LIES AN ENVELOPE.

ON THE CHEST BENEATH THE WINDOW CAN BE DISCERNED SMUDGES OF MUD.

HE THINKS IT BEST TO TOUCH NOTHING IN THE ROOM, PENDING THE ARRIVAL OF POLICE.

ANNE, WITH BETTY GOW AND ELSIE WHATELEY, GIVE THE REST OF THE HOUSE A THOROUGH SEARCH.

WHILE COL. LINDBERGH, RIFLE IN HAND, AND OLLY WHATELEY GO OVER THE GROUNDS.

IN QUICK SUCCESSION, THREE TELEPHONE CALLS ARE PLACED...

TO THE MERCER COUNTY SHERIFF'S OFFICE IN HOPEWELL...

TO HENRY BRECKINRIDGE, THE LINDBERGHS' ATTORNEY AND FAMILY FRIEND...

TO THE NEW JERSEY STATE POLICE.

AT ABOUT 10:40PM, THE FIRST SHERIFF DEPUTIES ARRIVE. OUTSIDE THE HOUSE, THEY FIND SEVERAL CLUES.

DIRECTLY BENEATH THE SOUTHEAST NURSERY WINDOW ARE TWO IMPRESSIONS IN THE MUD— APPARENTLY FROM A LADDER.

CLOSE BY IS WHAT LOOKS LIKE A SHOEPRINT.

UPON SCRUTINY, IT REVEALS UNEVEN EDGES AND A TEXTILE PATTERN, AS IF SOCKS OR BURLAP WERE WORN OVER SHOES.

SOME DISTANCE AWAY IS FOUND A THREE-QUARTER-INCH CARPENTER'S CHISEL ...

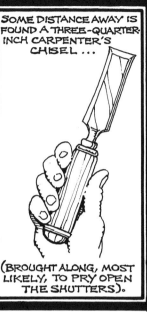

(BROUGHT ALONG, MOST LIKELY, TO PRY OPEN THE SHUTTERS).

A LITTLE FARTHER TO THE SOUTHEAST, WHAT WILL TURN OUT TO BE THE MOST IMPORTANT PIECE OF EVIDENCE: A THREE-PART EXTENSION LADDER, OBVIOUSLY HAND-MADE, LYING IN TWO SECTIONS.

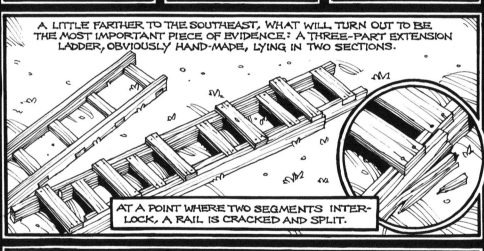

AT A POINT WHERE TWO SEGMENTS INTERLOCK, A RAIL IS CRACKED AND SPLIT.

TO THE EAST OF THE HOUSE IS A ROUGH ACCESS ROAD CALLED FEATHERBED LANE. COULD THIS HAVE BEEN THE KIDNAPPER'S ROUTE?

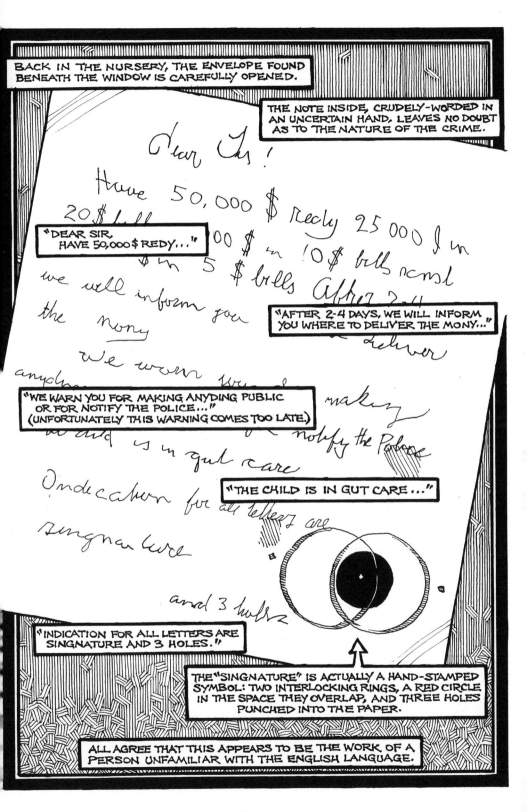

BACK IN THE NURSERY, THE ENVELOPE FOUND BENEATH THE WINDOW IS CAREFULLY OPENED.

THE NOTE INSIDE, CRUDELY-WORDED IN AN UNCERTAIN HAND, LEAVES NO DOUBT AS TO THE NATURE OF THE CRIME.

"DEAR SIR, HAVE 50,000$ REDY..."

"AFTER 2-4 DAYS, WE WILL INFORM YOU WHERE TO DELIVER THE MONY..."

"WE WARN YOU FOR MAKING ANYDING PUBLIC OR FOR NOTIFY THE POLICE..." (UNFORTUNATELY THIS WARNING COMES TOO LATE.)

"THE CHILD IS IN GUT CARE ..."

"INDICATION FOR ALL LETTERS ARE SINGNATURE AND 3 HOLES."

THE "SINGNATURE" IS ACTUALLY A HAND-STAMPED SYMBOL: TWO INTERLOCKING RINGS, A RED CIRCLE IN THE SPACE THEY OVERLAP, AND THREE HOLES PUNCHED INTO THE PAPER.

ALL AGREE THAT THIS APPEARS TO BE THE WORK OF A PERSON UNFAMILIAR WITH THE ENGLISH LANGUAGE.

23

BY 11:00 PM, POLICE HAVE ESTABLISHED STATEWIDE ROADBLOCKS.

ANY CAR CONTAINING A CHILD IS DETAINED FOR QUESTIONING.

RESIDENTS OF THE AREA DESCRIBE HAVING SEEN SUSPICIOUS-LOOKING CARS CARRYING SUSPICIOUS-LOOKING PEOPLE THROUGHOUT THE PREVIOUS DAY.

A MYSTERIOUS GREEN CAR IS MENTIONED BY MORE THAN ONE PERSON.

BY MIDNIGHT, THE AIRWAVES ARE ABUZZ WITH THE NEWS...

AND, THROUGHOUT THE MORNING, THE PRESS DESCENDS UPON TINY HOPEWELL.

WEDNESDAY, MARCH 2 —
BY MID-MORNING, THE NEW JERSEY STATE POLICE HAVE SET UP A HEADQUARTERS INSIDE THE LINDBERGHS' GARAGE.

THE INVESTIGATION IS HEADED BY THE STATE POLICE SUPERINTENDENT, COL. H. NORMAN SCHWARZKOPF.

THE JUSTICE DEPARTMENT'S BUREAU OF INVESTIGATION, DIRECTED BY J. EDGAR HOOVER, OFFERS ITS ASSISTANCE...

ALTHOUGH AT THIS TIME, THERE IS LITTLE, BY LAW, THAT IT CAN DO.

BY MID-DAY, THE ROADS INTO HOPEWELL ARE JAMMED.

JOURNALISTS AND THE CURIOUS PUBLIC ROAM FREELY ABOUT THE LINDBERGH PROPERTY...

UNTIL THEY ARE AT LAST CLEARED AWAY BY THE POLICE.

FORENSIC EXAMINERS CAN FIND NO FINGERPRINTS ON THE RANSOM NOTE, THE LADDER, THE CHISEL, OR ANYPLACE IN THE NURSERY—NOT EVEN THOSE OF THE FAMILY.

THIS IS DEEMED STRANGE BY ALL.

25

COL. LINDBERGH FEELS THAT THE KIDNAPPER'S INSTRUCTIONS MUST BE FOLLOWED FAITHFULLY, AS THE BEST WAY TO GET HIS SON BACK SAFELY.

IN THIS, THE POLICE ARE INCLINED TO LET HIM HAVE HIS WAY. NOTHING WILL BE DONE WITHOUT THE AVIATOR'S APPROVAL.

MRS. LINDBERGH MAKES UP A LIST OF THE BABY'S DIET REQUIREMENTS.

A half cup of orange juice or
One quart of milk during the
Three tablespoons of cooked ce
Two tablespoons of cooked ve
The yolk of one egg daily.
One baked potato or rice once a da
Two tablespoons of stewed fruit
A half-cup of prune juice after the e
Fourteen drops of viosterol, a vitam
during the day.

IT IS DISTRIBUTED TO EVERY MAJOR NEWSPAPER AND WIRE SERVICE.

LETTERS FROM OVER THE WORLD HAVE ALREADY BEGUN TO POUR IN . . .

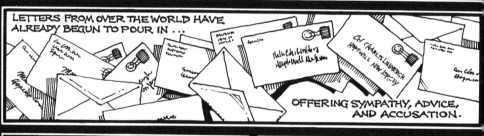

OFFERING SYMPATHY, ADVICE, AND ACCUSATION.

THE ASSUMPTION OF LINDBERGH AND BRECKINRIDGE AND SEVERAL OTHERS IS THAT THE CRIME WAS COMMITTED BY A GANG OF PROFESSIONALS.

THE LOCATION OF THE HOUSE, AFTER ALL, IS WELL KNOWN, ITS FLOOR PLAN HAVING BEEN PUBLISHED WIDELY.

KIDNAPPING IS LUCRATIVE WORK FOR GANGS DURING THESE DEPRESSION YEARS.

SEVERAL WEALTHY VICTIMS HAVE BEEN RELEASED UNHARMED AFTER PAYMENT OF THE RANSOM.

ANOTHER SCHOOL OF THOUGHT HOLDS THAT IT WAS CARRIED OUT BY A GROUP OF AMATEURS...

PERHAPS WITH THE AID OF A MEMBER OF THE LINDBERGHS' OR MORROWS' STAFF.

OTHERWISE, HOW WOULD THE KIDNAPPERS HAVE KNOWN THAT THE FAMILY HAD VARIED ITS ROUTINE AND STAYED AT HOPEWELL ANOTHER TWO NIGHTS?

WOULDN'T THE CHILD HAVE CRIED OUT IF PICKED UP BY UNFAMILIAR HANDS?

ALSO, THE LINDBERGHS' FOX TERRIER "WAGOOSH," KNOWN FOR BARKING AT THE SMALLEST INTRUSION, WAS STRANGELY SILENT LAST NIGHT.

THE RANSOM NOTE IS "UNPROFESSIONAL": IN A STILTED HAND, DEMANDING TOO LITTLE MONEY, AND MAKING NO DIRECT THREAT AGAINST THE CHILD.

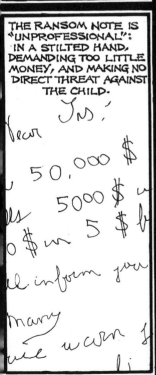

WHY DID THE CRIME OCCUR SO EARLY IN THE EVENING, WHILE THE ENTIRE HOUSE WAS STILL AWAKE?

LINDBERGH ALLOWS HIS WIFE AND HOUSEHOLD STAFF TO BE INTERVIEWED, BUT ONLY TO ESTABLISH THE EVENTS OF LAST EVENING.

AFTER THAT, HE CUTS OFF ACCESS.

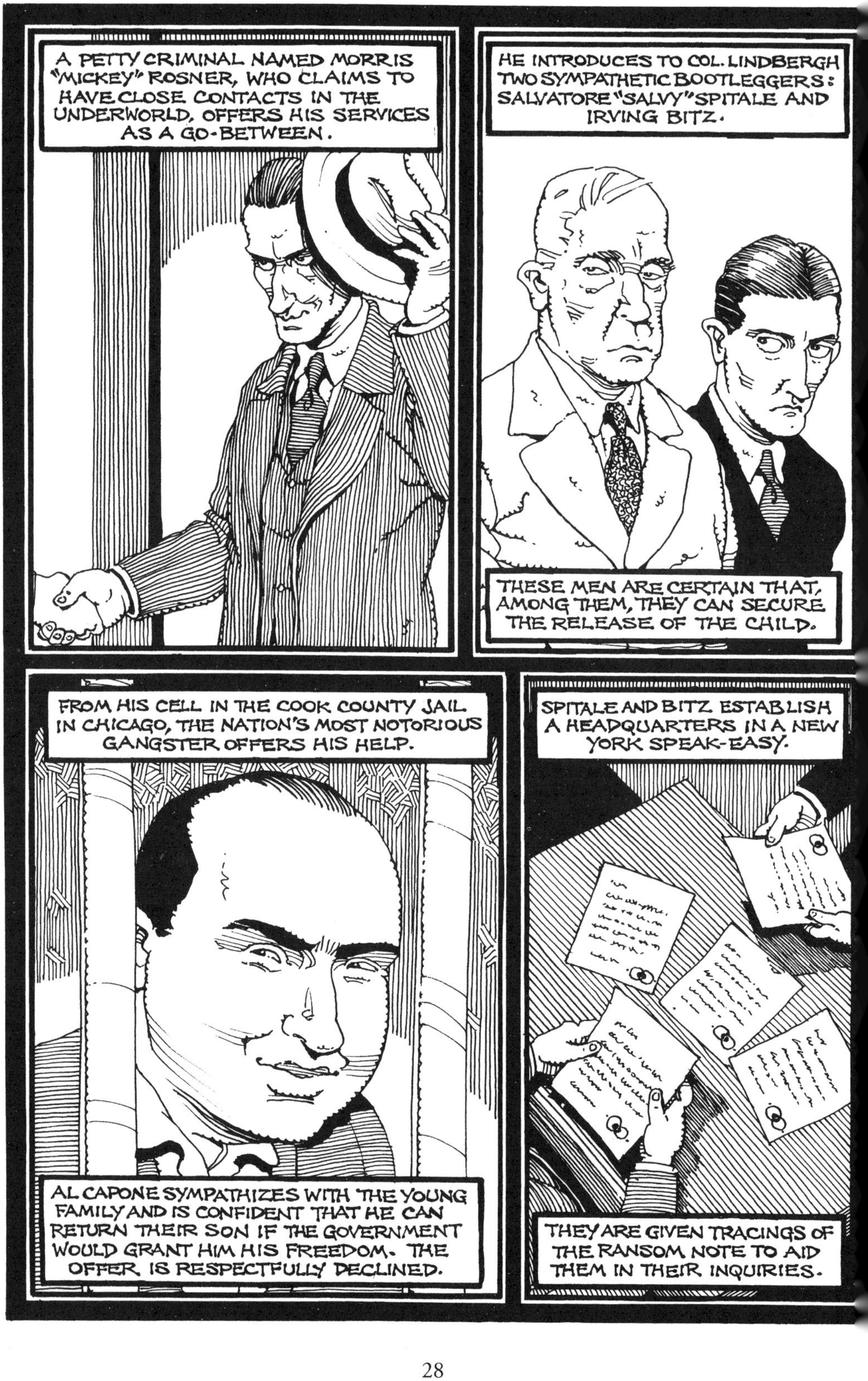
A PETTY CRIMINAL NAMED MORRIS "MICKEY" ROSNER, WHO CLAIMS TO HAVE CLOSE CONTACTS IN THE UNDERWORLD, OFFERS HIS SERVICES AS A GO-BETWEEN.
HE INTRODUCES TO COL. LINDBERGH TWO SYMPATHETIC BOOTLEGGERS: SALVATORE "SALVY" SPITALE AND IRVING BITZ.
THESE MEN ARE CERTAIN THAT, AMONG THEM, THEY CAN SECURE THE RELEASE OF THE CHILD.
FROM HIS CELL IN THE COOK COUNTY JAIL IN CHICAGO, THE NATION'S MOST NOTORIOUS GANGSTER OFFERS HIS HELP.
AL CAPONE SYMPATHIZES WITH THE YOUNG FAMILY AND IS CONFIDENT THAT HE CAN RETURN THEIR SON IF THE GOVERNMENT WOULD GRANT HIM HIS FREEDOM. THE OFFER IS RESPECTFULLY DECLINED.
SPITALE AND BITZ ESTABLISH A HEADQUARTERS IN A NEW YORK SPEAK-EASY.
THEY ARE GIVEN TRACINGS OF THE RANSOM NOTE TO AID THEM IN THEIR INQUIRIES.

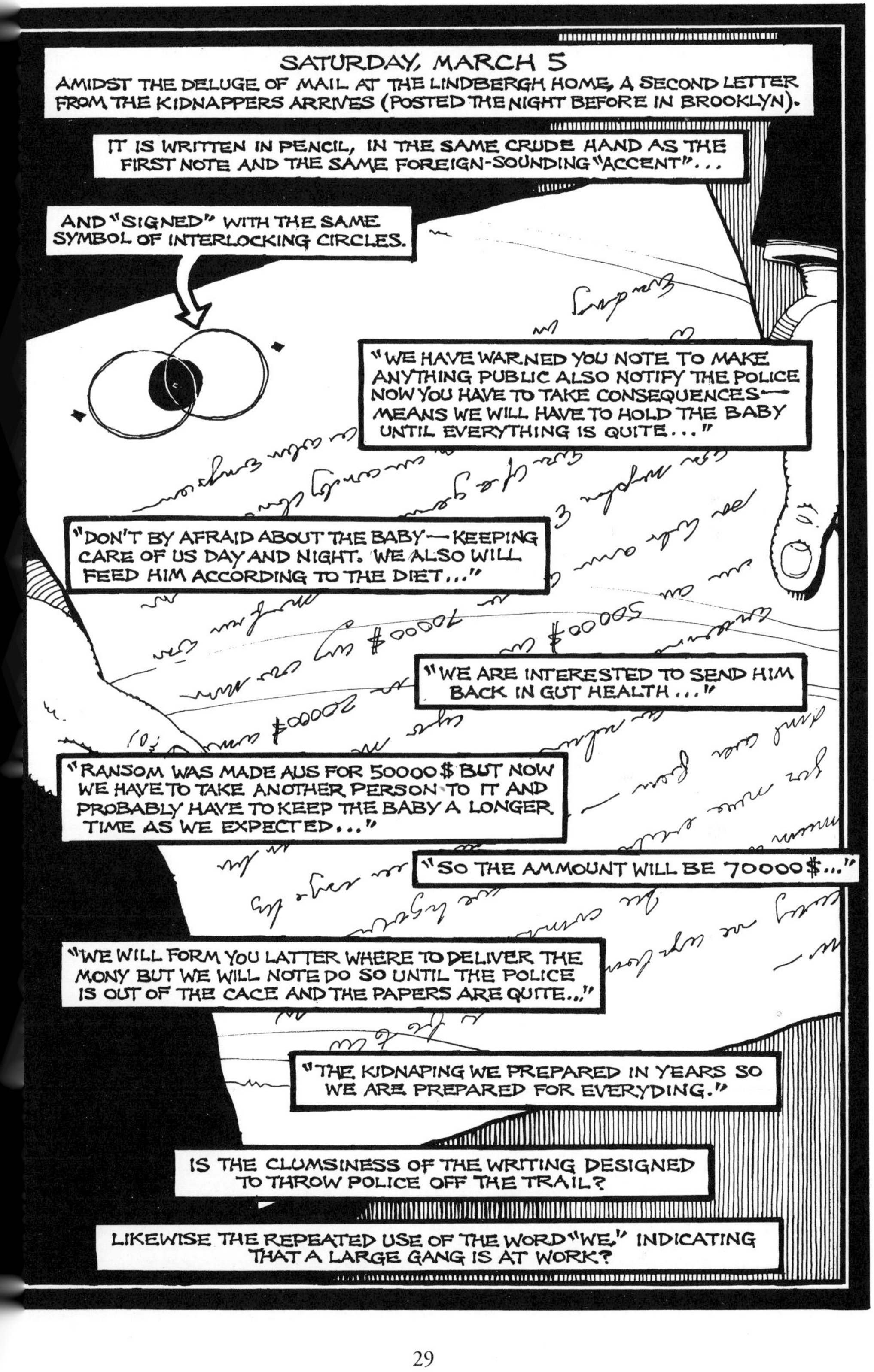
SATURDAY, MARCH 5
AMIDST THE DELUGE OF MAIL AT THE LINDBERGH HOME, A SECOND LETTER FROM THE KIDNAPPERS ARRIVES (POSTED THE NIGHT BEFORE IN BROOKLYN).
IT IS WRITTEN IN PENCIL, IN THE SAME CRUDE HAND AS THE FIRST NOTE AND THE SAME FOREIGN-SOUNDING "ACCENT"...
AND "SIGNED" WITH THE SAME SYMBOL OF INTERLOCKING CIRCLES.
"WE HAVE WARNED YOU NOTE TO MAKE ANYTHING PUBLIC ALSO NOTIFY THE POLICE NOW YOU HAVE TO TAKE CONSEQUENCES— MEANS WE WILL HAVE TO HOLD THE BABY UNTIL EVERYTHING IS QUITE..."
"DON'T BY AFRAID ABOUT THE BABY—KEEPING CARE OF US DAY AND NIGHT. WE ALSO WILL FEED HIM ACCORDING TO THE DIET..."
"WE ARE INTERESTED TO SEND HIM BACK IN GUT HEALTH..."
"RANSOM WAS MADE AUS FOR 50000 $ BUT NOW WE HAVE TO TAKE ANOTHER PERSON TO IT AND PROBABLY HAVE TO KEEP THE BABY A LONGER TIME AS WE EXPECTED..."
"SO THE AMMOUNT WILL BE 70000 $..."
"WE WILL FORM YOU LATTER WHERE TO DELIVER THE MONY BUT WE WILL NOTE DO SO UNTIL THE POLICE IS OUT OF THE CACE AND THE PAPERS ARE QUITE..."
"THE KIDNAPING WE PREPARED IN YEARS SO WE ARE PREPARED FOR EVERYDING."
IS THE CLUMSINESS OF THE WRITING DESIGNED TO THROW POLICE OFF THE TRAIL?
LIKEWISE THE REPEATED USE OF THE WORD "WE," INDICATING THAT A LARGE GANG IS AT WORK?

PART THREE
THE RANSOM

TUESDAY, MARCH 8, 1932
AT THIS POINT, A STRANGE AND COLORFUL
CHARACTER ENTERS THE CASE.

THE BRONX HOME NEWS

DR. JOHN F. CONDON, AGE 72, IS A RETIRED TEACHER, A PHYSICAL CULTURE DEVOTEE, AND A PROUD AMERICAN. LIKE MOST CITIZENS, HE IS SHOCKED AND OUTRAGED OVER THE ABDUCTION OF THE LINDBERGH CHILD.

HE LIVES WITH HIS WIFE MYRA IN THEIR HOME AT 2974 DECATUR AVE. IN THE NEW YORK BOROUGH OF THE BRONX.

HE IS PARTICULARLY HORRIFIED TO LEARN THAT COL. LINDBERGH IS RELYING UPON PROFESSIONAL CRIMINALS TO FIND HIS CHILD.

HE HAS SUBMITTED A LETTER TO THE LOCAL DAILY NEWSPAPER, THE BRONX HOME NEWS, WHICH IS PUBLISHED IN TODAY'S EDITION.

IN IT, HE ADDRESSES THE KIDNAPPERS, OFFERING HIMSELF AS GO-BETWEEN.

TO SWEETEN THE OFFER, HE PLEDGES $1000 OF HIS OWN MONEY ADDED TO THE RANSOM.

WEDNESDAY, MARCH 9 AN ANSWER ARRIVES AT THE CONDONS' DOOR.

MR DOCTOR JOHN F CONDON 2974 DECATUR AVENUE NEW YORK

CRUDELY LETTERED IN PENCIL, THE NOTE ACCEPTS CONDON AS GO-BETWEEN, WARNS HIM NOT TO NOTIFY THE PRESS OR THE POLICE AND INSTRUCTS HIM TO PLACE AN ANONYMOUS NOTICE IN THE NEW YORK AMERICAN WHEN THE MONEY IS READY.

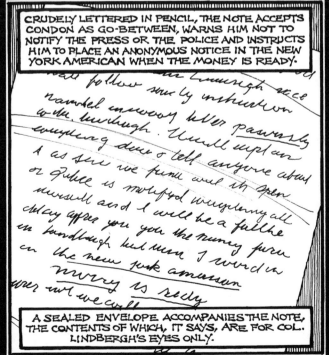

A SEALED ENVELOPE ACCOMPANIES THE NOTE, THE CONTENTS OF WHICH, IT SAYS, ARE FOR COL. LINDBERGH'S EYES ONLY.

CONDON TELEPHONES THE LINDBERGH HOUSE, SPEAKING TO BOTH COL. LINDBERGH AND HENRY BRECKINRIDGE.

THEY ASK HIM TO OPEN AND READ THE SEALED SECOND MESSAGE: IT AUTHORIZES DR. CONDON TO ACT AS GO-BETWEEN...

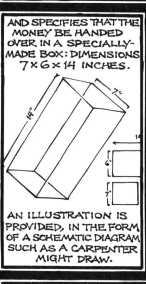

AND SPECIFIES THAT THE MONEY BE HANDED OVER IN A SPECIALLY-MADE BOX: DIMENSIONS 7 × 6 × 14 INCHES.

AN ILLUSTRATION IS PROVIDED, IN THE FORM OF A SCHEMATIC DIAGRAM SUCH AS A CARPENTER MIGHT DRAW.

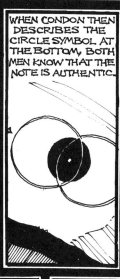

WHEN CONDON THEN DESCRIBES THE CIRCLE SYMBOL AT THE BOTTOM, BOTH MEN KNOW THAT THE NOTE IS AUTHENTIC.

THE OLDER GENTLEMAN IS THEN INVITED OUT TO THE LINDBERGH ESTATE. HE IS DRIVEN THERE BY HIS FRIENDS MILTON GAGLIO AND MAX ROSENHAIN.

ON THE WAY, THEY BECOME LOST SEVERAL TIMES, FINALLY ARRIVING IN THE EARLY HOURS OF THURSDAY, MARCH 10

CONDON ENDS UP SPENDING THE NIGHT ON THE FLOOR OF THE NURSERY...

WHILE HIS FRIENDS ARE SENT BACK TO THE BRONX.

IN THE MORNING, THE LINDBERGHS SIGN A STATEMENT AUTHORIZING HIM AS GO-BETWEEN.

DR. CONDON DESIRES NOTHING MORE THAN TO PERSONALLY DELIVER THE CHILD AGAIN INTO THE EMBRACE OF ITS MOTHER.

AS COL. LINDBERGH FOLLOWS THE RANSOM NOTES, POLICE FOLLOW DIFFERENT AVENUES OF INVESTIGATION.

OF PARTICULAR INTEREST IS THE BOYFRIEND OF BETTY GOW, FINN HENDRIK JOHNSEN, KNOWN AS HENRY "RED" JOHNSEN, A NORWEGIAN SEAMAN...

WHO WAS TOLD BY HER ON THE NIGHT OF THE KIDNAPPING THAT THE LINDBERGHS WOULD BE REMAINING AT HOPEWELL.

IT TURNS OUT THAT HE HAS WORKED ON SEVERAL LUXURY YACHTS AND IS IN THE UNITED STATES ILLEGALLY...

AND HE DRIVES A GREEN CAR.

IN THIS CAR IS FOUND AN EMPTY MILK BOTTLE. HE EXPLAINS THAT HE OFTEN DRINKS MILK WHILE DRIVING.

HIS WHEREABOUTS UPON THE NIGHT IN QUESTION— AT HIS BROTHER'S HOUSE IN WEST HARTFORD, CONNECTICUT—SEEM TO BE FIRMLY ESTABLISHED.

THURSDAY, MARCH 10
NEWARK POLICE INTERVIEW THE 29-PERSON STAFF OF NEXT DAY HILL.

ALL OF THEM ARE FOUND TO BE CO-OPERATIVE, EXCEPT FOR MISS VIOLET SHARPE, AN ENGLISH WOMAN, AGE 28, EMPLOYED AS A HOUSEMAID.

SHE IS SAID TO BE ROMANTICALLY INVOLVED WITH THE HEAD BUTLER, SEPTIMUS BANKS.

FOR HER INTERVIEW, SHE APPEARS NERVOUS AND INDIGNANT: WHY SHOULD THE POLICE BE PRYING INTO HER PRIVATE LIFE?

AS TO HER ACTIVITIES ON THE EVENING OF MARCH 1, SHE IS AT FIRST EVASIVE.

SHE THEN RELATES AN IMPLAUSIBLE STORY ABOUT GOING OUT TO A PICTURE SHOW WITH A GROUP OF PEOPLE SHE HAD ONLY MET THAT DAY.

NO, SHE COULD NOT RECALL WHAT PICTURE ... OR THE NAMES OF THE PEOPLE SHE WAS WITH.

FRIDAY, MARCH 11
A CLASSIFIED AD APPEARS IN THE NEW YORK AMERICAN.

I ACCEPT.
MONEY IS READY.
JAFSIE.

THE CODE NAME "JAFSIE" IS MADE UP OF JOHN F. CONDON'S INITIALS.

A REPLY ARRIVES THIS VERY DAY IN THE FORM OF A TELEPHONE CALL. A GUTTURAL VOICE INSTRUCTS DR. CONDON TO REMAIN AT HOME EVERY NIGHT, 6PM TO MIDNIGHT, AND SOON HE WILL RECEIVE ANOTHER NOTE. FOLLOW THE NOTE'S INSTRUCTIONS PRECISELY.

DURING THIS CONVERSATION, CONDON HEARS ANOTHER VOICE IN THE BACKGROUND. TO HIM, IT SOUNDS ITALIAN: "STATTI CITTO!" ("SHUT UP!")

HENRY BRECKINRIDGE TAKES UP RESIDENCE AT THE CONDONS' HOME, AWAITING THE KIDNAPPERS' NEXT MOVE. IT COMES ON THE EVENING OF:
SATURDAY, MARCH 12.

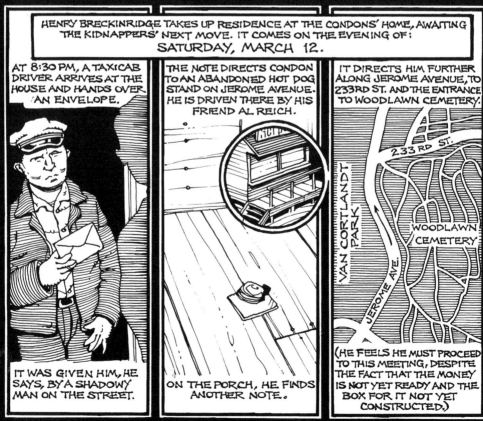

AT 8:30 PM, A TAXICAB DRIVER ARRIVES AT THE HOUSE AND HANDS OVER AN ENVELOPE.

IT WAS GIVEN HIM, HE SAYS, BY A SHADOWY MAN ON THE STREET.

THE NOTE DIRECTS CONDON TO AN ABANDONED HOT DOG STAND ON JEROME AVENUE. HE IS DRIVEN THERE BY HIS FRIEND AL REICH.

ON THE PORCH, HE FINDS ANOTHER NOTE.

IT DIRECTS HIM FURTHER ALONG JEROME AVENUE, TO 233RD ST. AND THE ENTRANCE TO WOODLAWN CEMETERY.

233 RD ST.

VAN CORTLANDT PARK

WOODLAWN CEMETERY

JEROME AVE.

(HE FEELS HE MUST PROCEED TO THIS MEETING, DESPITE THE FACT THAT THE MONEY IS NOT YET READY AND THE BOX FOR IT NOT YET CONSTRUCTED.)

DR. CONDON GETS OUT AND WALKS ALONG THE SIDEWALK BESIDE THE CEMETERY. AHEAD, A HAND EMERGES FROM THE BARS, WAVING A HANDKERCHIEF.

(THE ENSUING ENCOUNTER CAN ONLY BE ATTESTED TO BY THE RECOLLECTIONS OF JOHN F. CONDON.)

THE MAN SPEAKS IN A THICK GUTTURAL ACCENT, THE SAME VOICE AS ON THE TELEPHONE EARLIER.

YOU GOTTED THE MONEY WITH YOU?

NO, I CANNOT BRING THE MONEY UNTIL I SEE THE BABY.

THE MAN THEN VAULTS OVER THE FENCE...

AND LANDS BESIDE CONDON.

DID YOU BRING THE COPS?

I GAVE YOU MY WORD I WOULDN'T DO THAT.

DR. CONDON FOLLOWS THE STRANGER ACROSS THE STREET, INTO VAN CORTLANDT PARK.

IT'S TOO DANGEROUS!

COME BACK HERE! DON'T BE COWARDLY!

AT LAST, THEY SIT ON A PARK BENCH. THE MAN KEEPS HIS COLLAR UP AND HIS HAT PULLED DOWN, EFFECTIVELY CONCEALING HIS FACE.

IT'S TOO DANGEROUS. MIGHT BE TWENTY YEARS OR BURN. WOULD I BURN IF THE BABY WAS DEAD?

WHAT DO YOU MEAN? WHY WOULD WE BE CARRYING ON NEGOTIATIONS IF THE BABY IS DEAD?

THE BABY IS NOT DEAD. THE BABY IS BETTER THAN IT WAS. WE GIVE MORE FOR HIM TO EAT THAN WAS IN THE PAPER. TELL THE COLONEL NOT TO WORRY.

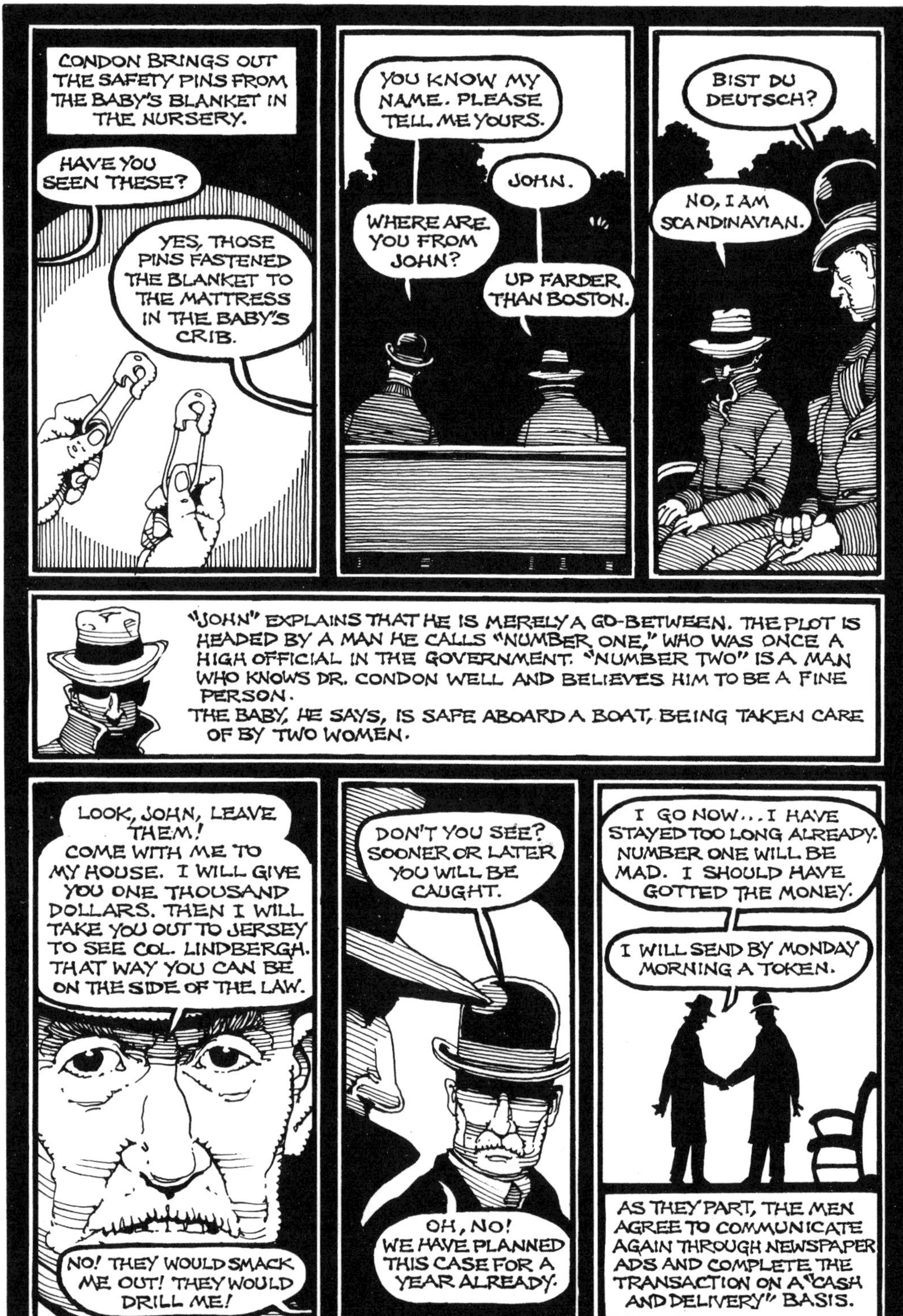

CONDON BRINGS OUT THE SAFETY PINS FROM THE BABY'S BLANKET IN THE NURSERY.
HAVE YOU SEEN THESE?
YES, THOSE PINS FASTENED THE BLANKET TO THE MATTRESS IN THE BABY'S CRIB.
YOU KNOW MY NAME. PLEASE TELL ME YOURS.
JOHN.
WHERE ARE YOU FROM JOHN?
UP FARDER THAN BOSTON.
BIST DU DEUTSCH?
NO, I AM SCANDINAVIAN.
"JOHN" EXPLAINS THAT HE IS MERELY A GO-BETWEEN. THE PLOT IS HEADED BY A MAN HE CALLS "NUMBER ONE," WHO WAS ONCE A HIGH OFFICIAL IN THE GOVERNMENT. "NUMBER TWO" IS A MAN WHO KNOWS DR. CONDON WELL AND BELIEVES HIM TO BE A FINE PERSON.
THE BABY, HE SAYS, IS SAFE ABOARD A BOAT, BEING TAKEN CARE OF BY TWO WOMEN.
LOOK, JOHN, LEAVE THEM! COME WITH ME TO MY HOUSE. I WILL GIVE YOU ONE THOUSAND DOLLARS. THEN I WILL TAKE YOU OUT TO JERSEY TO SEE COL. LINDBERGH. THAT WAY YOU CAN BE ON THE SIDE OF THE LAW.
NO! THEY WOULD SMACK ME OUT! THEY WOULD DRILL ME!
DON'T YOU SEE? SOONER OR LATER YOU WILL BE CAUGHT.
OH, NO! WE HAVE PLANNED THIS CASE FOR A YEAR ALREADY.
I GO NOW... I HAVE STAYED TOO LONG ALREADY. NUMBER ONE WILL BE MAD. I SHOULD HAVE GOTTED THE MONEY.
I WILL SEND BY MONDAY MORNING A TOKEN.
AS THEY PART, THE MEN AGREE TO COMMUNICATE AGAIN THROUGH NEWSPAPER ADS AND COMPLETE THE TRANSACTION ON A "CASH AND DELIVERY" BASIS.

SUNDAY, MARCH 13

POLICE BRING TO THE LINDBERGH HOME DR. ERASMUS M. HUDSON, PHYSICIAN AND FINGERPRINT EXPERT, IN THE HOPE THAT HE CAN FIND PRINTS WHERE THE POLICE TECHNICIAN DID NOT.

DR. HUDSON SPRAYS THE BABY'S TOYS WITH A FINE MIST OF SILVER NITRATE, AND THEN EXPOSES THEM TO THE SUN.

SEVERAL HUNDRED PARTIAL PRINTS EMERGE, OF WHICH THIRTEEN ARE IDENTIFIABLE AS THOSE OF THE CHILD.

THE KIDNAP LADDER UNDERGOES THE SAME PROCESS. OVER 500 SMUDGES ARE FOUND, OF WHICH 200 ARE USABLE PRINTS...

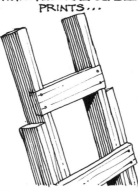

ATTESTING TO THE NUMBER OF OFFICIALS WHO HAVE SULLIED THIS IMPORTANT ITEM OF EVIDENCE.

PAINSTAKING SCRUTINY OF THE NURSERY REVEALS NO PRINTS FROM THE LINDBERGHS OR THEIR HOUSEHOLD STAFF.

THE SURFACES OF THE ROOM, IN FACT, APPEAR TO HAVE BEEN WIPED CLEAN.

TUESDAY, MARCH 15

ON THIS DAY, A PARCEL ARRIVES AT THE CONDON HOME. HENRY BRECKINRIDGE HURRIES THERE TO OPEN IT.

INSIDE IS A BABY'S SLEEPING SUIT — UNDOUBTEDLY THE "TOKEN" PROMISED BY THE MAN IN THE CEMETERY.

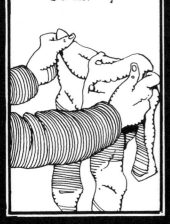

COL. LINDBERGH — IN DISGUISE — ARRIVES EARLY THE NEXT MORNING.

THE GARMENT HAS APPARENTLY BEEN LAUNDERED, BUT HE THINKS THAT, IN ALL PROBABILITY, IT IS HIS SON'S.

A NOTE IS ENCLOSED WITH THE SUIT DEMANDING THAT AN AD BE PLACED IN THE NEW YORK AMERICAN WHEN THE MONEY IS READY. THEN...

"AFTER 8 HOURS WE HAVE THE MONY RECEIVED, WE WILL NOTIFY YOU WHERE TO FIND THE BABY. IF THERE IS ANY TRAPP, YOU WILL BE RESPONSIBLE FOR WHAT FOLLOWS."

WEDNESDAY, MARCH 16
A SECOND CLASSIFIED AD RUNS IN THE NEW YORK AMERICAN.

I ACCEPT
MONEY IS READY.
JOHN, YOUR PACKAGE IS DELIVERED AND IS OK. DIRECT ME.
JAFSIE

DURING THIS TIME, COL. LINDBERGH HAS BEEN SELLING STOCKS AND BONDS, CLOSING OUT ACCOUNTS TO ACCUMULATE THE NECESSARY CASH.

A WOODEN BOX, BUILT TO THE KIDNAPPERS' SPECIFICATIONS, HAS BEEN COMPLETED BY A LOCAL CABINETMAKER.

MONDAY, MARCH 21
A LETTER IS AT LAST DELIVERED TO DR. CONDON...

"YOU AND MR. LINDBERGH KNOW OUR PROGRAM. IF YOU DON'T ACCEPT DEN WE WILL WAIT UNTIL YOU AGREE WITH OUR DEAL."

"WE WILL TELL YOU AGAIN: THIS KIDNAPPING CACE WAS PREPARED FOR A YEAR ALREADY SO THE POLICE WON'T HAVE ANY LUCK TO FIND US OR THE CHILD."

DID THE KIDNAPPERS MISS LAST WEEK'S AD? THEY SEEM TO THINK THAT LINDBERGH DOES NOT ACCEPT THEIR TERMS.

CONDON AND BRECKINRIDGE COMPOSE ANOTHER AD...
IT RUNS IN THE NEW YORK AMERICAN AND THE BRONX HOME NEWS FOR THREE CONSECUTIVE DAYS.

THANKS.
THAT LITTLE PACKAGE YOU SENT ME WAS IMMEDIATELY DELIVERED AND ACCEPTED AS THE REAL ARTICLE. SEE MY POSITION. OVER FIFTY YEARS IN BUSINESS AND CAN I PAY WITHOUT SEEING THE GOODS? COMMON SENSE MAKES ME TRUST YOU. CASE UNDERSTAND MY
JAFSIE.

THE CASH IS COLLECTED INTO THE DENOMINATIONS DEMANDED BY THE KIDNAPPERS.

ALSO IN ACCORDANCE WITH THEIR WISHES, COL. LINDBERGH REFUSES TO HAVE THE BILLS MARKED IN ANY WAY. HE IS CONVINCED, HOWEVER, BY AGENTS OF THE BUREAU OF INVESTIGATION TO HAVE THE SERIAL NUMBERS RECORDED.

ALSO AT THIS TIME, A NEW AVENUE TO THE KIDNAPPERS EMERGES, IN THE PERSON OF JOHN H. CURTIS, AGE 43, A WEALTHY AND RESPECTED BOAT-BUILDER OF NORFOLK, VIRGINIA.

TUESDAY, MARCH 22.

HE COMES TO THE LINDBERGH ESTATE IN THE COMPANY OF TWO LIKEWISE RESPECTABLE CITIZENS: ADMIRAL GUY BURRAGE AND THE REVEREND HAROLD DOBSON-PEACOCK, BOTH OF THEM ACQUAINTANCES OF THE LINDBERGH AND MORROW FAMILIES.

CURTIS RELATES TO COL. LINDBERGH A STRANGE AND COMPELLING STORY...

IT SEEMS THAT, BACK ON MARCH 9, HE WAS ACCOSTED BY A MYSTERIOUS MAN CALLING HIMSELF "SAM."

THE MAN EXPLAINED THAT HE WAS AN ASSOCIATE OF THE SCANDINAVIAN GANG THAT HAD STOLEN THE LINDBERGH BABY...

AND THAT THEY HAD CHOSEN CURTIS TO ACT AS A CONDUIT TO COL. LINDBERGH.

CURTIS WAS SHOCKED AND SPENT A NIGHT OF INDECISION.

THE NEXT MORNING, HE TOLD "SAM" THAT HE WOULD ACCEPT THE TASK.

COL. LINDBERGH HAS DOUBTS ABOUT THE STORY. COULD THESE BE THE SAME PEOPLE WHO CONTACTED DR. CONDON?

STILL, HE DOES NOT WANT TO CLOSE OFF ANY POSSIBILITY. HE ASKS CURTIS TO DEMAND FROM "SAM" PROOF THAT THE CHILD IS WELL—SUCH AS A RECENT PHOTOGRAPH.

AS THE MONTH OF MARCH CLOSES, YET A THIRD CONNECTION TO THE KIDNAPPERS IS IN PLAY...

INITIATED BY GASTON B. MEANS, AGE 53, A FORMER PRIVATE DETECTIVE AND AGENT FOR THE BUREAU OF INVESTIGATION.

THOUGH OF UNSAVORY REPUTATION, HE HAS MANAGED TO GAIN THE TRUST OF THE WEALTHY WASHINGTON HOSTESS EVALYN WALSH McLEAN, A FRIEND OF THE LINDBERGHS.

MEANS HAS TOLD HER OF HOW, BEFORE THE CRIME, HE WAS APPROACHED BY THE KIDNAP GANG AND ASKED TO JOIN THEM.

HE REFUSED, BUT WAS NOW APPOINTED TO HANDLE THE NEGOTIATIONS.

WITH COL. LINDBERGH'S APPROVAL, MRS. McLEAN HAS HANDED OVER $50,000 OF HER OWN MONEY TO PAY THE RANSOM.

THIS IS SHORTLY RAISED TO $100,000.

MEANS HAS COLLECTED THE FULL SUM FROM HER IN CASH — PLUS FURTHER AMOUNTS FOR HIS EXPENSES.

MRS. McLEAN NOW WAITS PATIENTLY WHILE HE GIVES HER EXCUSE AFTER EXCUSE AS TO WHY THE EXCHANGE CANNOT BE MADE.

FRIDAY, APRIL 1
WHILE WALKING ABOUT THE ESTATE, BETTY GOW AND ELSIE WHATELEY MAKE A SURPRISING DISCOVERY:

ONE OF THE BABY'S THUMB-GUARDS, LYING ALONG THE EDGE OF THE GRAVEL DRIVEWAY LEADING TO THE HOUSE.

DOES THIS MEAN THAT THE KIDNAPPERS USED THE MAIN DRIVEWAY AS THEIR ESCAPE ROUTE, RATHER THAN THE WOODS TO THE EAST?

FURTHER, COULD THE THUMB-GUARD HAVE LAIN THERE UNNOTICED FOR SO LONG BESIDE THE HEAVILY-TRAVELLED DRIVEWAY?

SATURDAY, APRIL 2
COL. LINDBERGH AND HENRY BRECKINRIDGE WAIT AT THE CONDONS' HOUSE FOR A RESPONSE TO THEIR ADVERTISEMENT.

AT ABOUT 7:45 PM, A TAXI DRIVER, AS BEFORE, LEAVES AN ENVELOPE ON THE FRONT PORCH.

THIS TIME, COL. LINDBERGH ACCOMPANIES THE DOCTOR.

OF THE $70,000 GATHERED, JUST $50,000 WILL FIT INTO THE SPECIALLY-BUILT CONTAINER.

THE NOTE DIRECTS THEM TO A GREENHOUSE AND NURSERY ON TREMONT AVENUE.

AT THE NURSERY, ANOTHER NOTE IS WAITING ON A TABLE OUTSIDE. IT SENDS THEM FURTHER EAST, TO ANOTHER CEMETERY: ST. RAYMOND'S.

THEY STOP AT THE CEMETERY'S ENTRANCE. CONDON GETS OUT, LEAVING LINDBERGH IN THE CAR.

BUT HE HESITATES TO ENTER THE DARK AND THREATENING INTERIOR.

A VOICE CALLS FROM THE DARKNESS, HEARD PLAINLY BY BOTH MEN.

HEY, DOCTOR— OVER HERE!

CONDON, DECIDING NOT TO CARRY THE BOX OF MONEY FOLLOWS THE VOICE INTO THE CEMETERY...

WHILE THE LONE EAGLE CAN DO NOTHING BUT WAIT.

THE FOLLOWING ENCOUNTER, AS BEFORE, CAN ONLY BE CONFIRMED BY THE RECOLLECTIONS OF DR. JOHN F. CONDON.

SUDDENLY, A MAN POPS UP FROM BEHIND A TOMBSTONE.

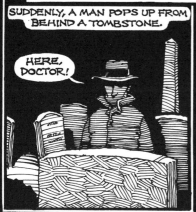

HERE, DOCTOR!

THE MAN LEADS CONDON DEEPER INTO THE CEMETERY. AT LAST THEY SPEAK WITH A HEDGE BETWEEN THEM. THE DOCTOR RECOGNIZES HIM AS THE SAME "JOHN" HE SPOKE WITH BEFORE.

YOU GOT IT, THE MONEY?

NO, IT'S UP IN THE CAR.

WHO IS UP THERE?

COL. LINDBERGH.

CONDON REFUSES TO GIVE UP THE MONEY WITHOUT A "RECEIPT" TELLING WHERE THE CHILD IS.

"JOHN" GOES OFF TO GET ONE WHILE CONDON RETURNS TO THE CAR FOR THE BOX OF CASH.

FIFTEEN MINUTES LATER, THEY FIND EACH OTHER AGAIN. BY CONDON'S WATCH: 9:29 PM.

NOW GIVE ME THE NOTE.

DON'T OPEN IT YET, NOT FOR SIX HOURS.

THE TWO MEN, ONCE AGAIN, SHAKE HANDS AND PART.

IF YOU GIVE ME A CHANCE TO GET THAT BABY, EVERYTHING WILL BE ALL RIGHT BUT IF YOU DON'T, I WILL FOLLOW YOU TO AUSTRALIA DON'T TRY TO DOUBLE-CROSS ME.

BACK AT THE CAR, CONDON GIVES THE ENVELOPE TO LINDBERGH.

I PROMISED NOT TO OPEN IT FOR SIX HOURS, BUT THAT DOESN'T MEAN THAT YOU CAN'T.

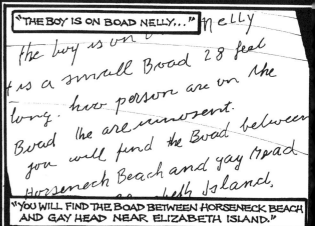

"THE BOY IS ON BOAD NELLY..."

"YOU WILL FIND THE BOAD BETWEEN HORSENECK BEACH AND GAY HEAD NEAR ELIZABETH ISLAND."

THE NOTE REFERS TO THE AREA NORTH OF MARTHA'S VINEYARD, AND, FOR THE NEXT SEVERAL DAYS, POLICE SEARCH THE LOCAL HARBORS AND LANDINGS THOROUGHLY.

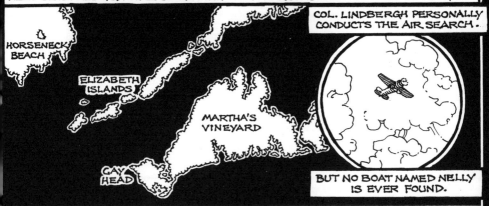

HORSENECK BEACH

ELIZABETH ISLANDS

MARTHA'S VINEYARD

GAY HEAD

COL. LINDBERGH PERSONALLY CONDUCTS THE AIR SEARCH.

BUT NO BOAT NAMED NELLY IS EVER FOUND.

WEDNESDAY, APRIL 6
THE UNITED STATES TREASURY DEPARTMENT BEGINS TO CIRCULATE A LIST OF THE RECORDED RANSOM BILLS TO BANKS ACROSS THE NATION.

TWO DAYS LATER, THE FIRST OF THE NOTES TURNS UP AT A BANK IN THE BRONX.

NO FURTHER MESSAGES ARE RECEIVED BY JOHN F. CONDON, BUT LINDBERGH REFUSES TO GIVE UP HOPE.

HE RETURNS HIS ATTENTION TO THE AVENUE OFFERED BY JOHN H. CURTIS.

CURTIS CLAIMS THAT, THROUGH HIS CONTACT "SAM," HE HAS MET WITH THE CAPTAIN OF THE SCHOONER ON WHICH THE CHILD IS BEING KEPT.

AMONG THE GROUP IS A MAN CALLED "JOHN," WHO SPEAKS WITH A HEAVY ACCENT.

FOR THE NEXT SEVERAL WEEKS, RENDEZVOUS POINTS ARE ARRANGED, ONLY FOR THEM TO FALL THROUGH AT THE LAST MOMENT.

ALSO BY THIS TIME, THE SCHEME INITIATED BY GASTON MEANS HAS BEGUN TO UNRAVEL. HAVING LED MRS. McLEAN AROUND THE COUNTRY—TO SOUTH CAROLINA AND TEXAS—HE KEEPS REASSURING HER THAT THEY ARE ON THE VERY BRINK OF FINDING THE CHILD.

BY THE END OF APRIL, HOWEVER, SHE HAS GROWN WEARY OF THE CHASE AND DEMANDS THAT HER MONEY BE RETURNED.

IN THE MEANTIME, THE PRESS HAS GOTTEN WIND OF THE FACT THAT THE RANSOM HAS BEEN PAID BUT THE CHILD NOT RETURNED.

MONDAY, APRIL 11
THE NEW YORK TIMES REVEALS THAT THE MYSTERIOUS "JAFSIE" IS DR. JOHN F. CONDON OF THE BRONX.

CROWDS SURROUND HIS HOME ON DECATUR AVENUE. AT FIRST HE BASKS IN THE CELEBRITY...

BUT SOON HE MUST OBTAIN AN UNLISTED TELEPHONE NUMBER.

AT POLICE HEADQUARTERS, HE PERUSES COUNTLESS "MUG" SHOTS.

A POLICE ARTIST DRAWS A SKETCH FROM HIS DESCRIPTION OF "JOHN."

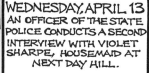

WEDNESDAY, APRIL 13
AN OFFICER OF THE STATE POLICE CONDUCTS A SECOND INTERVIEW WITH VIOLET SHARPE, HOUSEMAID AT NEXT DAY HILL.

SHE IS NO LESS ANGRY AND EVASIVE THAN DURING HER FIRST, MORE THAN A MONTH AGO.

HER STORY HAS CHANGED SOMEWHAT: SHE DID NOT ATTEND A PICTURE SHOW ON MARCH 1, SHE SAYS, BUT WENT TO A ROADHOUSE CALLED THE PEANUT GRILL.

HER COMPANION WAS A MAN NAMED "ERNIE," WHOM SHE HAD MET THAT DAY. NO, SHE CANNOT REMEMBER HIS LAST NAME.

TO THE POLICE, HER STORY STILL RINGS HOLLOW. ISN'T SHE PRACTICALLY ENGAGED TO THE BUTLER, SEPTIMUS BANKS?

A SEARCH OF HER ROOM FINDS A STACK OF BUSINESS CARDS FROM A LOCAL TAXICAB SERVICE.

THURSDAY, MAY 12
ON THIS DAY,
EVERYTHING CHANGES.

HOPEWELL

JUST OUTSIDE OF HOPEWELL,
THEY STOP BY THE ROAD
SO THAT ALLEN CAN
RELIEVE HIMSELF IN
THE WOODS.

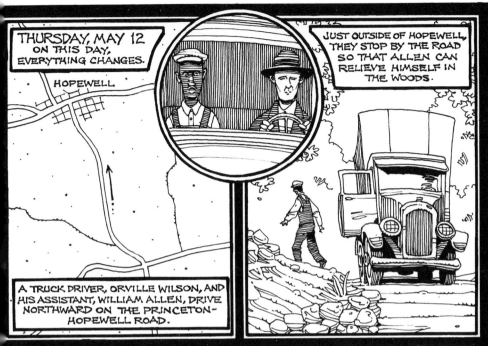

A TRUCK DRIVER, ORVILLE WILSON, AND
HIS ASSISTANT, WILLIAM ALLEN, DRIVE
NORTHWARD ON THE PRINCETON-
HOPEWELL ROAD.

HE WALKS TO THE TOP OF A RISE AND THERE
COMES UPON, TO HIS HORROR, WHAT LOOK LIKE THE
BADLY DECOMPOSED REMAINS OF A SMALL CHILD.

AUTHORITIES ARE SUMMONED, AND THE BODY
IS REMOVED TO THE SWAYZE AND MARGERUM
FUNERAL HOME IN TRENTON, WHICH SERVES
AS THE MERCER COUNTY MORGUE.

A MESSAGE IS SENT TO COL. LINDBERGH.

AT THIS MOMENT, THE AVIATOR IS ABOARD
JOHN CURTIS' YACHT, THE "CACHALOT" OFF CAPE
MAY, NEW JERSEY — IN HOPES OF A
MEETING WITH THE KIDNAPPERS.

THEY HAVE REPEATEDLY ASSURED HIM,
THROUGH CURTIS, THAT HIS SON IS IN
FINE HEALTH.

THE BODY IS IN A HORRIBLE STATE, MUCH OF IT EATEN AWAY BY FOREST CREATURES. IT HAS OBVIOUSLY LAIN IN THE WOODS FOR QUITE SOME TIME, PERHAPS SINCE THE NIGHT OF THE KIDNAPPING.

NEVERTHELESS, FRAGMENTS OF CLOTHING ARE STILL IDENTIFIABLE.

BETTY GOW RECOGNIZES THE FABRIC AND THREAD SHE USED TO SEW THE BABY A NIGHTSHIRT ON THE EVENING OF THE CRIME.

FURTHER, THE LABEL OF THE T-SHIRT IS THE SAME AS IN THOSE PURCHASED FOR HIM BY MRS. LINDBERGH.

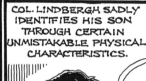

COL. LINDBERGH SADLY IDENTIFIES HIS SON THROUGH CERTAIN UNMISTAKABLE PHYSICAL CHARACTERISTICS.

THE AUTOPSY CONCLUDES THAT THE BOY MET HIS DEATH BY A FRACTURE OF THE SKULL CAUSED BY EXTERNAL VIOLENCE.

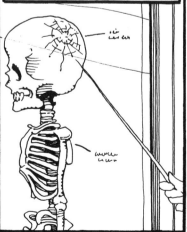

SPECULATION ARISES THAT THE CHILD WAS DROPPED ACCIDENTALLY AS IT WAS BEING CARRIED DOWN THE LADDER, PERHAPS IN A BAG OF SOME SORT...

THE THIRTY POUNDS OF EXTRA WEIGHT CAUSING THE FLIMSY LADDER TO BREAK AT ITS LEAST STABLE JUNCTURE.

PART FOUR
THE MANHUNT

THE SHOCKING NEWS SPREADS THROUGHOUT THE WORLD. THE CASE OF KIDNAPPING IS NOW ONE OF MURDER.

COL. LINDBERGH NOW RELINQUISHES HIS LEADING ROLE IN THE INVESTIGATION. HE AND HIS WIFE — NOW PREGNANT WITH THEIR SECOND CHILD — GO INTO DEEP SECLUSION.

THE MANHUNT IS NOW TAKEN UP IN EARNEST BY THE NEW JERSEY STATE POLICE, COMMANDED BY COL. H. NORMAN SCHWARZKOPF, ASSISTED BY LOCAL AGENCIES OF A SEVERAL-STATE AREA.

TUESDAY, MAY 17
UNDER PROMPTING BY THE POLICE, JOHN H. CURTIS CONFESSES THAT HIS ENTIRE SCENARIO WAS A HOAX.

HE WILL EVENTUALLY BE TRIED FOR FRAUD.

GASTON MEANS WILL ALSO BE PUT ON TRIAL FOR HIS DEVIOUS EXTORTION OF MONEY FROM MRS. EVALYN McLEAN.

THE LADY WILL SEE ONLY A FRACTION OF IT RETURNED TO HER.

THE UNFORTUNATE VIOLET SHARPE COMES TO A BAD END.

THURSDAY, JUNE 9
SHE IDENTIFIES A PHOTOGRAPH OF A TAXI-SERVICE OPERATOR NAMED ERNEST BRINKERT AS THE MAN WITH WHOM SHE WENT TO THE ROADHOUSE.

SHE THEN BECOMES HYSTERICAL AND REFUSES TO ANSWER ANY FURTHER QUESTIONS.

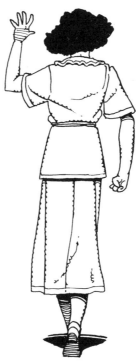

POLICE PLAN TO RETURN THE NEXT DAY, BUT BEFORE THEY CAN...

FRIDAY, JUNE 10
VIOLET SHARPE COMMITS SUICIDE BY SWALLOWING A MIXTURE OF WATER AND CYANIDE CHLORIDE, IN THE FORM OF A POWDERED SILVER POLISH.

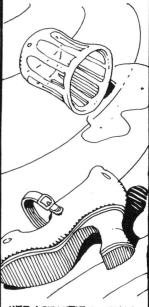

HER ACTIVITIES ON THE NIGHT OF THE KIDNAPPING ARE LATER FOUND TO HAVE BEEN PERFECTLY INNOCENT, LEAVING ANOTHER MYSTERY AMONG THE MANY IN THIS CASE.

DURING THE SUMMER OF 1932, THE LINDBERGHS LEAVE THE HOUSE AT HOPEWELL, NEVER TO RESIDE THERE AGAIN.

WEDNESDAY, JUNE 22. CONGRESS PASSES THE "LINDBERGH LAW," MAKING KIDNAPPING A FEDERAL CRIME — ALTHOUGH TOO LATE TO HELP IN THIS CASE.

TUESDAY, AUGUST 16. IN NEW YORK CITY, ANNE LINDBERGH GIVES BIRTH TO THEIR SECOND CHILD, A SON THEY NAME JON.

THE WRITTEN MESSAGES FROM THE KIDNAPPER — THIRTEEN IN ALL — HAVE BEEN PLACED UNDER THE SCRUTINY OF SEVERAL HANDWRITING EXPERTS...

INCLUDING PROF. ALBERT OSBORNE, CALLED THE DEAN OF AMERICAN FORENSIC GRAPHOLOGISTS.

THEIR CONSENSUS IS THAT THE NOTES WERE ALL WRITTEN BY THE SAME HAND. THE MISSPELLINGS AND GRAMMATICAL ANOMALIES ARE CONSISTENT THROUGHOUT.

THE WRITER IS MOST LIKELY GERMAN.

THE MESSAGES ARE ALSO STUDIED BY A NEW YORK PSYCHIATRIST, DR. DUDLEY SCHOENFELD.

HIS CONCLUSIONS:

THE KIDNAPPER IS A MAN WITH DELUSIONS OF OMNIPOTENCE, WHO NEVERTHELESS OCCUPIES A LOW STATION IN LIFE...

AND BLAMES OTHERS FOR HIS FAILURES AND INADEQUACIES.

THIS MAN FOCUSES ALL OF HIS ANGER AND FRUSTRATION ON COL. LINDBERGH, THE UNIVERSALLY ADORED HERO, AND SCHEMES TO OUTSMART AND HUMILIATE HIM.

SUCH A MAN WOULD WORK ALONE AND TAKE GREAT PERSONAL RISKS.

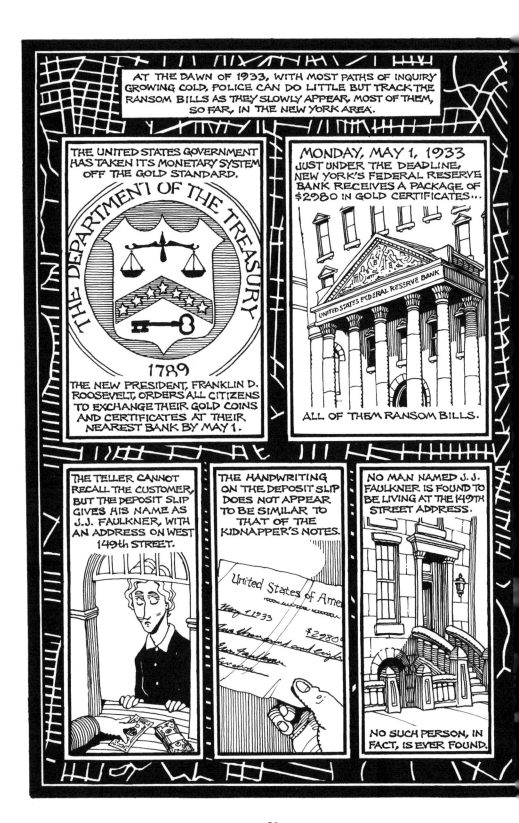

AT THE DAWN OF 1933, WITH MOST PATHS OF INQUIRY GROWING COLD, POLICE CAN DO LITTLE BUT TRACK THE RANSOM BILLS AS THEY SLOWLY APPEAR, MOST OF THEM, SO FAR, IN THE NEW YORK AREA.

THE UNITED STATES GOVERNMENT HAS TAKEN ITS MONETARY SYSTEM OFF THE GOLD STANDARD.

THE DEPARTMENT OF THE TREASURY

1789

THE NEW PRESIDENT, FRANKLIN D. ROOSEVELT, ORDERS ALL CITIZENS TO EXCHANGE THEIR GOLD COINS AND CERTIFICATES AT THEIR NEAREST BANK BY MAY 1.

MONDAY, MAY 1, 1933 JUST UNDER THE DEADLINE, NEW YORK'S FEDERAL RESERVE BANK RECEIVES A PACKAGE OF $2980 IN GOLD CERTIFICATES...

UNITED STATES FEDERAL RESERVE BANK

ALL OF THEM RANSOM BILLS.

THE TELLER CANNOT RECALL THE CUSTOMER, BUT THE DEPOSIT SLIP GIVES HIS NAME AS J.J. FAULKNER, WITH AN ADDRESS ON WEST 149th STREET.

THE HANDWRITING ON THE DEPOSIT SLIP DOES NOT APPEAR TO BE SIMILAR TO THAT OF THE KIDNAPPER'S NOTES.

United States of Ame

May 1 1933

$2980

NO MAN NAMED J.J. FAULKNER IS FOUND TO BE LIVING AT THE 149th STREET ADDRESS.

NO SUCH PERSON, IN FACT, IS EVER FOUND.

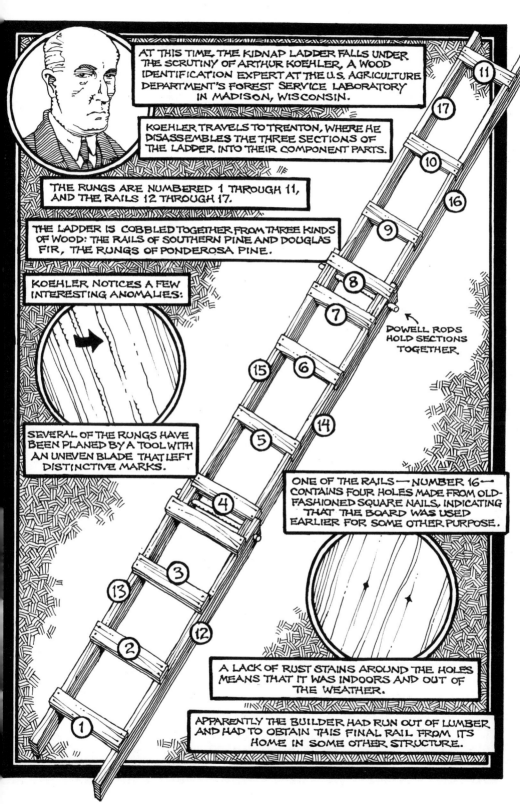

AT THIS TIME, THE KIDNAP LADDER FALLS UNDER THE SCRUTINY OF ARTHUR KOEHLER, A WOOD IDENTIFICATION EXPERT AT THE U.S. AGRICULTURE DEPARTMENT'S FOREST SERVICE LABORATORY IN MADISON, WISCONSIN.

KOEHLER TRAVELS TO TRENTON, WHERE HE DISASSEMBLES THE THREE SECTIONS OF THE LADDER INTO THEIR COMPONENT PARTS.

THE RUNGS ARE NUMBERED 1 THROUGH 11, AND THE RAILS 12 THROUGH 17.

THE LADDER IS COBBLED TOGETHER FROM THREE KINDS OF WOOD: THE RAILS OF SOUTHERN PINE AND DOUGLAS FIR, THE RUNGS OF PONDEROSA PINE.

KOEHLER NOTICES A FEW INTERESTING ANOMALIES:

DOWELL RODS HOLD SECTIONS TOGETHER

SEVERAL OF THE RUNGS HAVE BEEN PLANED BY A TOOL WITH AN UNEVEN BLADE THAT LEFT DISTINCTIVE MARKS.

ONE OF THE RAILS — NUMBER 16 — CONTAINS FOUR HOLES MADE FROM OLD-FASHIONED SQUARE NAILS, INDICATING THAT THE BOARD WAS USED EARLIER FOR SOME OTHER PURPOSE.

A LACK OF RUST STAINS AROUND THE HOLES MEANS THAT IT WAS INDOORS AND OUT OF THE WEATHER.

APPARENTLY THE BUILDER HAD RUN OUT OF LUMBER AND HAD TO OBTAIN THIS FINAL RAIL FROM ITS HOME IN SOME OTHER STRUCTURE.

IN THE SIDE-RAILS MADE OF SOUTHERN PINE, KOEHLER DISCERNS THE MARKINGS OF A DEFECTIVE BLADE IN THE PLANING PROCESS AT THE SAWMILL WHERE THE LUMBER ORIGINATED.

HE BEGINS A LABORIOUS INVESTIGATION INTO THE SOURCE OF THE PINE BOARDS.

AS A FIRST STEP, HE SENDS A FORM LETTER TO EVERY LUMBER MILL ON THE EASTERN SEABOARD, 1598 IN ALL.

TWENTY-FIVE MILLS RESPOND THAT, YES, THEY USE THE KIND OF PLANERS THAT KOEHLER DESCRIBES.

HE REQUESTS FROM THESE MILLS SMALL SAMPLES OF THE LUMBER RUN THROUGH THE PLANERS TWO YEARS AGO.

WOOD FROM A MILL IN SOUTH CAROLINA SHOWS REMARKABLE SIMILARITIES TO THE BOARDS IN THE LADDER.

KOEHLER TRAVELS TO THE MILL, AND, AFTER MUCH TESTING, CONCLUDES THAT THE LADDER'S RAILS WERE MILLED THERE AFTER SEPTEMBER, 1929.

HE THEN SPENDS SEVERAL MONTHS FOLLOWING EVERY SHIPMENT OF 1"x 4" SOUTHERN PINE BOARDS FROM THE MILL TO RETAILERS IN THE NORTHEAST.

ONE LUMBER YARD AFTER ANOTHER TELLS HIM THAT THEIR STOCK FROM THAT TIME PERIOD HAS SOLD OUT.

R & MILLWOR

AT LAST, THE TRAIL BRINGS HIM TO THE NATIONAL LUMBER AND MILLWORK CO. IN THE WILLIAMSBRIDGE SECTION OF THE BRONX.

SOME BOARDS FROM THAT TIME HAPPEN TO HAVE BEEN SAVED. KOEHLER DECLARES THEM TO BE THE SAME AS THOSE USED IN THE LADDER.

THE LUMBER YARD HAS NO RECORD OF WHO BOUGHT THE WOOD TWO YEARS AGO, SO HERE THE INVESTIGATION STALLS.

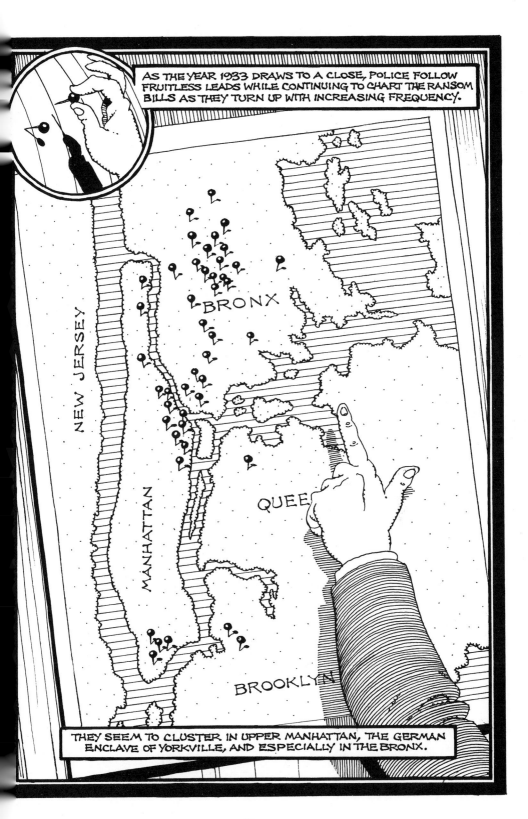

AS THE YEAR 1933 DRAWS TO A CLOSE, POLICE FOLLOW FRUITLESS LEADS WHILE CONTINUING TO CHART THE RANSOM BILLS AS THEY TURN UP WITH INCREASING FREQUENCY.

THEY SEEM TO CLUSTER IN UPPER MANHATTAN, THE GERMAN ENCLAVE OF YORKVILLE, AND ESPECIALLY IN THE BRONX.

SUNDAY, NOVEMBER 26
THE CASHIER AT A GREENWICH VILLAGE PICTURE HOUSE IS CONFRONTED BY AN UNUSUAL CUSTOMER.

IN A HEAVY ACCENT, HE ASKS FOR A SINGLE TICKET AND TOSSES HER A SMALL SQUARE OF PAPER.

IT IS A $5.00 BILL, TIGHTLY FOLDED INTO EIGHT SECTIONS.

IT WILL TURN OUT TO BE ONE OF THE RANSOM BILLS.

THE CASHIER CLEARLY REMEMBERS THE MAN'S FACE...

HIGH CHEEKBONES, FLAT CHEEKS, POINTED CHIN, AND VACANT BLUE EYES.

WELL INTO THE YEAR 1934, THE RANSOM MONEY—OFTEN AS MUCH AS $40 PER WEEK — CONTINUES TO APPEAR. NONE OF THE BILLS THUS FAR CAN BE TRACED TO ITS SOURCE.

SATURDAY, SEPTEMBER 15, 1934
THE BREAK COMES AT LAST...

AT A FILLING STATION AT 127TH ST. AND LEXINGTON AVE. IN UPPER MANHATTAN.

A MAN IN A BLUE DODGE PAYS FOR HIS GAS WITH A $10 GOLD CERTIFICATE.

SUSPICIOUS OF THE BILL, THE ATTENDANT RECORDS THE LICENSE NUMBER OF THE CAR AS IT LEAVES THE STATION.

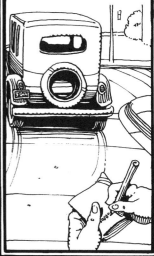

PART FIVE.
THE ACCUSED

WEDNESDAY, SEPTEMBER 19, 1934
NEW YORK POLICE HAVE TRACED THE OWNER OF THE CAR TO A
HOUSE AT 1279 E. 222ND STREET IN THE BRONX.

THE UPPER FLOOR IS THE HOME OF
RICHARD HAUPTMANN, AGE 35, A CARPENTER BY TRADE.

OFFICERS SURROUND THE HOUSE IN THE EARLY MORNING, WATCHING
FOR ANY MOVEMENT.

AT ABOUT 8:15 AM, A MAN EMERGES.

INSTEAD OF ARRESTING HIM ON THE SPOT, POLICE WATCH AS HE WALKS TO A GARAGE ACROSS THE ALLEY.

AND DRIVES OFF IN THE BLUE DODGE.

THE MAN IS STOPPED AS HE DRIVES DOWN PARK AVENUE IN THE FORDHAM SECTION OF THE BRONX.

WHAT IS THIS?

A SEARCH OF HIS PERSON YIELDS A $20 GOLD CERTIFICATE, FOLDED INTO EIGHT SECTIONS.

IT WILL TURN OUT TO BE ONE OF THE RANSOM BILLS.

POLICE BRING HAUPTMANN BACK TO HIS SECOND-FLOOR APARTMENT.

THERE, HE REJOINS HIS WIFE, ANNA, AND THEIR 1-YEAR-OLD SON MANFRED.

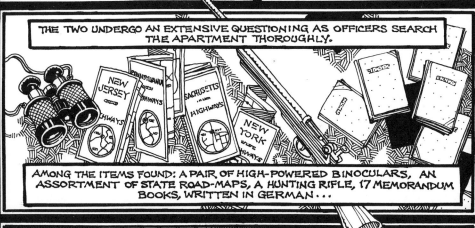

THE TWO UNDERGO AN EXTENSIVE QUESTIONING AS OFFICERS SEARCH THE APARTMENT THOROUGHLY.

AMONG THE ITEMS FOUND: A PAIR OF HIGH-POWERED BINOCULARS, AN ASSORTMENT OF STATE ROAD-MAPS, A HUNTING RIFLE, 17 MEMORANDUM BOOKS, WRITTEN IN GERMAN...

AND A STACK OF RAW SEAL-SKINS (THE MAN EXPLAINS THAT, AS A A SIDE-LINE, HE BUYS AND SELLS FURS).

IN THE AFTERNOON, HAUPTMANN IS BROUGHT DOWNTOWN TO THE NYPD'S 2ND PRECINCT STATION AT 130 GREENWICH STREET FOR A THOROUGH INTERROGATION.

THIS WILL INCLUDE A CERTAIN AMOUNT OF PHYSICAL "PERSUASION."

NEVERTHELESS, THE MAN FORCEFULLY DENIES HAVING HAD ANY PART IN EITHER THE KIDNAPPING OR THE EXTORTION OF THE RANSOM MONEY.

HIS FULL NAME IS:
BRUNO RICHARD HAUPTMANN.

HE IS AN IMMIGRANT FROM GERMANY AND SPEAKS WITH A HEAVY ACCENT.

HE PREFERS TO BE CALLED RICHARD OR DICK.

HE SUBMITS SAMPLES OF HIS HANDWRITING IN A TEST DEVISED BY ALBERT S. OSBORNE.

AMONG THOSE CALLED TO IDENTIFY HIM ARE...

CAB DRIVER JOSEPH PERRONE, WHO DELIVERED THE KIDNAPPER'S NOTE TO THE CONDON HOME ON MARCH 12, 1932.

CECILE M. BARR, THEATRE CASHIER, WHO RECEIVED THE FOLDED RANSOM BILL ON NOVEMBER 26, 1933.

THE SERVICE STATION ATTENDANT WHO COPIED HAUPTMANN'S LICENSE PLATE NUMBER ON SEPTEMBER 15, 1934.

AND, MOST CRUCIALLY, DR. JOHN F. CONDON.

ALL PICK HAUPTMANN READILY ENOUGH EXCEPT FOR THE EVER-ECCENTRIC CONDON. HE FEELS HE NEEDS MORE TIME.

HE SLOWLY SCRUTINIZES EACH MAN, THEN TALKS PRIVATELY WITH HAUPTMANN, INCLUDING A FEW SENTENCES OF GERMAN.

HE ASKS THE PRISONER TO READ SEVERAL PHRASES ALOUD.

IT IS TOO DANGEROUS!

HE WOULD SMACK ME UP!

TO THE EXASPERATION OF POLICE, CONDON REFUSES TO IDENTIFY THE MAN AT THIS PARTICULAR PLACE AND TIME.

HIS ROUNDABOUT PLOY, HE WILL LATER CLAIM, IS TO CONVINCE HAUPTMANN TO CONFESS HIS CRIME.

THURSDAY, SEPTEMBER 20
AT THE HAUPTMANN RESIDENCE, THE SEARCHERS HAVE BY NOW SHIFTED THEIR ATTENTION TO THE RAMSHACKLE WOODEN GARAGE ACROSS THE ALLEY.

INSIDE, THERE IS A CARPENTER'S WORK-BENCH.

THE TOOL SET IS MISSING A THREE-QUARTER-INCH CHISEL, THE SAME SIZE AS WAS FOUND AT THE LINDBERGH HOUSE.

BEHIND A BOARD NAILED ACROSS TWO UPRIGHTS ARE FOUND TWO PACKAGES OF $10 GOLD CERTIFICATES, ABOUT $1830, ALL OF THEM RANSOM BILLS.

ANOTHER BUNDLE OF BILLS IS FOUND IN A 1-GALLON SHELLAC CAN: TWELVE PACKAGES, ADDING UP TO $11,960.

OVER THE NEXT SEVERAL DAYS, THE GARAGE WILL BE SLOWLY DISMANTLED.

A FURTHER $840 WILL BE FOUND, FOR A TOTAL OF $14,600 — A MERE FRACTION OF THE FULL RANSOM PAYMENT.

AT THE PRECINCT HOUSE, AFTER NEARLY 24 HOURS OF "GRILLING," HAUPTMANN CONTINUES TO MAINTAIN HIS INNOCENCE.

HE HAS GIVEN THE POLICE HIS ALIBIS FOR THREE IMPORTANT DATES...

ON TUESDAY, MARCH 1, 1932, THE DAY OF THE KIDNAPPING, HE WAS IN MANHATTAN, SEARCHING FOR WORK AT VARIOUS BUILDING SITES.

AT 7:00 PM, HE MET HIS WIFE AT HER PLACE OF EMPLOYMENT, FREDERICK'S BAKERY IN THE BRONX.

THEY ATE DINNER THERE AND THEN WENT HOME TO BED.

ON SATURDAY, APRIL 2, 1932, THE NIGHT OF THE RANSOM PAYMENT, HE WAS AT HOME ENJOYING A MUSICAL EVENING WITH HIS FRIEND HANS KLOPPENBURG.

THEY GET TOGETHER ON THE FIRST SATURDAY OF EVERY MONTH TO PLAY AND SING THEIR FAVORITE GERMAN SONGS.

SUNDAY, NOVEMBER 26, 1933, THE NIGHT THE MYSTERIOUS PATRON TOSSED THE FOLDED BILL TO THE THEATRE CASHIER, HAPPENED TO HAVE BEEN HAUPTMANN'S BIRTHDAY.

HE CELEBRATED AT HOME WITH HIS WIFE AND A FEW FRIENDS.

HOW DID HAUPTMANN SUPPORT HIS FAMILY, HE IS ASKED, SINCE HE QUIT HIS JOB, IN APRIL OF 1932, AT THE MAJESTIC APARTMENTS IN MANHATTAN?

HOW DID HE AFFORD SUCH RECENT INDULGENCES AS A NEW VICTROLA AND A TRIP TO GERMANY FOR HIS WIFE?

THE PRISONER EXPLAINS THAT HE BEGAN TO INVEST IN THE STOCK MARKET AROUND THAT TIME...

AND HAD DONE SO WELL THAT THE FAMILY COULD LIVE DECENTLY ON THE EARNINGS.

HOW DID HAUPTMANN COME INTO POSSESSION OF SO MUCH OF THE LINDBERGH RANSOM MONEY?

FISCH

HE SAYS THAT HE FOUND IT AMONG SEVERAL BOXES OF PERSONAL ITEMS LEFT TO HIM BY HIS FRIEND AND BUSINESS PARTNER ISADOR FISCH.

HE AND FISCH ENGAGED IN SEVERAL VENTURES TOGETHER, INCLUDING THE FUR-IMPORTING ENTERPRISE.

BUT FISCH, SUFFERING FROM TUBERCULOSIS, RETURNED TO GERMANY IN DECEMBER OF 1933, AND DIED IN LIEPZIG ON MARCH 29, 1934.

ONE OF THE BOXES WAS STORED BY HAUPTMANN ON THE TOP SHELF OF A KITCHEN CLOSET...

UNTIL ONE DAY, DURING A HEAVY RAIN, A LEAK IN THE ROOF SOAKED THE CONTAINER.

INSIDE, HE WAS SHOCKED TO FIND STACKS AND STACKS OF CASH!

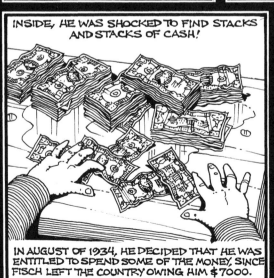

IN AUGUST OF 1934, HE DECIDED THAT HE WAS ENTITLED TO SPEND SOME OF THE MONEY, SINCE FISCH LEFT THE COUNTRY OWING HIM $7000.

DESPITE HIS DENIALS, THE PRISONER IS CHARGED THIS AFTERNOON WITH EXTORTION.

BUT COL. SCHWARZKOPF BELIEVES THAT THE STATE OF NEW JERSEY WILL BE ABLE TO NAB HIM FOR THE GREATER CRIME.

AS HAUPTMANN'S PAST LIFE IN GERMANY IS SLOWLY UNCOVERED, IT REFLECTS UPON HIM POORLY.

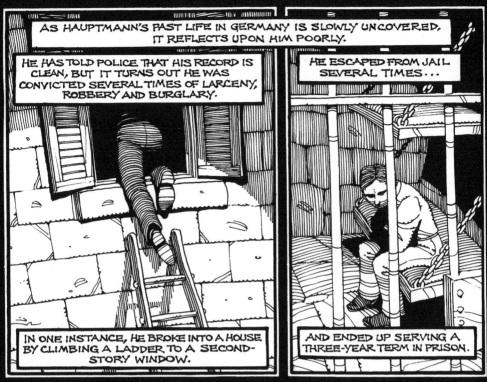

HE HAS TOLD POLICE THAT HIS RECORD IS CLEAN, BUT IT TURNS OUT HE WAS CONVICTED SEVERAL TIMES OF LARCENY, ROBBERY AND BURGLARY.

HE ESCAPED FROM JAIL SEVERAL TIMES...

IN ONE INSTANCE, HE BROKE INTO A HOUSE BY CLIMBING A LADDER TO A SECOND-STORY WINDOW.

AND ENDED UP SERVING A THREE-YEAR TERM IN PRISON.

HE MADE THREE ATTEMPTS TO FLEE TO AMERICA, FINALLY MAKING IT—AS A STOWAWAY—IN 1923.

HE SETTLED INTO NEW YORK'S GERMAN COMMUNITY AND HAS SINCE LIVED A SEEMINGLY ORDINARY LIFE.

ON OCTOBER 10, 1925, HE MARRIED ANNA SCHOEFFLER, AN IMMIGRANT LIKE HIMSELF. IN 1933, THEIR SON MANFRED WAS BORN.

MONDAY, SEPTEMBER 24

OFFICERS STILL SEARCHING THE HAUPTMANN HOME COME ACROSS A NEW PIECE OF EVIDENCE.

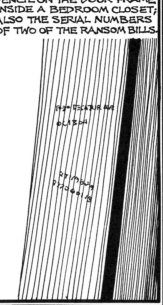

THE ADDRESS AND TELEPHONE NUMBER OF JOHN F. CONDON ARE FOUND WRITTEN IN PENCIL ON THE DOOR FRAME INSIDE A BEDROOM CLOSET; ALSO THE SERIAL NUMBERS OF TWO OF THE RANSOM BILLS.

HAUPTMANN RESPONDS THAT HE DOESN'T RECALL HAVING WRITTEN THE NUMBERS... BUT HE MIGHT HAVE, SINCE HE WAS FOLLOWING THE CASE AT THE TIME.

NYC POLICE
128221
9 | 2 | 34

WEDNESDAY, SEPTEMBER 26

HAUPTMANN IS INDICTED FOR EXTORTION BY A BRONX GRAND JURY. LATER IN THE DAY, OFFICERS OF THE NEW JERSEY STATE POLICE, WHILE SEARCHING THE ATTIC OF THE PRISONER'S HOME, FIND A PUZZLING DISCREPANCY

ONE OF THE FLOOR-BOARDS IS MISSING... APPARENTLY SAWN AWAY.

SEVERAL OFFICERS HAVE LOOKED HERE ALREADY, BUT NONE NOTICED THIS GAP IN THE FLOOR. IS IT SIGNIFICANT?

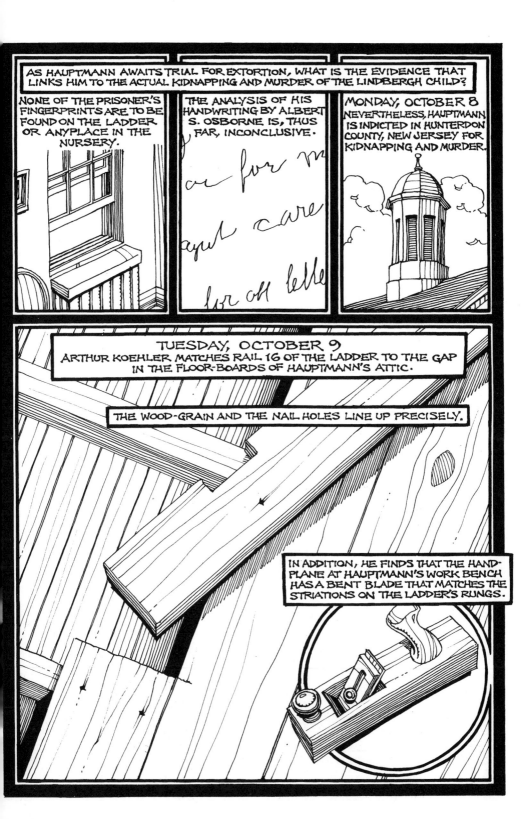

AS HAUPTMANN AWAITS TRIAL FOR EXTORTION, WHAT IS THE EVIDENCE THAT LINKS HIM TO THE ACTUAL KIDNAPPING AND MURDER OF THE LINDBERGH CHILD?

NONE OF THE PRISONER'S FINGERPRINTS ARE TO BE FOUND ON THE LADDER OR ANYPLACE IN THE NURSERY.

THE ANALYSIS OF HIS HANDWRITING BY ALBERT S. OSBORNE IS, THUS FAR, INCONCLUSIVE.

MONDAY, OCTOBER 8
NEVERTHELESS, HAUPTMANN IS INDICTED IN HUNTERDON COUNTY, NEW JERSEY FOR KIDNAPPING AND MURDER.

TUESDAY, OCTOBER 9
ARTHUR KOEHLER MATCHES RAIL 16 OF THE LADDER TO THE GAP IN THE FLOOR-BOARDS OF HAUPTMANN'S ATTIC.

THE WOOD-GRAIN AND THE NAIL HOLES LINE UP PRECISELY.

IN ADDITION, HE FINDS THAT THE HAND-PLANE AT HAUPTMANN'S WORK BENCH HAS A BENT BLADE THAT MATCHES THE STRIATIONS ON THE LADDER'S RUNGS.

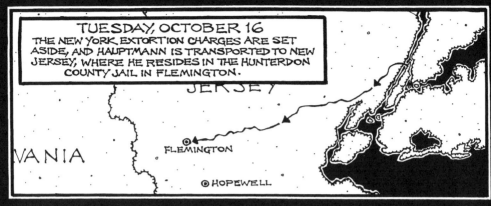

TUESDAY, OCTOBER 16
THE NEW YORK EXTORTION CHARGES ARE SET ASIDE, AND HAUPTMANN IS TRANSPORTED TO NEW JERSEY, WHERE HE RESIDES IN THE HUNTERDON COUNTY JAIL IN FLEMINGTON.

JERSEY

VANIA

FLEMINGTON

HOPEWELL

FRIDAY, NOVEMBER 2
HE ACQUIRES A HIGH-PROFILE DEFENCE ATTORNEY IN THE PERSON OF THE FLAMBOYANT VETERAN EDWARD J. REILLY OF BROOKLYN...

WHOSE SERVICES ARE PAID FOR BY WILLIAM RANDOLPH HEARST'S NEW YORK JOURNAL — IN EXCHANGE FOR MRS. HAUPTMANN'S EXCLUSIVE STORY.

REILLY WILL BE ASSISTED BY THREE NEW YORK ATTORNEYS: C. LLOYD FISHER, FREDERICK A. POPE AND EGBERT ROSECRANS.

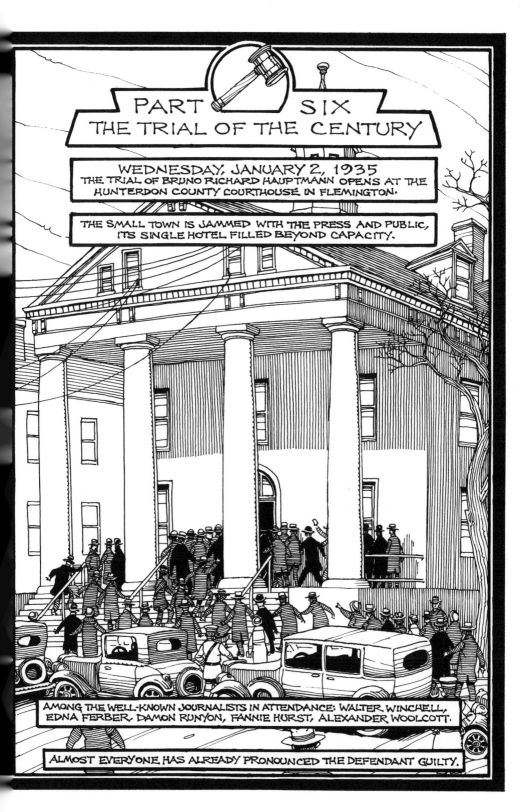

PART SIX
THE TRIAL OF THE CENTURY

WEDNESDAY, JANUARY 2, 1935
THE TRIAL OF BRUNO RICHARD HAUPTMANN OPENS AT THE
HUNTERDON COUNTY COURTHOUSE IN FLEMINGTON.

THE SMALL TOWN IS JAMMED WITH THE PRESS AND PUBLIC,
ITS SINGLE HOTEL FILLED BEYOND CAPACITY.

AMONG THE WELL-KNOWN JOURNALISTS IN ATTENDANCE: WALTER WINCHELL,
EDNA FERBER, DAMON RUNYON, FANNIE HURST, ALEXANDER WOOLCOTT.

ALMOST EVERYONE HAS ALREADY PRONOUNCED THE DEFENDANT GUILTY.

THE COURTROOM IS CALLED TO ORDER BY JUDGE THOMAS TRENCHARD.

THE PROSECUTION TEAM IS HEADED BY NEW JERSEY'S ATTORNEY GENERAL, DAVID T. WILENTZ.

THE FIRST DAY IS TAKEN UP BY THE SELECTION OF A JURY.

A PANEL OF EIGHT MEN AND FOUR WOMEN—SOLID CITIZENS ALL—IS AGREED UPON.

IN AN UNPRECEDENTED DECISION, NEWSREEL CAMERAS WILL BE ALLOWED TO RECORD CERTAIN PORTIONS OF THE PROCEEDINGS.

SINCE THERE WERE NO EYEWITNESSES TO THE CRIME, THE PROSECUTION PLANS TO INTRODUCE A MOUNTAIN OF CIRCUMSTANTIAL EVIDENCE.

WILENTZ PRESENTS HIS CASE IN TWO PHASES: THE FIRST IS TO ESTABLISH THAT HAUPTMANN HAD OBTAINED AND SPENT THE RANSOM MONEY.

AMONG THE FIRST TO TAKE THE WITNESS STAND IS CHARLES A. LINDBERGH HIMSELF.

HE INSISTS THAT IT WAS THE DEFENDANT'S VOICE HE HEARD FROM THE CEMETERY ON THE NIGHT THE RANSOM WAS PAID.

JOHN F. CONDON ENDURES TWO DAYS ON THE STAND.

HE CANNOT BE SHAKEN FROM HIS IDENTIFICATION OF HAUPTMANN AS THE MAN CALLING HIMSELF "JOHN," WITH WHOM HE TALKED PERSONALLY ON TWO SEPARATE OCCASIONS.

THE THEATRE CASHIER CECILE BARR...

ESTABLISHES THAT THE DEFENDANT WAS IN POSSESSION OF RANSOM BILLS LONG BEFORE HE CLAIMED TO HAVE RECOVERED THEM FROM HIS CLOSET.

THE CAB DRIVER JOSEPH PERRONE...

POINTS TO HAUPTMANN AS HAVING HANDED HIM AN ENVELOPE TO DELIVER TO THE CONDON HOME ON MARCH 12, 1932.

THE HANDWRITING CASE IS SECURED BY ALBERT S. OSBORNE AND SEVEN OTHER DOCUMENT EXPERTS.

ALL CONFIRM THAT HAUPTMANN ALONE WROTE THE KIDNAPPING NOTES.

THE PROSECUTION'S SECOND PHASE IS AN ATTEMPT TO PLACE HAUPTMANN IN THE VICINITY OF THE LINDBERGH HOUSE ON MARCH 1, 1933. THREE MEN TESTIFY AS TO HAVING SEEN HIM ON THAT DAY.

MILLARD WHITED AND AMANDUS HOCHMUTH, WHO LIVE NEAR THE LINDBERGH ESTATE...

AND CHARLES ROSSITER, A TRAVELLING SALESMAN WHO HAPPENED TO BE IN THE AREA.

THE RECOLLECTIONS OF ALL THREE ARE PUT INTO DOUBT BY THE DEFENSE. HOCHMUTH, IN FACT, IS NEARLY BLIND FROM CATARACTS.

THE FINAL WITNESS FOR THE STATE IS THE WOOD EXPERT ARTHUR KOEHLER. HE SHOWS THE JURY HOW RAIL 16 OF THE KIDNAP LADDER LINES UP WITH THE FLOOR-BOARD IN THE DEFENDANT'S ATTIC.

AND HE DEMONSTRATES HOW THE PLANE FROM HAUPTMANN'S WORK-BENCH MATCHES THE TOOL-MARKS ON THE LADDER'S RUNGS.

WITH THIS, THE PROSECUTION RESTS ITS CASE.

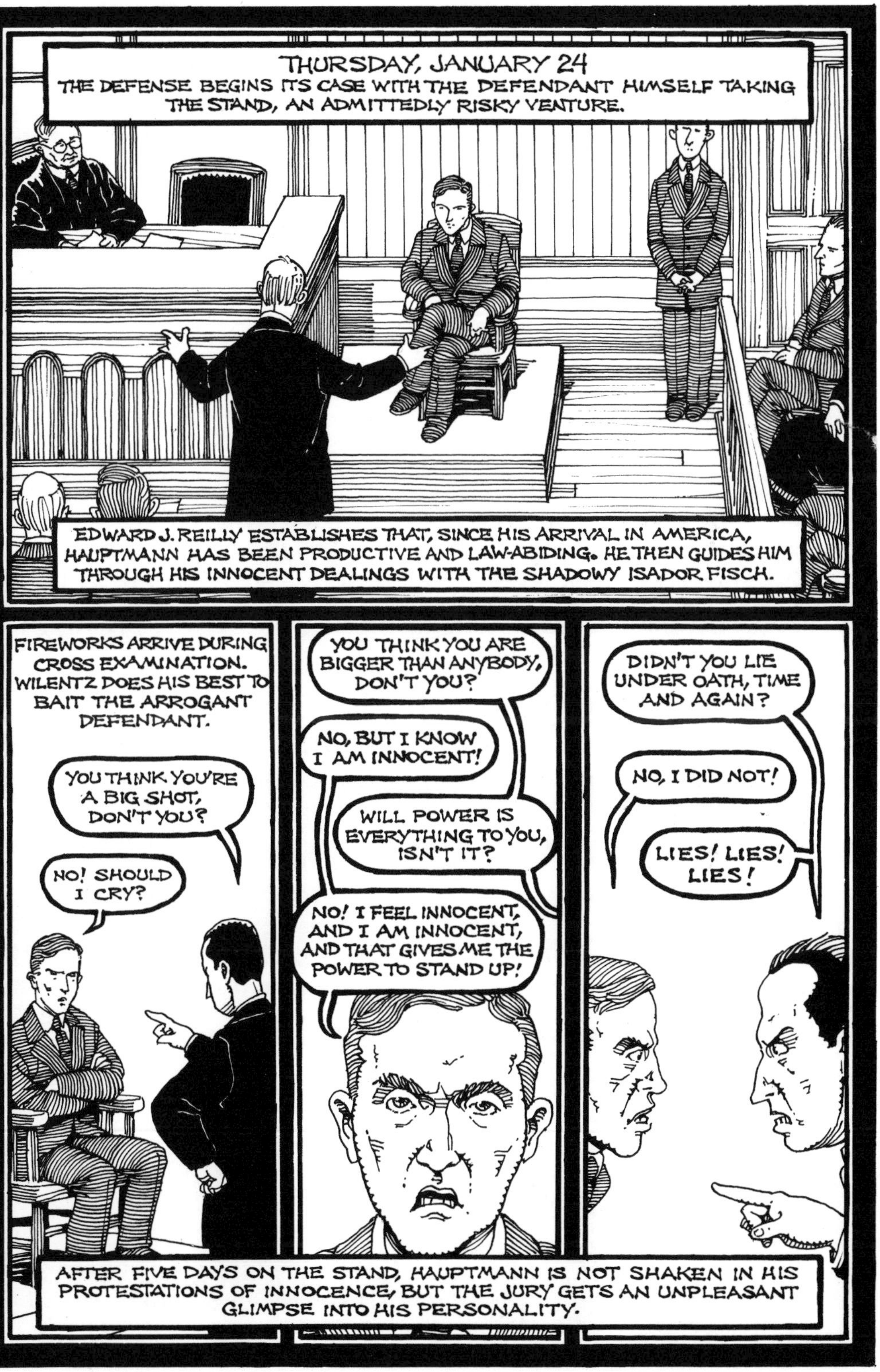
THURSDAY, JANUARY 24
THE DEFENSE BEGINS ITS CASE WITH THE DEFENDANT HIMSELF TAKING THE STAND, AN ADMITTEDLY RISKY VENTURE.
EDWARD J. REILLY ESTABLISHES THAT, SINCE HIS ARRIVAL IN AMERICA, HAUPTMANN HAS BEEN PRODUCTIVE AND LAW-ABIDING. HE THEN GUIDES HIM THROUGH HIS INNOCENT DEALINGS WITH THE SHADOWY ISADOR FISCH.
FIREWORKS ARRIVE DURING CROSS EXAMINATION. WILENTZ DOES HIS BEST TO BAIT THE ARROGANT DEFENDANT.
YOU THINK YOU'RE A BIG SHOT, DON'T YOU?
NO! SHOULD I CRY?
YOU THINK YOU ARE BIGGER THAN ANYBODY, DON'T YOU?
NO, BUT I KNOW I AM INNOCENT!
WILL POWER IS EVERYTHING TO YOU, ISN'T IT?
NO! I FEEL INNOCENT, AND I AM INNOCENT, AND THAT GIVES ME THE POWER TO STAND UP!
DIDN'T YOU LIE UNDER OATH, TIME AND AGAIN?
NO, I DID NOT!
LIES! LIES! LIES!
AFTER FIVE DAYS ON THE STAND, HAUPTMANN IS NOT SHAKEN IN HIS PROTESTATIONS OF INNOCENCE, BUT THE JURY GETS AN UNPLEASANT GLIMPSE INTO HIS PERSONALITY.

THE REMAINDER OF THE DEFENSE CASE CONSISTS OF SEVERAL DUBIOUS WITNESSES AND "EXPERTS."

THESE INCLUDE CHRISTIAN AND KATIE FREDERICKSON, PROPRIETORS OF FREDERICKSON'S BAKERY, AND CERTAIN OF THEIR CUSTOMERS, WHO CLAIM TO HAVE SEEN HAUPTMANN THERE ON THE EVENING OF MARCH 1, 1932.

TWO GENTLEMEN, BEN LUPICA AND WILLIAM BOLMER, WERE IN THE VICINITY OF THE LINDBERGH ESTATE ON THAT NIGHT.

THEY EACH DESCRIBE HAVING SEEN A MYSTERIOUS CAR, CONTAINING A MAKESHIFT-LOOKING LADDER, AND DRIVEN BY A MAN WHO LOOKED NOTHING LIKE THE DEFENDANT.

FRIENDS OF THE HAUPTMANNS, INCLUDING HANS KLOPPENBURG AND GRETA HENKEL TESTIFY AS TO THE DEFENDANT'S GOOD CHARACTER...

AND REPORT HAVING SEEN ISADOR FISCH IN HIS COMPANY UPON SEVERAL OCCASIONS.

THE DEFENSE CALLS ITS SINGLE HANDWRITING AUTHORITY IN THE PERSON OF JOHN TRENDLEY.

HE INSISTS THAT HAUPTMANN DID NOT WRITE THE RANSOM NOTES, DISPLAYING SEVERAL POINTS OF DISSIMILARITY.

LIKEWISE A LONE "WOOD EXPERT," CHARLES DE BISSCHOP, A LUMBERMAN, NURSERYMAN AND GENERAL CONTRACTOR.

HE MAINTAINS THAT RAIL 16 DOES NOT MATCH THE FLOOR-BOARD IN HAUPTMANN'S ATTIC.

MONDAY, FEBRUARY 11

EDWARD J. REILLY SUMS UP FOR THE DEFENSE.

THE CASE IS TOO PERFECT FROM THE PROSECUTION'S POINT OF VIEW. THERE ISN'T A MAN IN THE WORLD WITH BRAINS ENOUGH TO PLAN THIS KIDNAPPING ALONE, AND NOT WITH A GANG, AND THEN SIT DOWN AND MAKE THE FOOLISH MISTAKE OF RIPPING A BOARD OUT OF HIS ATTIC AND LEAVING THE OTHER HALF OF IT THERE.

I BELIEVE RICHARD HAUPTMANN IS ABSOLUTELY INNOCENT OF MURDER.

TUESDAY, FEBRUARY 12

DAVID WILENTZ, IN HIS SUMMATION FOR THE STATE, ABANDONS ANY PRETENSE OF THE VICTIM HAVING DIED ACCIDENTALLY.

WHAT TYPE OF MAN WOULD MURDER THE CHILD OF CHARLES AND ANNE LINDBERGH? HE WOULDN'T BE AN AMERICAN. NO AMERICAN GANGSTER EVER SANK TO THE LEVEL OF KILLING BABIES.

NO, IT HAD TO BE A FELLOW WHO HAD ICE WATER, NOT BLOOD, IN HIS VEINS. IT HAD TO BE A FELLOW WHO HAD A PECULIAR MENTAL MAKE-UP, WHO THOUGHT HE WAS BIGGER THAN LINDY. AN EGOMANIAC, WHO THOUGHT HE WAS OMNIPOTENT.

WEDNESDAY, FEBRUARY 13

THE TRIAL COMES TO AN END, AFTER 29 SESSIONS, 162 WITNESSES AND 381 EXHIBITS, AS THE JURY RETIRES TO CONSIDER ITS DECISION.

11½ HOURS LATER, THEY RETURN WITH THE NOT-UNEXPECTED VERDICT OF...

GUILTY.

WITH NO RECOMMENDATION OF MERCY — MEANING THAT THE JUDGE IS REQUIRED BY LAW TO SENTENCE THE DEFENDANT TO DEATH.

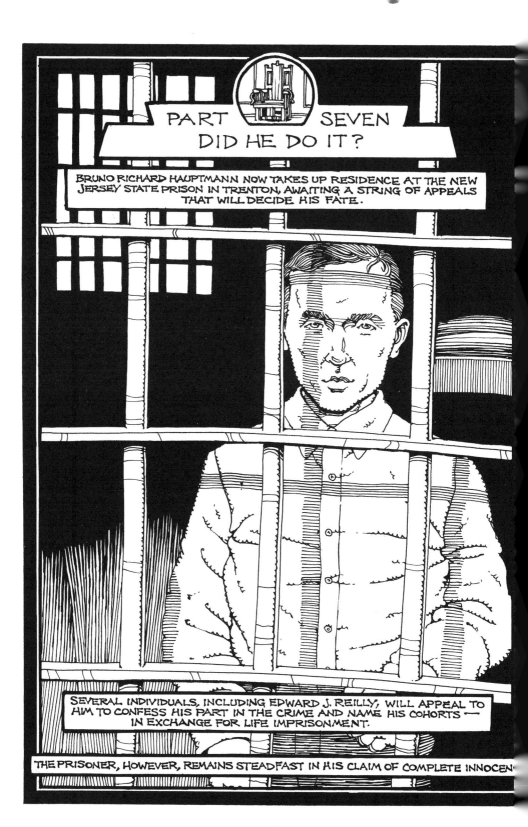

PART SEVEN
DID HE DO IT?

BRUNO RICHARD HAUPTMANN NOW TAKES UP RESIDENCE AT THE NEW JERSEY STATE PRISON IN TRENTON, AWAITING A STRING OF APPEALS THAT WILL DECIDE HIS FATE.

SEVERAL INDIVIDUALS, INCLUDING EDWARD J. REILLY, WILL APPEAL TO HIM TO CONFESS HIS PART IN THE CRIME AND NAME HIS COHORTS — IN EXCHANGE FOR LIFE IMPRISONMENT.

THE PRISONER, HOWEVER, REMAINS STEADFAST IN HIS CLAIM OF COMPLETE INNOCEN

OF THE DEFENSE TEAM, ONLY C. LLOYD FISHER REMAINS LOYAL TO THE CONVICTED MAN. HE PREPARES A BRIEF CITING INSTANCES OF PROSECUTORIAL MISCONDUCT.

DONE BY THE PROSECUTION AND HINDER THE DEFENSE.
1. DEFENSE WAS DENIED AN UP-TO-THE MINUTE COPY OF THE TRIAL TRANSCRIPT.
2. DEFENSE WAS NOT GIVEN ADEQUATE OPPORTUNITY TO EXAMINE THE RANSOM NOTES AND OTHER HANDWRITING EXHIBITS.
3. DEFENSE COUNSEL WAS DENIED PRIVATE CONFERENCE WITH THE DEFENDANT.
4. (a) DEFENSE WAS DENIED ACCESS TO THE HAUPTMANN HOME.
   (b) DEFENSE WAS DENIED ACCESS TO THE LINDBERGH HOUSE AND GROUNDS.
5. CROWDING THE PROSECUTION TABLE WITH INFLUENTIAL AND WELL-KNOWN THE STATE'S CASE

THE NEW JERSEY COURT OF APPEALS, HOWEVER, DENIES HIS PETITION, AND THE U.S. SUPREME COURT DECLINES TO REVIEW THE CASE.

HAUPTMANN'S CAUSE IS TAKEN UP BY NEW JERSEY'S NEW GOVERNOR, HAROLD HOFFMAN, WHO PUBLICLY STATES HIS BELIEF THAT THE LINDBERGH CASE IS STILL NOT SOLVED.

SUNDAY, JANUARY 12, 1936
HE GRANTS THE PRISONER A 30-DAY REPRIEVE AND ORDERS THE STATE POLICE TO RE-OPEN THE CASE.

ELLIS PARKER, SENIOR DETECTIVE OF BURLINGTON COUNTY, AND THE STATE'S MOST FAMOUS CRIME-BUSTER, SHARES THE GOVERNOR'S DOUBTS ABOUT HAUPTMANN'S GUILT.

PARKER'S THEORY IS THAT THE REMAINS FOUND IN THE WOODS WERE ERRONEOUSLY IDENTIFIED AND THAT THE LINDBERGH CHILD IS STILL ALIVE ...

AND IN THE HANDS OF THE ACTUAL KIDNAPPER, A DISBARRED TRENTON ATTORNEY AND EX-CONVICT NAMED PAUL H. WENDEL.

WEDNESDAY, FEBRUARY 13
PARKER AND A GROUP OF OTHERS ABDUCT WENDEL AND BEAT A CONFESSION OUT OF HIM.

BUT UPON HIS RELEASE SEVERAL WEEKS LATER, WENDEL RETRACTS THE CONFESSION, AND PARKER WILL LATER, IRONICALLY, BE TRIED FOR KIDNAPPING.

SPECULATION CONTINUES AMONG THE PUBLIC AND THE PRESS AS TO WHETHER HAUPTMANN WAS THE SOLE PERPETRATOR OF THE "CRIME OF THE CENTURY"... OR WAS HE PART OF A LARGER GANG — PERHAPS WITH THE AID OF SOMEONE WITHIN THE LINDBERGH HOUSEHOLD... OR IS HE AN INNOCENT MAN "FRAMED" BY THE AUTHORITIES?

THESE ARE THE IMPORTANT LINGERING QUESTIONS —

HOW WOULD HAUPTMANN HAVE KNOWN THAT THE LINDBERGHS HAD DECIDED TO LENGTHEN THEIR STAY AT THE HOPEWELL HOUSE THROUGH MARCH 1, 1932, INSTEAD OF RETURNING TO THE MORROW ESTATE, AS WAS THEIR ROUTINE?

MORE THAN HALF OF THE RANSOM PAYMENT HAS NEVER BEEN RECOVERED. COULD HAUPTMANN HAVE SPENT IT ALL? OR IS IT IN THE HANDS OF OTHERS? (AFTER HIS ARREST, THE BILLS STOPPED TURNING UP.)

ISADOR FISCH HAS PROVED TO BE A QUESTIONABLE CHARACTER WHO COULD VERY WELL HAVE BEEN IN THE BUSINESS OF "LAUNDERING" ILLEGALLY-OBTAINED CASH. DID HAUPTMANN RECEIVE THE MONEY QUITE INNOCENTLY AMONG THE POSSESSIONS HE LEFT BEHIND?

WHAT WAS THE ORIGIN OF THE "ITALIAN" VOICE HEARD IN THE BACKGROUND BY JOHN F. CONDON DURING HIS TELEPHONE CONVERSATION WITH "JOHN?" (ONE ANSWER: SINCE HAUPTMANN HAD NO TELEPHONE AT HIS HOME, HE MIGHT HAVE MADE THE CALL FROM AN ITALIAN RESTAURANT IN THE NEIGHBORHOOD.)

WHO WAS THE MYSTERIOUS "J. J. FAULKNER," WHO EXCHANGED $2980 OF RANSOM MONEY IN MAY OF 1933? THE HANDWRITING ON THE DEPOSIT SLIP HAS NEVER BEEN POSITIVELY LINKED TO HAUPTMANN.

WHO CONSTRUCTED THE KIDNAP LADDER? MANY HAVE DEEMED IT TOO PRIMITIVE AND SLAPDASH TO HAVE BEEN BUILT BY AN EXPERIENCED CARPENTER LIKE HAUPTMANN.

WHY WERE NONE OF HAUPTMANN'S FINGERPRINTS FOUND ON THE LADDER OR ANYPLACE IN THE NURSERY? INDEED, WHY WERE NO PRINTS FROM ANYBODY, SAVE THE CHILD HIMSELF, FOUND IN THE BABY'S ROOM?

IF SO, IT IS THE PRODUCT OF A MASSIVE POLICE CONSPIRACY, PERPETRATED BY MANY OFFICERS OF COMPETING AGENCIES...

OR COULD A SMALL CABAL HAVE MANAGED IT ALL?

REGARDING RAIL 16 OF THE LADDER: CERTAIN WITNESSES CLAIM TO HAVE SEEN NO NAIL HOLES IN THE WOOD WHEN IT WAS FIRST RECOVERED.

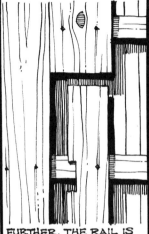

FURTHER, THE RAIL IS CONSIDERABLY SHORTER AND NARROWER THAN THE PLANKS IN HAUPTMANN'S ATTIC.

WOULD IT NOT HAVE BEEN EASIER FOR A KIDNAPPER TO PURCHASE THE CORRECT-SIZED BOARD, RATHER THAN TO LABORIOUSLY PRY ONE FROM THE ATTIC, CUT AND PLANE IT TO FIT?

WAS THIS CRUCIAL PIECE OF EVIDENCE MANUFACTURED WHEN NOTHING ELSE EMERGED TO PLACE THE DEFENDANT AT THE CRIME SCENE?

REGARDING THE ADDRESS AND TELEPHONE NUMBER OF JOHN F. CONDON, FOUND INSIDE A CLOSET DOOR-FRAME AT HAUPTMANN'S HOUSE...

HE AT FIRST ADMITTED THAT HE "COULD HAVE" WRITTEN IT, BUT LATER DENIED IT.

IT IS LATER CLAIMED TO HAVE BEEN PUT THERE BY AN UNSCRUPULOUS NEW YORK JOURNALIST — AS A PRANK THAT WENT AWRY...

AT LEAST THAT IS HOW THE MAN HIMSELF TELLS THE STORY.

THERE IS LITTLE DOUBT THAT HAUPTMANN RECEIVED BRUTAL TREATMENT AT THE HANDS OF THE NEW YORK AND NEW JERSEY POLICE...

AND THAT HIS TRIAL WAS TAINTED BY MISCONDUCT ON THE PART OF THE STATE.

77

IF HAUPTMANN DID NOT DO IT, WHO DID?	
THE MOST PERSISTENT THEORY POINTS TO A GANG OF PROFESSIONAL CRIMINALS, WORKING WITH THE "INSIDE" HELP OF A MEMBER OF THE LINDBERGH OR MORROW HOUSEHOLD STAFF...  SUCH AS VIOLET SHARPE... THE WHATELEYS... OR BETTY GOW, IN LEAGUE WITH HER NORWEGIAN SWEETHEART HENRY "RED" JOHNSEN.	IN THIS SCENARIO, THE LADDER IS PLACED AS MISDIRECTION...  AS THE KIDNAPPER IS SIMPLY HANDED THE SLEEPING CHILD BY THE INSIDE ACCOMPLICE.

LATER THEORIES WILL PROPOSE MORE UNLIKELY CULPRITS ... SUCH AS COL. LINDBERGH HIMSELF!

THE AVIATOR DROPS THE CHILD ACCIDENTALLY DURING ONE OF THE PRACTICAL JOKES OF WHICH HE IS SAID TO BE FOND.

THE CHILD IS BURIED IN THE WOODS, AND THE ENTIRE KIDNAPPING STORY IS MANUFACTURED BY LINDBERGH AND BRECKINRIDGE...

WHO PLANT A LADDER NEAR THE HOUSE AND SCRAWL A "RANSOM" NOTE.

TO THEIR MINDS, WITH NO FURTHER WORD FROM AN ABDUCTOR, THE INCIDENT WOULD EVENTUALLY BLOW OVER.

BUT AN ENTERPRISING CRIMINAL SEES A COPY OF THE NOTE AND INITIATES AN EXTORTION SCHEME BY FORGING OTHERS IN THE SAME HANDWRITING.

A VARIATION OF THIS THEORY HAS THE CHILD KILLED — ACCIDENTALLY OR DELIBERATELY — BY ANNE LINDBERGH'S UNBALANCED OLDER SISTER ELISABETH.

NONE OF THESE SCENARIOS, HOWEVER, ACCOUNTS FOR THE LADDER: WHERE DID IT COME FROM?

OBVIOUSLY HOME-MADE, BUT NOBODY HAS EVER COME FORWARD CLAIMING TO HAVE BUILT IT.

IN ANY CASE, WHY WOULD THE PUBLICITY-SHY LINDBERGH CONCOCT A FICTION THAT WOULD BRING HIM MAXIMUM PUBLIC EXPOSURE?

AN ADJUNCT TO THE THEORIES CITED ABOVE MAINTAINS THAT THE LINDBERGH CHILD IS ALIVE YET.

THE REMAINS WERE, AFTER ALL, TOO DECOMPOSED TO PERMIT POSITIVE IDENTIFICATION.

THEY WERE EITHER THOSE OF A BOY RUN AWAY FROM A NEARBY ORPHANS' ASYLUM...

OR AN ANONYMOUS CORPSE PLACED BY GANGSTERS TO TAKE THE "HEAT" OFF OF THEM.

BETTY GOW "IDENTIFIES" THE BODY BECAUSE SHE IS PART OF THE PLOT...

THE LONE EAGLE FROM HIS DESIRE TO END THE SEARCH AND CLOSE THE CASE.

THE CHILD COULD HAVE FALLEN INTO THE HANDS OF A "BABY BROKER"...

THE RANSOM MONEY USED TO SET THE BOY UP WITH A FAMILY FAR AWAY, WHERE HE WILL GROW TO MANHOOD WITH NO IDEA OF HIS ORIGIN.

IF, AS THE WEIGHT OF THE EVIDENCE SUGGESTS, HAUPTMANN IS THE SOLE PERPETRATOR — HOW DID HE DO IT?

AS HE STATES IN THE RANSOM NOTES, THE PLAN HAS BEEN IN THE WORKS FOR ONE YEAR.

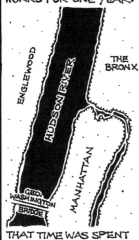

THE BRONX

ENGLEWOOD

HUDSON RIVER

MANHATTAN

GEO. WASHINGTON BRIDGE

THAT TIME WAS SPENT SCRUTINIZING THE MORROW ESTATE IN ENGLEWOOD, JUST ACROSS THE HUDSON RIVER FROM THE BRONX.

HE GETS TO KNOW THE COMINGS AND GOINGS OF THE FAMILY,

THE 3-PART LADDER, WHEN EXTENDED TO ITS FULL LENGTH, REACHES TO THE SECOND-STORY WINDOW OF THE BABY'S NURSERY.

ON THE EVENING OF MARCH 1, 1932, HAVING HEARD THAT COL. LINDBERGH WILL BE IN NEW YORK ALL EVENING, HE DRIVES TO ENGLEWOOD...

FULLY INTENDING TO WAIT INTO THE NIGHT TO MAKE HIS MOVE.

ALONG THE WAY, HOWEVER, HE CATCHES A STRAY BIT OF GOSSIP, PERHAPS FROM AN EMPLOYEE OF THE HOUSE: THE LINDBERGHS ARE STILL AT HOPEWELL.

BUT NOW HE CANNOT BACK AWAY — HE HAS WORKED HIMSELF INTO A FEVER. TONIGHT HAS TO BE THE NIGHT!

SO HE DRIVES THE 50 MILES TO THE HOPEWELL ESTATE (WHICH HE HAS NO DOUBT VISITED BEFORE)

AND HERE HE SEIZES THE MOMENT.

DOES HE INTEND TO KILL THE CHILD? IF NOT, WHERE WOULD HE KEEP IT? NO ANSWER HAS YET ARISEN.

IN ANY CASE, THE MAN'S ARROGANCE WILL PREVENT HIM FROM EVER CONFESSING TO THE CRIME.

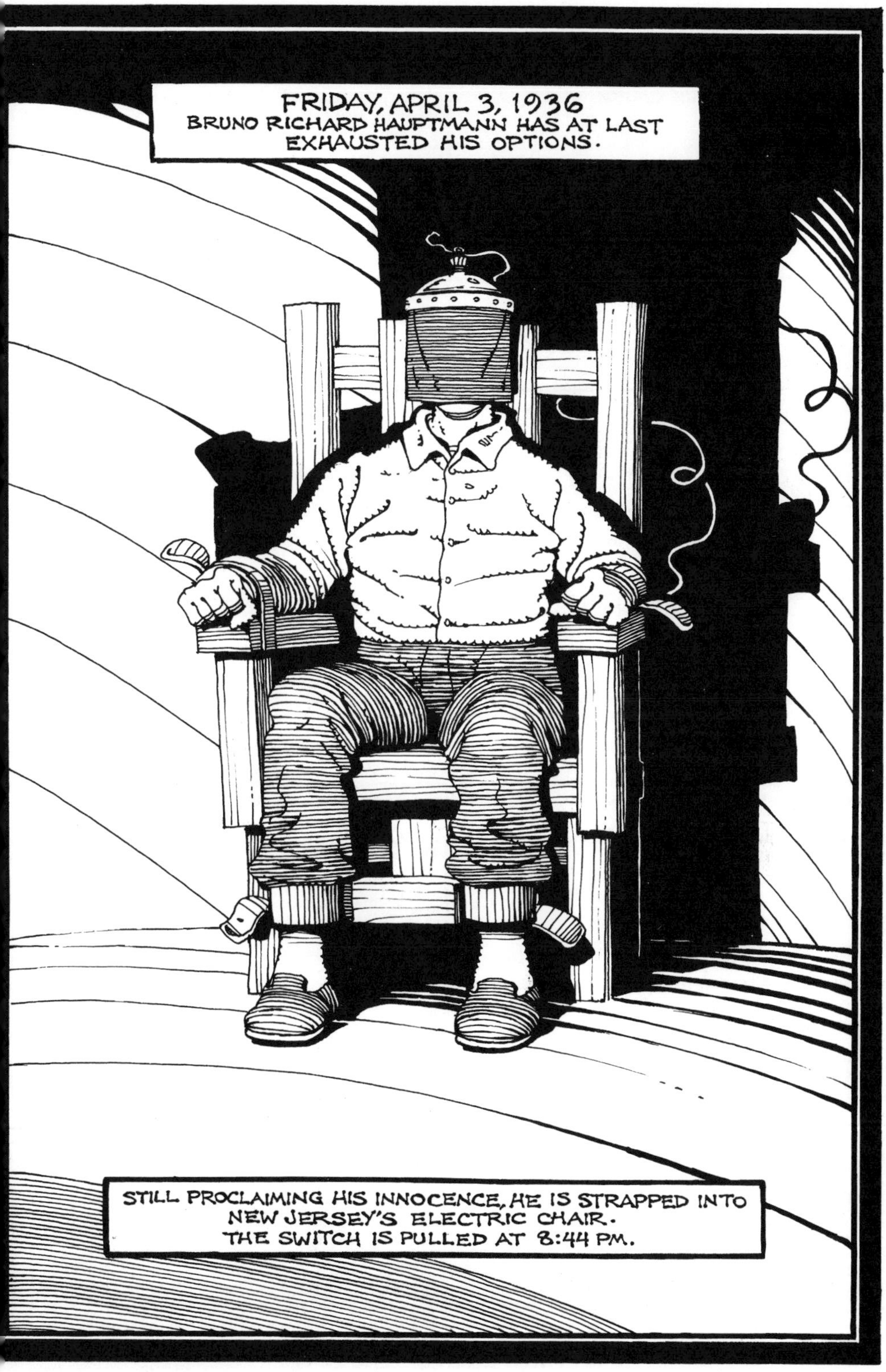
FRIDAY, APRIL 3, 1936
BRUNO RICHARD HAUPTMANN HAS AT LAST EXHAUSTED HIS OPTIONS.
STILL PROCLAIMING HIS INNOCENCE, HE IS STRAPPED INTO NEW JERSEY'S ELECTRIC CHAIR.
THE SWITCH IS PULLED AT 8:44 PM.

OVER THE YEARS, HAUPTMANN'S LOYAL WIDOW ANNA PROVES QUITE STEADFAST IN KEEPING HIS CAUSE ALIVE.

SHE TWICE SUES THE STATE OF NEW JERSEY: IN 1981 FOR HAVING WRONGFULLY EXECUTED HER HUSBAND, AND IN 1986 FOR HAVING FRAMED HIM FOR MURDER.

BOTH SUITS ARE DISMISSED. HER APPEAL TO THE U.S. SUPREME COURT IS LIKEWISE REJECTED.

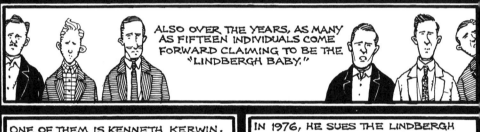

ALSO OVER THE YEARS, AS MANY AS FIFTEEN INDIVIDUALS COME FORWARD CLAIMING TO BE THE "LINDBERGH BABY."

ONE OF THEM IS KENNETH KERWIN.

IN THE 1960s, HE CONFRONTS COL. LINDBERGH IN DARIEN, CONNECTICUT AND MUST BE TAKEN AWAY BY POLICE.

IN 1976, HE SUES THE LINDBERGH ESTATE FOR HIS RIGHTFUL INHERITANCE.

BUT HIS CLAIM, AND THOSE OF THE OTHERS, IS PROVED FALSE THROUGH FINGERPRINTS AND SIMPLE BLOOD TESTS.

DR. JOHN F. CONDON RELATES HIS ADVENTURES ON THE LINDBERGH CASE IN A 1936 ACCOUNT SERIALIZED IN LIBERTY MAGAZINE.

HE DIES IN 1945 AT AGE 85.

OTHERS WHO WRITE OF THEIR ASSOCIATION WITH THE CASE INCLUDE —

- NEW JERSEY GOVERNOR HAROLD HOFFMAN
- DEFENSE ATTORNEY C. LLOYD FISHER
- MRS. EVALYN WALSH McLEAN
- KIDNAP VICTIM PAUL H. WENDEL
- FINGERPRINT EXPERT ALBERT S. OSBORNE
- ANNE MORROW LINDBERGH, IN TWO VOLUMES OF HER LETTERS AND JOURNALS

Liberty 5¢

WANTED

JAFSIE TELLS ALL!

HOUR OF GOLD HOUR OF LEAD

ANNE MORROW LINDBERGH

AFTER THE TRIAL, CHARLES LINDBERGH MOVES WITH HIS WIFE AND SON TO ENGLAND.

HE AND ANNE WILL PRODUCE FOUR MORE OFFSPRING.

THE LONE EAGLE NEVER SPEAKS OF THE KIDNAPPING FOR THE REMAINDER OF HIS LIFE. HE DIES ON AUGUST 25, 1974 AT AGE 72...

AND IS BURIED ON THE HAWAIIAN ISLAND OF MAUI.

HIS WIDOW, AGE 94, DIES IN 2001.

ANNA HAUPTMANN, STILL MAINTAINING HER HUSBAND'S INNOCENCE, DIES IN 1994, AT AGE 95.

AS WITH HER HUSBAND, HER REMAINS ARE CREMATED, THE ASHES SCATTERED IN AN UNDISCLOSED LOCATION.

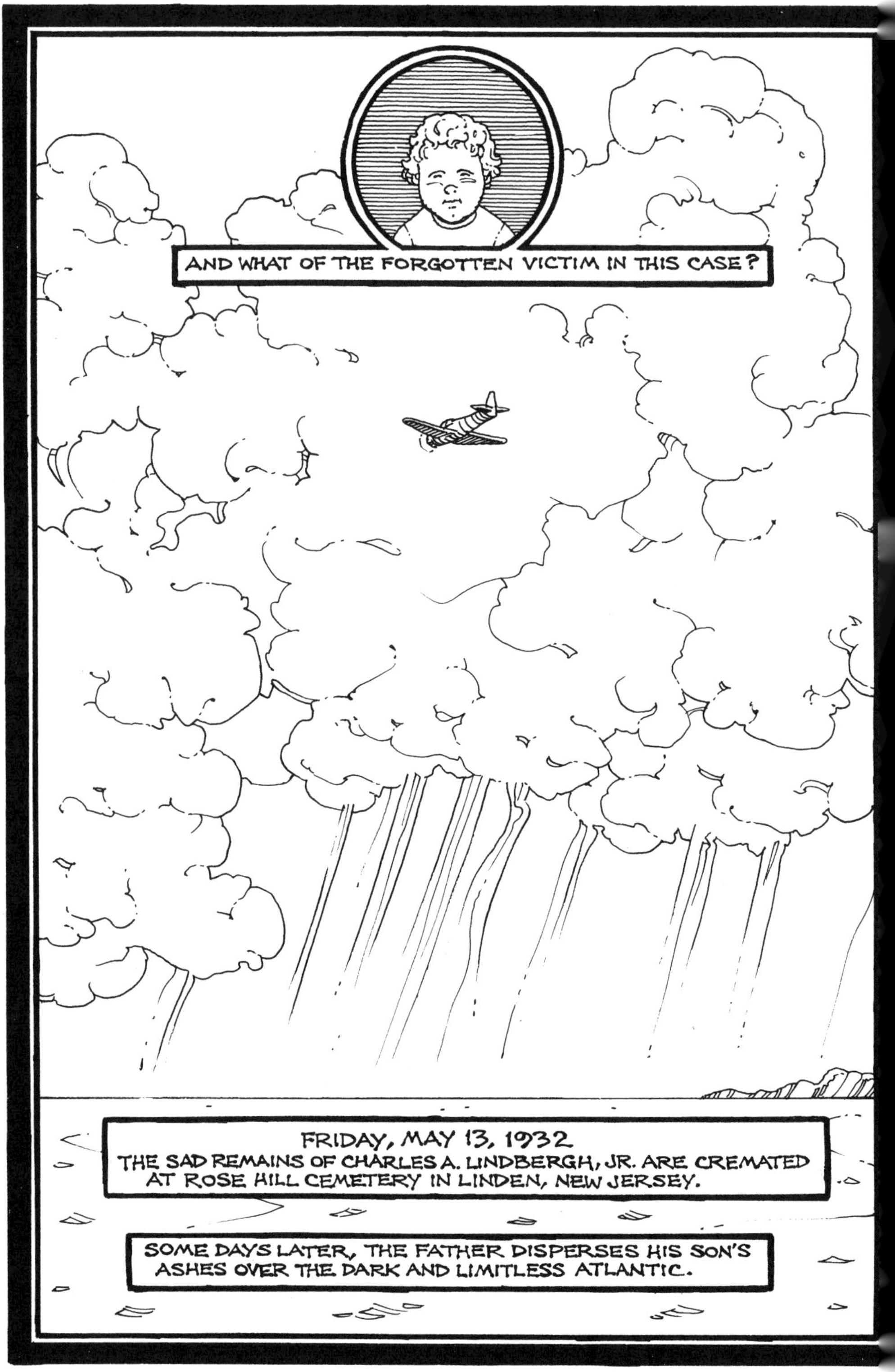
AND WHAT OF THE FORGOTTEN VICTIM IN THIS CASE?
FRIDAY, MAY 13, 1932
THE SAD REMAINS OF CHARLES A. LINDBERGH, JR. ARE CREMATED AT ROSE HILL CEMETERY IN LINDEN, NEW JERSEY.
SOME DAYS LATER, THE FATHER DISPERSES HIS SON'S ASHES OVER THE DARK AND LIMITLESS ATLANTIC.

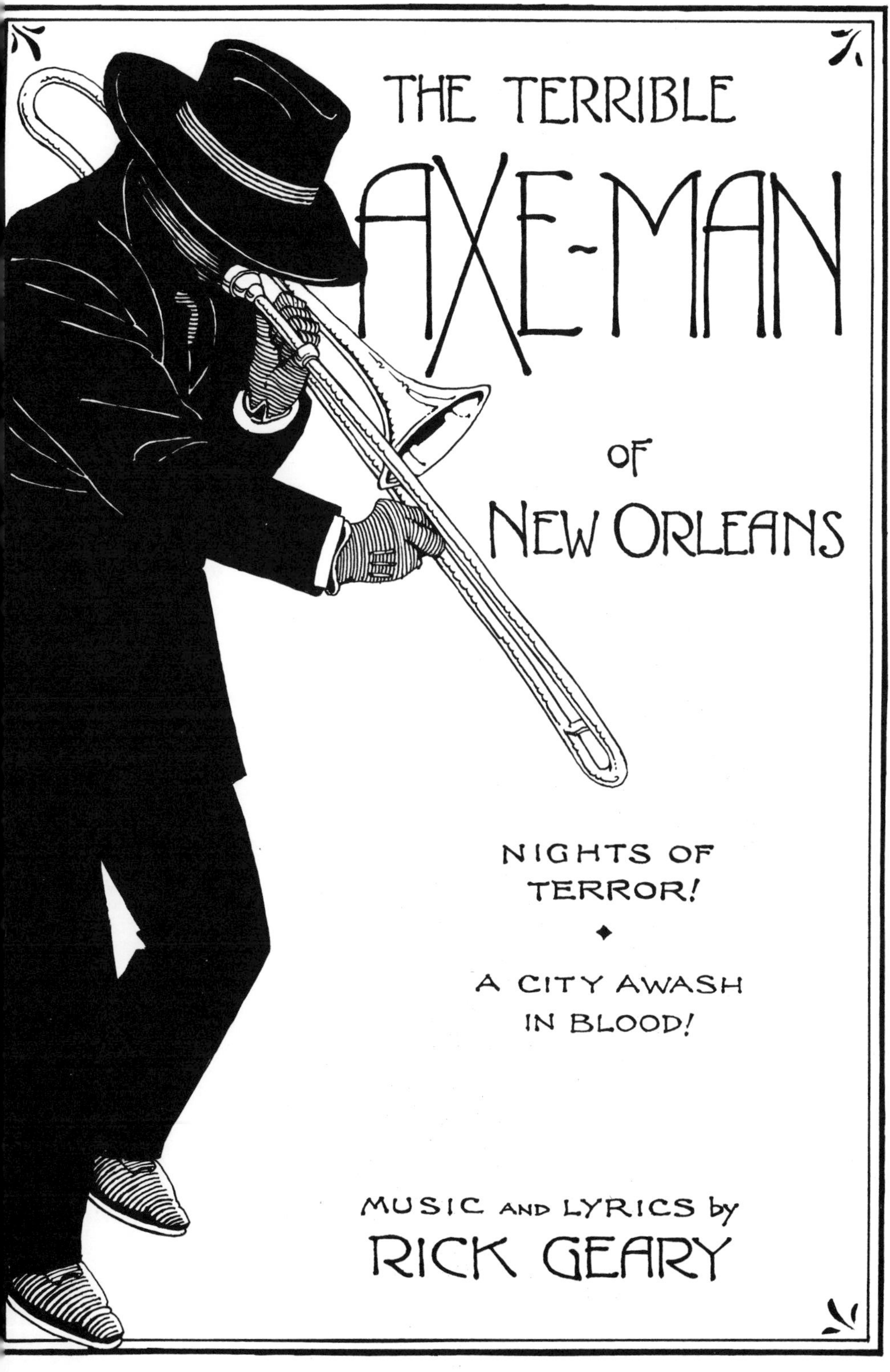
THE TERRIBLE
AXE-MAN
OF
NEW ORLEANS
NIGHTS OF TERROR!
A CITY AWASH IN BLOOD!
MUSIC AND LYRICS by
RICK GEARY

THE TERRIBLE AXE-MAN OF NEW ORLEANS

BIBLIOGRAPHY

Arthur, Stanley Clisby, *Old New Orleans*. (Gretna LA, Pelican Publishing Co., 1995)

New Orleans. (London, Dorling Kindersley Limited, 2005)

Purvis, James, "The Axeman of New Orleans," reprinted in *The Mammoth Book of Murder*, Richard Glyn Jones, ed. (New York, Carroll & Graf Publishers, Inc, 1989)

Saxon, Lyle, Edward Dreyer and Robert Tallant, *Gumbo Ya Ya; Folk Tales of Louisiana*. (Gretna LA, Pelican Publishing Co., 1987)

Schechter, Harold, *The Serial Killer Files*. (New York, Ballantine Books, 2004)

Times-Picayune (New Orleans LA), selected issues, Friday, May 24, 1918-Tuesday, October 28, 1919.

Special thanks to Mark Rosenbohm and Stacey Salamone

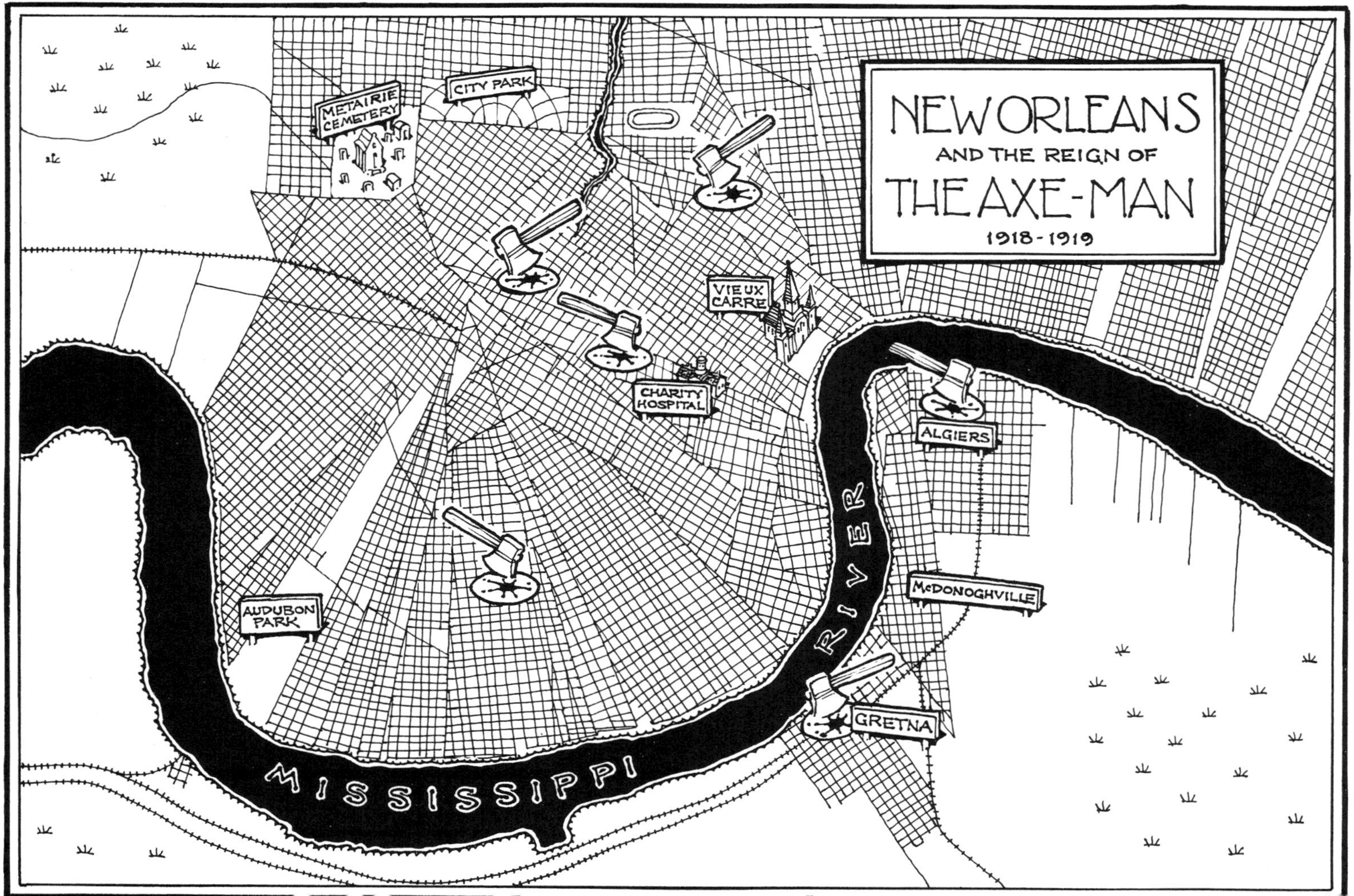
NEW ORLEANS
AND THE REIGN OF
THE AXE-MAN
1918-1919
CITY PARK
METAIRIE CEMETERY
VIEUX CARRE
CHARITY HOSPITAL
ALGIERS
AUDUBON PARK
McDONOGHVILLE
GRETNA
MISSISSIPPI RIVER

PART I

THE CRESCENT CITY
1918

THE CITY OF NEW ORLEANS WAS BORN FROM THE SWAMPY WILDERNESS ...

AT A SPOT WHERE, FOR UNCOUNTED CENTURIES, NATIVE HUNTERS FOUND A PORTAGE BETWEEN THE GREAT RIVER ("MISI SIPI") AND THE BIG LAKE ("OKWATA") TO THE NORTH.

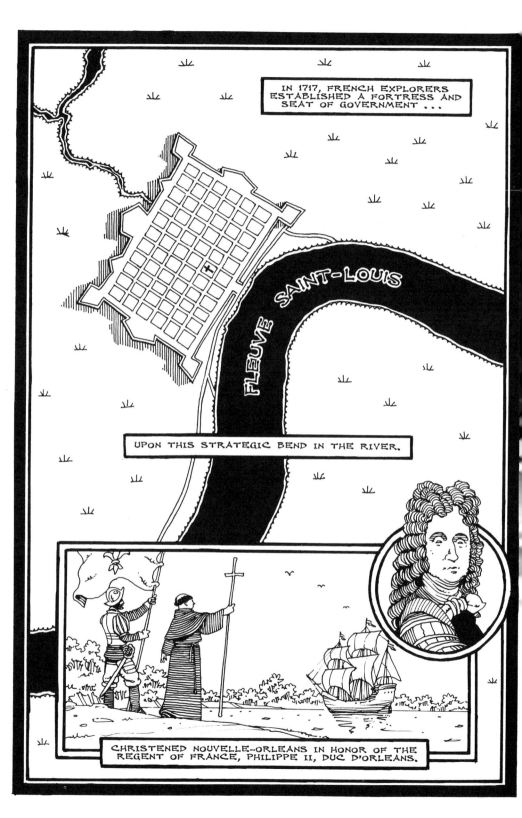

IN 1717, FRENCH EXPLORERS ESTABLISHED A FORTRESS AND SEAT OF GOVERNMENT ...

FLEUVE SAINT-LOUIS

UPON THIS STRATEGIC BEND IN THE RIVER.

CHRISTENED NOUVELLE-ORLEANS IN HONOR OF THE REGENT OF FRANCE, PHILIPPE II, DUC D'ORLEANS.

IN 1763, FOLLOWING ITS DEFEAT BY THE BRITISH IN THE SEVEN YEARS' WAR, FRANCE WAS COMPELLED TO RELINQUISH MOST OF ITS HOLDINGS IN NORTH AMERICA.

THESE INCLUDED THE TERRITORY OF LOUISIANA AND THE CITY OF NEW ORLEANS, WHICH WERE HANDED OVER TO SPAIN.

MUCH OF THE CITY'S DISTINCTIVE ARCHITECTURE IS THE PRODUCT OF ITS 40 YEARS AS A SPANISH COLONY.

IN 1802, NAPOLEON RETOOK LOUISIANA...

LOUISIANA PURCHASE

ONLY TO SELL IT THE VERY NEXT YEAR TO THE RAPIDLY-EXPANDING UNITED STATES OF AMERICA.

NEW ORLEANS WAS NOW AN AMERICAN CITY, BUT OF A DECIDEDLY EUROPEAN FLAVOR.

AN AMERICAN, UPON VISITING, WOULD IN FACT FIND HIMSELF IN FOREIGN TERRITORY.

THE FRENCH COLONIAL SETTLERS, KNOWN AS "CREOLES," RETAINED THEIR UNIQUE IDENTITY ...

AS DID THOSE LATER FRENCH EMIGRES, WHO CALLED THEMSELVES "ACADIANS," DRIVEN FROM NOVA SCOTIA BY THE BRITISH IN THE MID-1700S.

THEY SETTLED THROUGHOUT THE REGION AND CAME TO BE KNOWN AS "CAJUNS."

AS A PORT OPEN TO THE WORLD, THE CITY BECAME HOME TO IMMIGRANTS OF EVERY NATION.

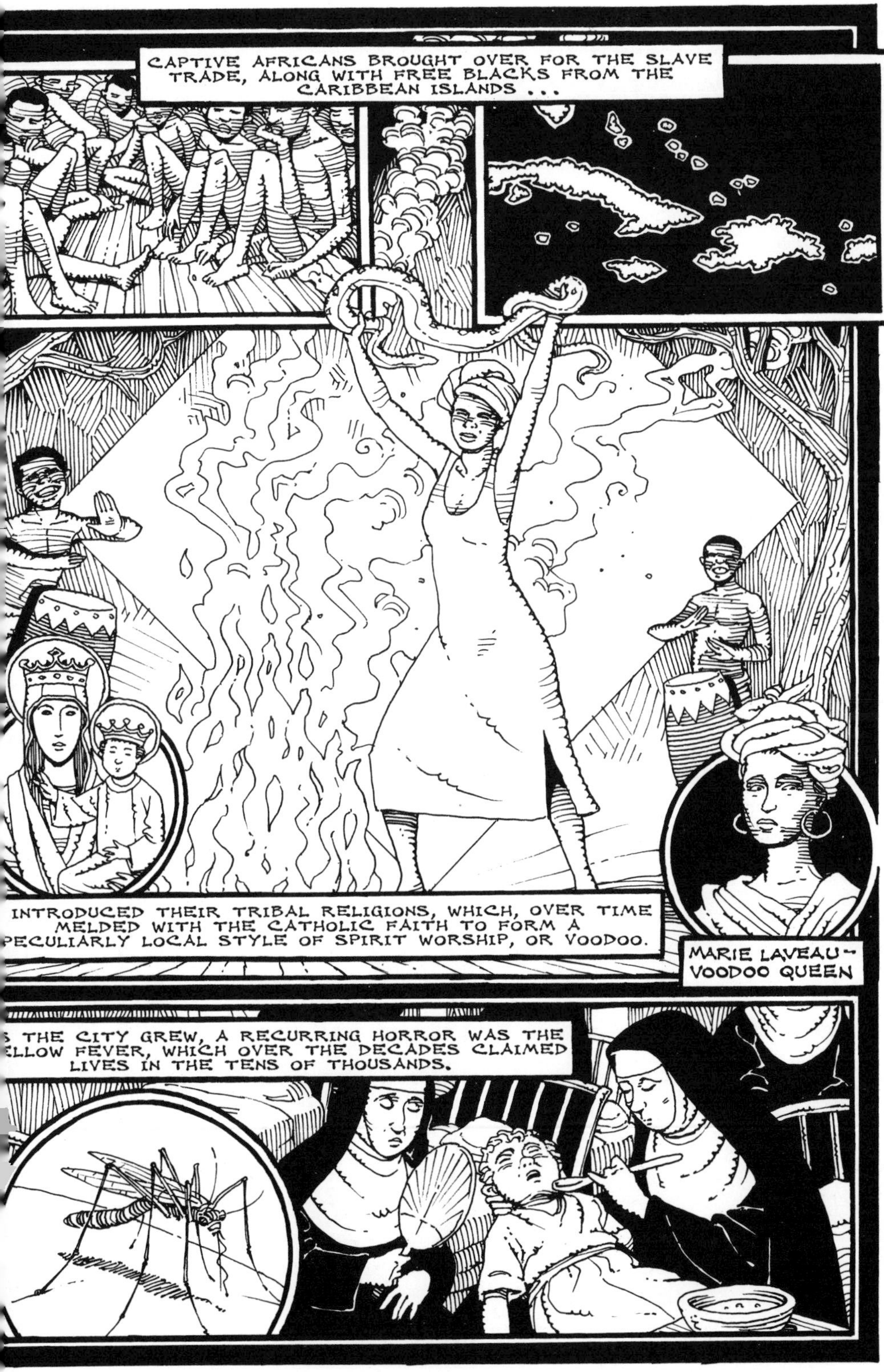
CAPTIVE AFRICANS BROUGHT OVER FOR THE SLAVE TRADE, ALONG WITH FREE BLACKS FROM THE CARIBBEAN ISLANDS ...
INTRODUCED THEIR TRIBAL RELIGIONS, WHICH, OVER TIME MELDED WITH THE CATHOLIC FAITH TO FORM A PECULIARLY LOCAL STYLE OF SPIRIT WORSHIP, OR VOODOO.
MARIE LAVEAU - VOODOO QUEEN
S THE CITY GREW, A RECURRING HORROR WAS THE ELLOW FEVER, WHICH OVER THE DECADES CLAIMED LIVES IN THE TENS OF THOUSANDS.

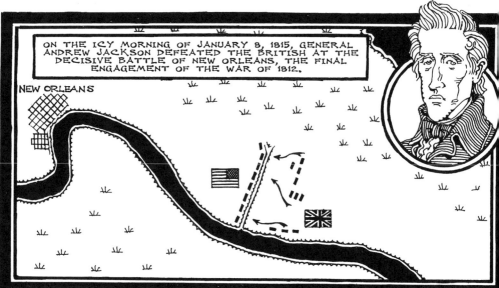

ON THE ICY MORNING OF JANUARY 8, 1815, GENERAL ANDREW JACKSON DEFEATED THE BRITISH AT THE DECISIVE BATTLE OF NEW ORLEANS, THE FINAL ENGAGEMENT OF THE WAR OF 1812.

NEW ORLEANS

THE ENSUING YEARS SAW THE CITY GROW AND PROSPER ASTONISHINGLY

THE COTTON CAPITAL OF THE WORLD!

NATCHEZ

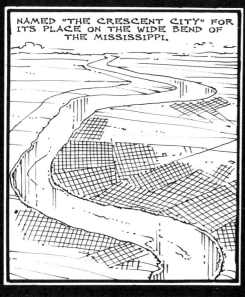

NAMED "THE CRESCENT CITY" FOR ITS PLACE ON THE WIDE BEND OF THE MISSISSIPPI.

BY THE EVE OF THE CIVIL WAR, IT WAS ONE OF THE MOST IMPORTANT STRATEGIC POINTS IN THE ENTIRE NATION.

EARLY ON, HOWEVER, THE UNION SECURED NEW ORLEANS AND OCCUPIED IT FOR THE REMAINDER OF THE CONFLICT.

THE CELEBRATION OF "MARDI GRAS" (FAT TUESDAY) HAS BEEN AN OFFICIAL TRADITION IN THE CITY SINCE 1838, ONE THAT GREW OVER THE YEARS INTO A GIANT PARTY FOR THE NATION ...

AND SYMBOLIC OF NEW ORLEANS AS THE CENTER FOR CAREFREE GOOD TIMES ...

REFLECTED IN ITS SEVERAL NICKNAMES:

"THE BIG EASY"

"THE CITY THAT CARE FORGOT"

"CITY OF FESTIVALS"

"PARIS OF THE SOUTH"

"CITY OF MYSTERY"

THE CITY HAS LIKEWISE PUT ITS STAMP UPON THE MUSICAL STYLES THAT EMERGED OVER TWO CENTURIES ...

BEGINNING IN "CONGO SQUARE," WHERE SLAVES GATHERED ON SUNDAYS FOR MUSIC AND DANCING ...

MANY STREAMS FLOWED INTO A VAST RIVER:

THE EMERGENCE OF LOCAL MARCHING BANDS ...

THE SONGS FROM THE COTTON AND CANE FIELDS OF THE DELTA THAT CAME TO BE KNOWN AS THE "BLUES."

THE "RAGGED" TEMPOS OF MUSICIANS IN THE BORDELLOS OF THE STORYVILLE DISTRICT.

THESE STRAINS MELDED TO CREATE A NEW STYLE, BASED UPON IMPROVISATION, AND CALLED, ORIGINALLY, "JASS."

THE LOCAL VARIETY CAME TO BE CALLED "DIXIELAND."

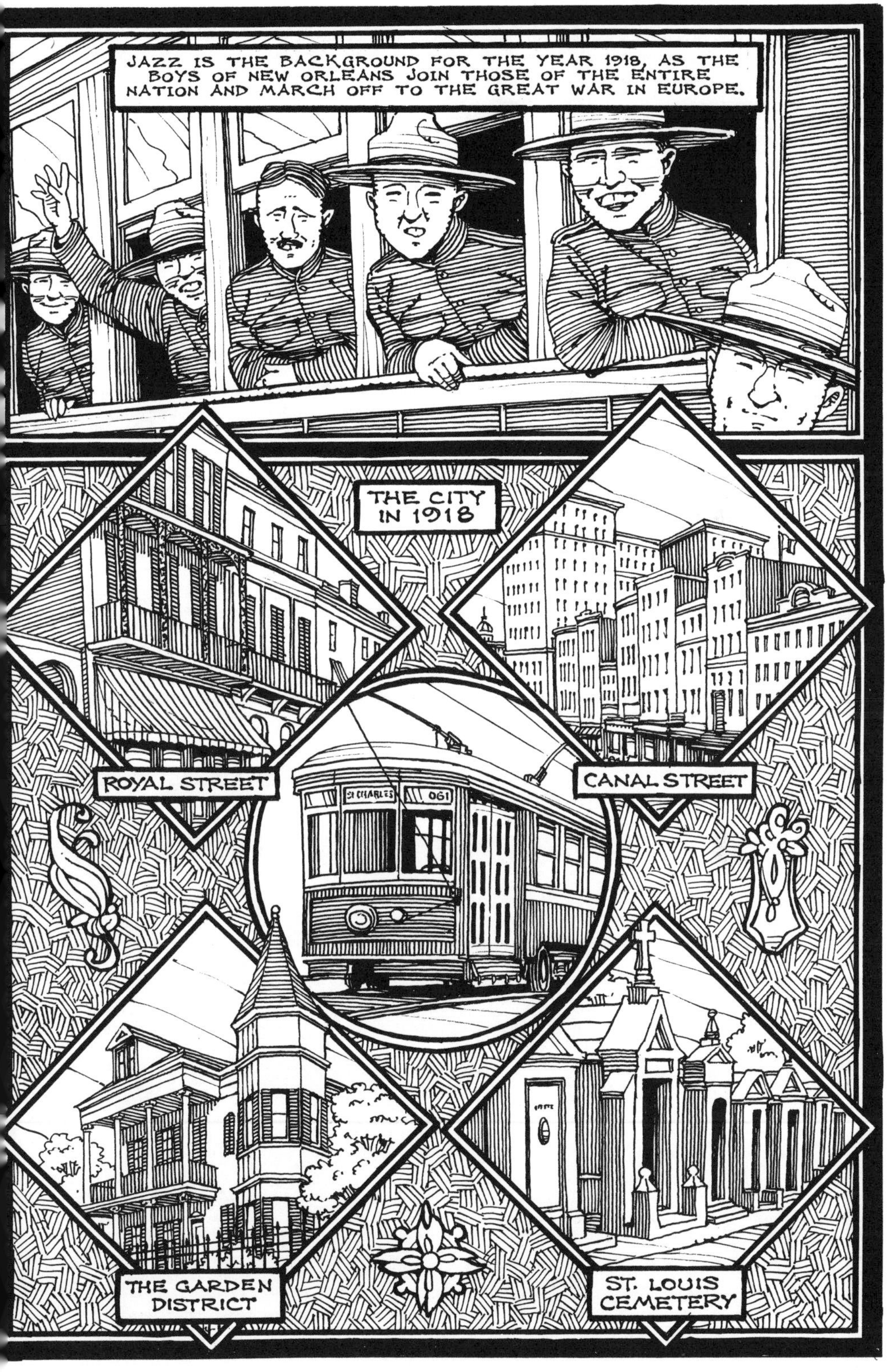
JAZZ IS THE BACKGROUND FOR THE YEAR 1918, AS THE BOYS OF NEW ORLEANS JOIN THOSE OF THE ENTIRE NATION AND MARCH OFF TO THE GREAT WAR IN EUROPE.
THE CITY IN 1918
ROYAL STREET
ST CHARLES
061
CANAL STREET
THE GARDEN DISTRICT
ST. LOUIS CEMETERY

NEW ORLEANS IS ALSO FAMOUS FOR THE SEVERAL MYSTERIOUS AND LEGENDARY CRIMINALS WHO PREY UPON CITIZENS ON THE PUBLIC STREETS.

"NEEDLEMEN" AND "BLACK BOTTLE MEN" WHO GIVE THEIR UNSUSPECTING VICTIMS A QUICK DOSE OF POISON . . .

MEN ARRAYED IN GOWNS OR ROBES, WHO DROP FROM TREES OR JUMP FROM AROUND CORNERS AND GIVE CHASE TO TERRIFIED WOMEN.

"JACK THE CLIPPER" SNIPS THE LOCKS OF SCHOOLGIRLS ON STREETCARS OR IN THEATRES.

THESE ARE BUT HARMLESS AND CURIOUS PRELUDES TO THE ACTUAL MENACE THAT STALKS THE CITY IN THE YEARS 1918 AND 1919.

THE TERRIBLE AXE-MAN!

PART II

BLOOD EVERYWHERE!

JOSEPH AND CATHERINE MAGGIO, ITALIAN IMMIGRANTS, RUN A GROCERY AND TAVERN AT THE CORNER OF UPPERLINE AND MAGNOLIA STREETS.

GROCERY and BAR | JOE MAGGIO

THEY KEEP A HOME BEHIND THE STORE. AN ADJOINING APARTMENT IS OCCUPIED BY JOSEPH'S BROTHERS JAKE AND ANDREW.

THURSDAY, MAY 23, 1918
AT ABOUT 5:00AM, ANDREW MAGGIO IS AWAKENED BY HORRIFYING THUDS AND MOANS THROUGH THE WALL.

HE POUNDS UPON THE PARTITION BUT RECEIVES NO RESPONSE.

WITH GREAT DIFFICULTY, HE ROUSES HIS BROTHER JAKE, WHO WAS OUT DRINKING LAST NIGHT AND STILL NOT COMPLETELY CLEAR OF MIND.

THEY RUSH NEXT DOOR TO THE APARTMENT OF THEIR BROTHER.

IN THE COUPLE'S BEDROOM, A BLOOD-SOAKED SCENE AWAITS THEM.

(IT WILL BE DESCRIBED AS AMONG THE MOST GRUESOME IN NEW ORLEANS POLICE ANNALS.)

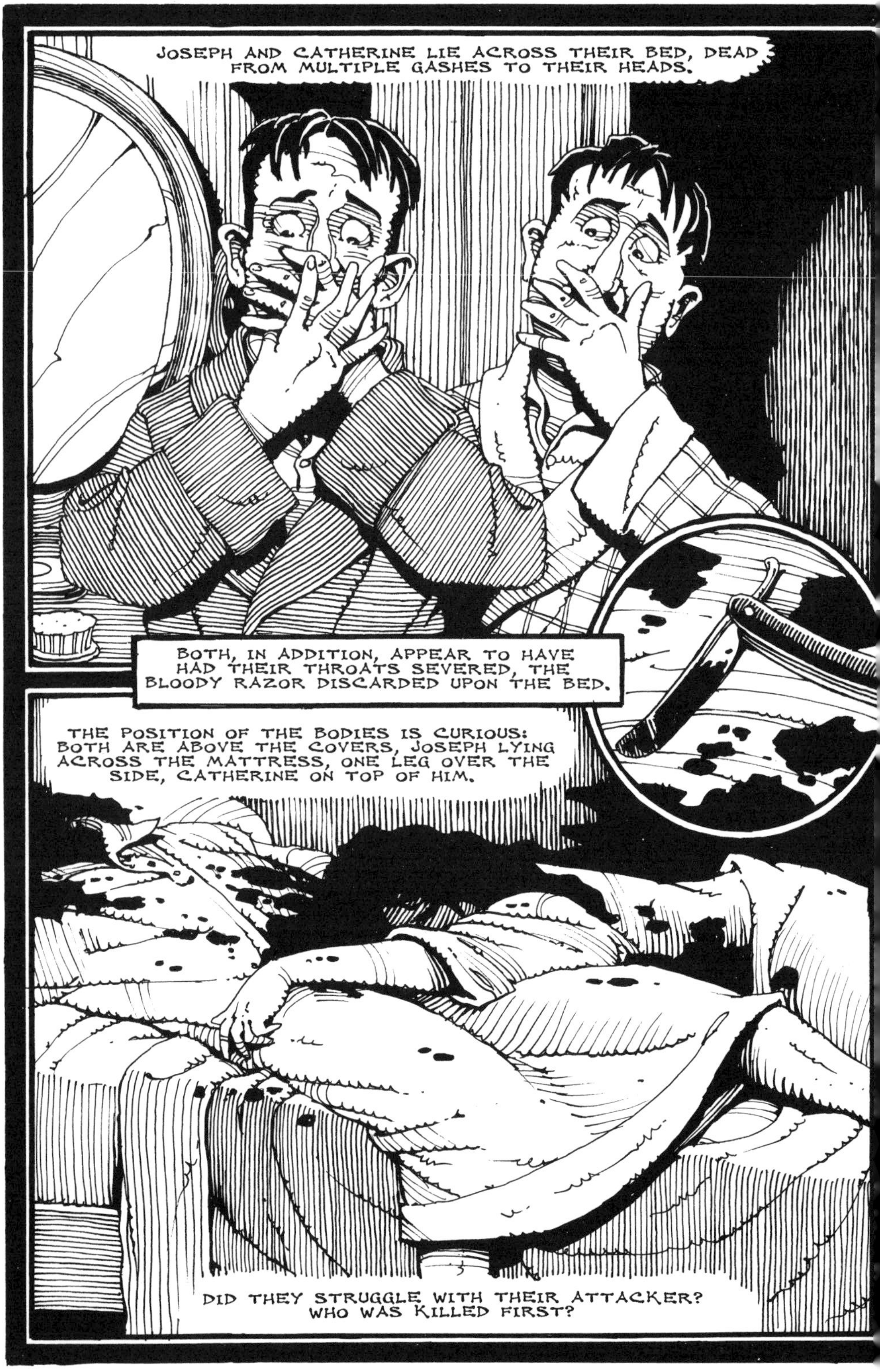
JOSEPH AND CATHERINE LIE ACROSS THEIR BED, DEAD FROM MULTIPLE GASHES TO THEIR HEADS.
BOTH, IN ADDITION, APPEAR TO HAVE HAD THEIR THROATS SEVERED, THE BLOODY RAZOR DISCARDED UPON THE BED.
THE POSITION OF THE BODIES IS CURIOUS: BOTH ARE ABOVE THE COVERS, JOSEPH LYING ACROSS THE MATTRESS, ONE LEG OVER THE SIDE, CATHERINE ON TOP OF HIM.
DID THEY STRUGGLE WITH THEIR ATTACKER? WHO WAS KILLED FIRST?

THE NEW ORLEANS POLICE ARE SUMMONED. FIRST TO ARRIVE IS CORPORAL ARTHUR HATENER.

THE KILLER APPARENTLY GAINED ENTRY BY HACKING AWAY THE LOWER PANEL OF THE REAR DOOR BY MEANS OF A CHISEL.

THE HOME IS THOROUGHLY SEARCHED AND THE BROTHERS QUESTIONED.

THE IMPLEMENT IS FOUND NEARBY.

A BLOOD-SMEARED AXE, OBVIOUSLY THE MURDER WEAPON, STANDS DISCARDED IN THE CAST IRON BATHTUB.

JAKE AND ANDREW IDENTIFY IT AS BELONGING TO THEIR BROTHER.

A SAFE IN THE APARTMENT LIES OPEN AND ITS CONTENTS RIFLED, BUT NOTHING APPEARS TO HAVE BEEN REMOVED.

A BOX OF CASH AND GEMS UNDER THE BED IS UNTOUCHED.

THE CORONER ARRIVES. HE PLACES THE TIME OF DEATH AT 2:00 TO 3:00AM.

THE BODIES ARE THEN REMOVED TO THE MORGUE.

SUSPICION IMMEDIATELY FALLS UPON THE YOUNGER BROTHER ANDREW, A BARBER WHOSE SHOP IS LOCATED ON CAMP STREET NEAR JULIA STREET.

HE ADMITS THAT THE STRAIGHT RAZOR FOUND ON THE BED IS HIS. HE BROUGHT IT HOME A FEW DAYS AGO TO HONE OUT A NICK.

HOW DID IT GET INTO HIS BROTHER'S APARTMENT?

THE MURDERER, POLICE CONCLUDE, MUST HAVE BEEN SOMEONE FAMILIAR WITH THE PREMISES.

THE BROTHER JAKE RECEIVED HIS DRAFT NOTICE YESTERDAY AND SPENT THE NIGHT DRINKING. HE CAME HOME, IN AN ADVANCED STATE OF INTOXICATION, AT ABOUT 2:00AM.

A NEIGHBOR CONFIRMS HAVING SEEN HIM ARRIVE AT THAT HOUR.

BOTH BROTHERS ARE PLACED UNDER ARREST AND TAKEN TO THE SEVENTH PRECINCT STATION.

JAKE IS SOON RELEASED, BUT ANDREW IS KEPT LONGER, IN HOPES OF BUILDING A CASE AGAINST HIM.

BUT WITH NO PHYSICAL EVIDENCE LINKING HIM TO THE CRIME, THERE IS LITTLE THAT THE POLICE CAN DO.

LATER IN THE DAY, HE IS RELUCTANTLY SET FREE AS WELL.

THE NEXT DAY, JAKE MAGGIO IS INTERVIEWED BY A REPORTER FOR THE TIMES-PICAYUNE.

HE BEMOANS HIS FOUL LUCK IN LOSING HIS BROTHER AND SISTER-IN-LAW, RECEIVING HIS DRAFT NOTICE, AND BEING PLACED UNDER ARREST, ALL WITHIN THE SAME 24-HOUR PERIOD.

ONE BLOCK FROM THE MURDER SCENE, AT UPPERLINE AND ROBERTSON STREETS, A PUZZLING INSCRIPTION IS FOUND SCRAWLED IN CHALK ON THE SIDEWALK.

MRS MAGGIO IS GOING TO SIT UP TONIGHT JUST LIKE MRS TONEY

IS THIS A CHILDISH PRANK? A MESSAGE LEFT BY THE KILLER? A WARNING LEFT BY AN ACCOMPLICE?

WAS IT WRITTEN BEFORE OR AFTER THE DEED?

MANY OBSERVERS, INCLUDING POLICE OFFICERS, SEE IN THIS THE WORK OF THE BLACK HAND, THE INFAMOUS UNDERGROUND FORCE THAT PREYS UPON ITALIAN IMMIGRANTS.

WHO IS "MRS. TONEY?" THE NAME PUTS SOME PEOPLE IN MIND OF A SERIES OF CRIMES COMMITTED SEVERAL YEARS AGO ...

110

ACCORDING TO A RETIRED POLICE DETECTIVE, JOSEPH D'ANTONIO, AT LEAST THREE ITALIAN GROCERS AND THEIR WIVES WERE MURDERED IN MUCH THE SAME WAY IN 1911.

ROSETTI

CRUTI

SCHIAMBRIA

THIS LAST VICTIM BORE THE FIRST NAME OF TONY. COULD HIS WIFE HAVE BEEN "SITTING UP" THAT NIGHT AND THUS HAVE POSED A HINDRANCE TO THE ASSASSIN?

ALL OF THEM WERE CHOPPED TO PIECES BY AN AXE-WIELDING INTRUDER WHO ENTERED THROUGH A DOOR PANEL.

THE MAFIA IS WELL KNOWN FOR EXTORTING "PROTECTION" PAYMENTS FROM IMMIGRANT MERCHANTS ...

AND DEALING VIOLENTLY WITH THOSE WHO REFUSE TO "COME ACROSS."

JOURNALISTS WHO DO NOT RECALL THESE EARLIER CRIMES CAN FIND NO RECORD OF THEM IN NEWSPAPER OR POLICE ARCHIVES.

WERE THEY KEPT SECRET BY OFFICIALS WARY OF FRIGHTENING THE PUBLIC, OR WHO WERE THEMSELVES IN THE EMPLOY OF ORGANIZED CRIME?

IT DOES NOT TAKE LONG FOR THE KILLER TO STRIKE AGAIN.

AT THE CORNER OF DORGENOIS AND LA HARPE STREETS IS THE SMALL GROCERY OWNED BY LOUIS BESUMER, AGE 59, A NATIVE OF POLAND.

MARKET

HE LIVES BEHIND THE BUSINESS WITH HIS COMPANION, ANNA HARRIET LOWE, AGE 28.

112

SATURDAY, JUNE 6, 1918
ON THIS MORNING, A BAKER NAMED JOHN BANZA ARRIVES AT THE STORE WITH A CONSIGNMENT OF BREAD AND CAKES.

FINDING THE FRONT DOOR LOCKED, HE GOES AROUND TO THE SIDE ENTRANCE AND KNOCKS.

HE IS HORRIFIED TO SEE IT OPENED BY MR. BESUMER, HIS FACE AWASH IN BLOOD FROM A DEEP GASH TO THE HEAD.

WE WERE ATTACKED!

IN THE BEDROOM, BANZA FINDS MISS LOWE LIKEWISE MUTILATED.

SHE CLINGS BARELY TO LIFE.

BLOODY FOOTPRINTS LEAD FROM THE BED TO A SWATCH OF FALSE HAIR ON THE FLOOR.

113

POLICE AND AN AMBULANCE ARE SUMMONED, AND THE VICTIMS ARE RUSHED TO CHARITY HOSPITAL.

SCRUTINY OF THE APARTMENT FINDS A SCENE MUCH LIKE THAT OF THE PREVIOUS CRIME.

ONCE AGAIN, ENTRY WAS EFFECTED THROUGH A PANEL OF THE REAR DOOR, PRIED OUT BY MEANS OF A WOOD CHISEL.

THE WEAPON, THIS TIME A RUSTY HATCHET, WILL BE IDENTIFIED BY BESUMER AS HIS OWN.

HE WILL ALSO CONFIRM THAT NO MONEY OR VALUABLES ARE MISSING.

AT THE HOSPITAL, BESUMER TALKS TO POLICE. HIS INJURIES DO NOT APPEAR TO BE LIFE-THREATENING.

HE REGRETS THAT HE CANNOT DESCRIBE HIS ASSAILANT, THE ATTACK HAVING OCCURRED IN THE MIDDLE OF THE NIGHT.

HE ALSO ADMITS THAT ANNA LOWE IS NOT HIS WIFE, AS IS ASSUMED BY THEIR FRIENDS AND NEIGHBORS.

SHE LIES IN A DELIRIUM FROM HER WOUNDS AND CLAIMS TO HAVE BEEN ATTACKED BY A "MULATTO."

ACCORDINGLY, A BLACK MAN IS DETAINED AND QUESTIONED: A FORMER HELPER AT THE STORE WHO QUIT HIS JOB A WEEK AGO.

HE TELLS CONFLICTING STORIES ABOUT HIS WHEREABOUTS LAST NIGHT AND IS INCARCERATED BRIEFLY BEFORE BEING EXONERATED AND RELEASED.

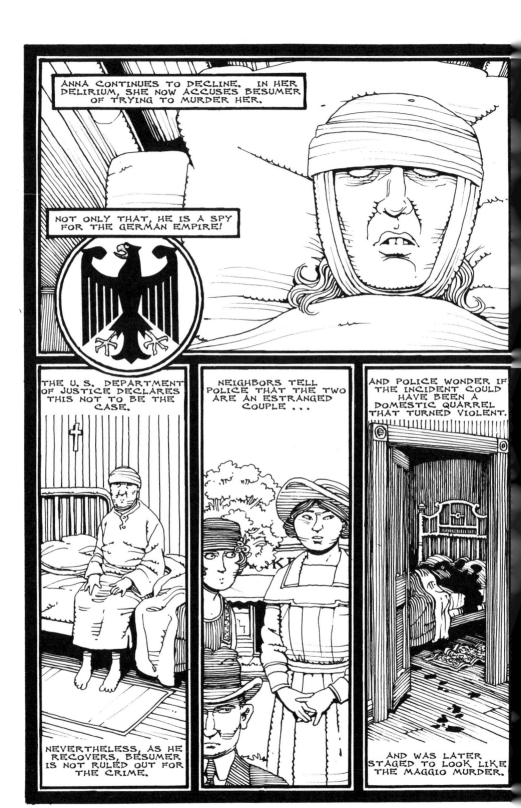

ANNA CONTINUES TO DECLINE. IN HER DELIRIUM, SHE NOW ACCUSES BESUMER OF TRYING TO MURDER HER.

NOT ONLY THAT, HE IS A SPY FOR THE GERMAN EMPIRE!

THE U. S. DEPARTMENT OF JUSTICE DECLARES THIS NOT TO BE THE CASE.

NEIGHBORS TELL POLICE THAT THE TWO ARE AN ESTRANGED COUPLE . . .

AND POLICE WONDER IF THE INCIDENT COULD HAVE BEEN A DOMESTIC QUARREL THAT TURNED VIOLENT.

NEVERTHELESS, AS HE RECOVERS, BESUMER IS NOT RULED OUT FOR THE CRIME.

AND WAS LATER STAGED TO LOOK LIKE THE MAGGIO MURDER.

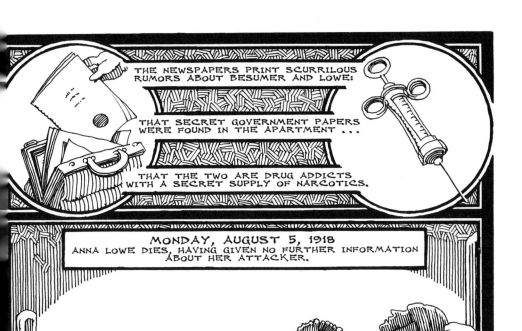

THE NEWSPAPERS PRINT SCURRILOUS RUMORS ABOUT BESUMER AND LOWE:

THAT SECRET GOVERNMENT PAPERS WERE FOUND IN THE APARTMENT ...

THAT THE TWO ARE DRUG ADDICTS WITH A SECRET SUPPLY OF NARCOTICS.

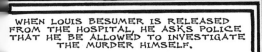

MONDAY, AUGUST 5, 1918
ANNA LOWE DIES, HAVING GIVEN NO FURTHER INFORMATION ABOUT HER ATTACKER.

WHEN LOUIS BESUMER IS RELEASED FROM THE HOSPITAL, HE ASKS POLICE THAT HE BE ALLOWED TO INVESTIGATE THE MURDER HIMSELF.

THIS MAKES THEM EVEN MORE SUSPICIOUS, AND HE IS PLACED UNDER ARREST.

(HE WILL BE PUT ON TRIAL IN APRIL OF 1919 ...

AND ACQUITTED AFTER A TEN-MINUTE DELIBERATION.)

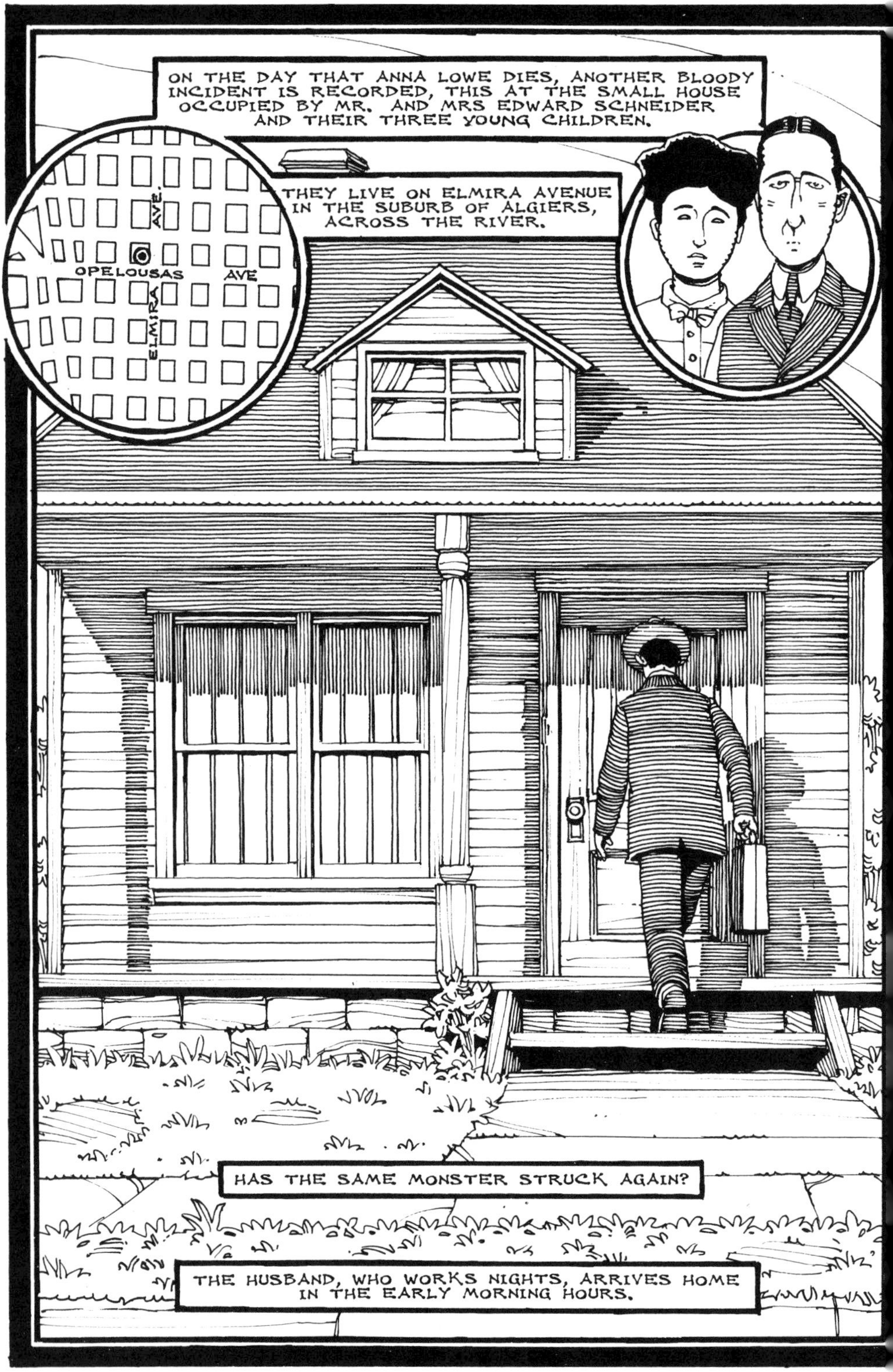
ON THE DAY THAT ANNA LOWE DIES, ANOTHER BLOODY INCIDENT IS RECORDED, THIS AT THE SMALL HOUSE OCCUPIED BY MR. AND MRS EDWARD SCHNEIDER AND THEIR THREE YOUNG CHILDREN.
THEY LIVE ON ELMIRA AVENUE IN THE SUBURB OF ALGIERS, ACROSS THE RIVER.
OPELOUSAS AVE
ELMIRA AVE.
HAS THE SAME MONSTER STRUCK AGAIN?
THE HUSBAND, WHO WORKS NIGHTS, ARRIVES HOME IN THE EARLY MORNING HOURS.

UPON ENTERING THE HOUSE, HE SENSES AN UNUSUAL ATMOSPHERE. THE PLACE IS TOO QUIET.

HE CALLS OUT TO HIS WIFE, WHO IS IN HER EIGHTH MONTH OF PREGNANCY, BUT RECEIVES NO RESPONSE.

HE FINDS HER LYING ON THEIR BED, BLEEDING PROFUSELY FROM SEVERAL CUTS TO THE HEAD -- BUT STILL ALIVE.

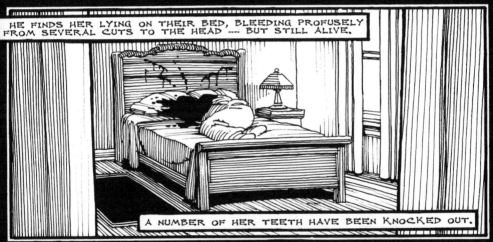

A NUMBER OF HER TEETH HAVE BEEN KNOCKED OUT.

POLICE AND AN AMBULANCE ARE CALLED AT ONCE.

AN EXAMINATION OF THE SCENE, HOWEVER, FINDS LITTLE THAT CONNECTS IT TO THE PREVIOUS CRIMES.

MRS. SCHNEIDER RECOVERS CONSCIOUSNESS A FEW DAYS LATER BUT CAN RECALL LITTLE OF THE ATTACK.

SHE WAS SLEEPING, SHE SAYS, AND AWOKE TO SEE A DARK, HULKING FIGURE LOOMING OVER HER.

IN THREE WEEKS, SHE GIVES BIRTH TO A HEALTHY BABY GIRL.

WHAT ARE WE TO MAKE OF THIS LATEST INCIDENT?

NO SIGN OF A BREAK-IN IS FOUND, EITHER BY DOOR OR WINDOW.

MR. SCHNEIDER'S AXE IS MISSING, AND HIS HATCHET IS FOUND IN THE YARD NEXT DOOR.

THE COUPLE, HOWEVER, ARE NEITHER GROCERS NOR ITALIAN NOR IMMIGRANTS OF ANY KIND.

120

JOSEPH ROMANO, AGE 30, IS A BARBER AND ITALIAN IMMIGRANT WHO KEEPS A HOME WITH HIS TWO YOUNG NIECES, PAULINE AND MARY BRUNO, AGES 18 AND 13.

THEY LIVE BEHIND A GROCERY AT THE CORNER OF TONTI AND GRAVIER STREETS.

SATURDAY, AUGUST 10, 1918
AT ABOUT 3:00AM, THE TWO GIRLS ARE JOLTED AWAKE BY SOUNDS OF A STRUGGLE IN THEIR UNCLE'S ROOM NEXT DOOR.

THEY SIT UP TO SEE A DARK FIGURE STANDING AT THE FOOT OF THEIR BED.

THE SISTERS SCREAM, AND THE MAN BOLTS FROM THE ROOM.

DESPITE HIS BULK, HE IS ASTONISHINGLY LIGHT ON HIS FEET.

HE FAIRLY FLIES DOWN THE HALL AND OUT OF THE BUILDING.

PAULINE LATER DESCRIBES THE MAN AS HEAVY-SET, WEARING A DARK SUIT AND AN "ALPINE" HAT.

THEIR UNCLE STAGGERS INTO THE GIRLS' ROOM.

SOMETHING HAS HAPPENED...

THEY FOLLOW HIM INTO THE KITCHEN...

MY HEAD HURTS...

WHERE HE COLLAPSES INTO A CHAIR.

CALL AN AMBULANCE...

HER UNCLE WAS A GOOD MAN, PAULINE WILL RECALL, WITHOUT A SINGLE ENEMY.

I...DON'T KNOW... WHO DID THIS...

HE LAPSES INTO UNCONSCIOUSNESS AND IS TAKEN TO CHARITY HOSPITAL...

WHERE HE DIES A SHORT TIME LATER.

THE FIRST POLICEMAN ON THE SCENE IS PATROLMAN CHISHOLM OF THE FIRST PRECINCT STATION, JUST TWO BLOCKS AWAY.

HE IS ALERTED BY THE SCREAMS OF THE BRUNO GIRLS.

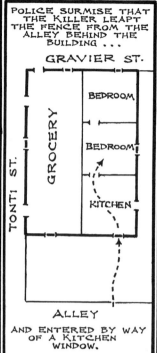

POLICE SURMISE THAT THE KILLER LEAPT THE FENCE FROM THE ALLEY BEHIND THE BUILDING ...

GRAVIER ST.

TONTI ST.

GROCERY

BEDROOM

BEDROOM

KITCHEN

ALLEY

AND ENTERED BY WAY OF A KITCHEN WINDOW.

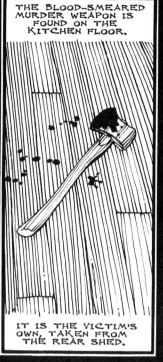

THE BLOOD-SMEARED MURDER WEAPON IS FOUND ON THE KITCHEN FLOOR.

IT IS THE VICTIM'S OWN, TAKEN FROM THE REAR SHED.

HIS ROOM IS TORN APART FROM HIS STRUGGLE WITH THE ASSASSIN, BUT THERE APPEARS TO HAVE BEEN NO ROBBERY.

THEIR UNCLE EARNED BUT A SMALL SALARY, THE NIECES CONFIRM.

"WHO'LL BE NEXT?" IS THE QUESTION CIRCULATING THROUGH THE TERRIFIED ITALIAN COMMUNITY.

SUPERINTENDENT OF POLICE MOONEY DECLARES:

I AM OF THE BELIEF THAT THE MURDERER IS A DEPRAVED CRIMINAL WITH NO REGARD FOR HUMAN LIFE ...

AND WE WILL GET HIM!

PART III

A CITY IN TERROR

WITH THEIR CITY FLOWING RED, CITIZENS GIVE WAY TO NERVOUSNESS AND PANIC.

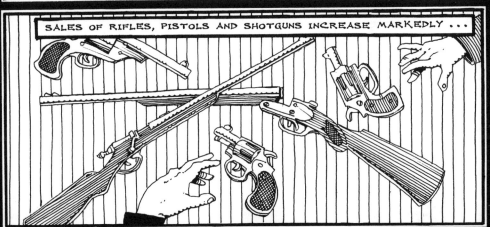

SALES OF RIFLES, PISTOLS AND SHOTGUNS INCREASE MARKEDLY...

AS DOES THE INSTALLATION OF BARS, GRATES AND GRILLES.

AS DARKNESS FALLS, FAMILIES HUDDLE INDOORS.

HUSBANDS AND FATHERS SIT UP NIGHTS, LISTENING FOR THE SLIGHTEST SOUND . . .

OR ELSE SLEEP FITFULLY, A LOADED FIREARM WITHIN EASY REACH.

POLICE ARE INUNDATED WITH REPORTS OF SUSPICIOUS-LOOKING MEN . . .

OF AXES AND CHISELS DISCARDED ON THE STREET.

THE INNOCENT STRANGER HAD BEST BE WARY OF WANDERING INTO AN UNFAMILIAR NEIGHBORHOOD.

HE IS APT TO BE CHASED DOWN AND BEATEN.

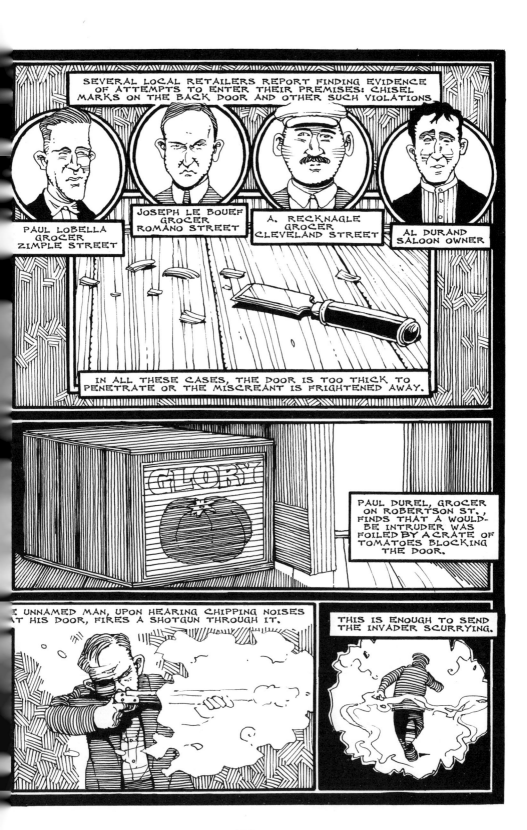

SEVERAL LOCAL RETAILERS REPORT FINDING EVIDENCE OF ATTEMPTS TO ENTER THEIR PREMISES: CHISEL MARKS ON THE BACK DOOR AND OTHER SUCH VIOLATIONS.

PAUL LOBELLA
GROCER
ZIMPLE STREET

JOSEPH LE BOUEF
GROCER
ROMANO STREET

A. RECKNAGLE
GROCER
CLEVELAND STREET

AL DURAND
SALOON OWNER

IN ALL THESE CASES, THE DOOR IS TOO THICK TO PENETRATE OR THE MISCREANT IS FRIGHTENED AWAY.

GLORY

PAUL DUREL, GROCER ON ROBERTSON ST., FINDS THAT A WOULD-BE INTRUDER WAS FOILED BY A CRATE OF TOMATOES BLOCKING THE DOOR.

E UNNAMED MAN, UPON HEARING CHIPPING NOISES T HIS DOOR, FIRES A SHOTGUN THROUGH IT.

THIS IS ENOUGH TO SEND THE INVADER SCURRYING.

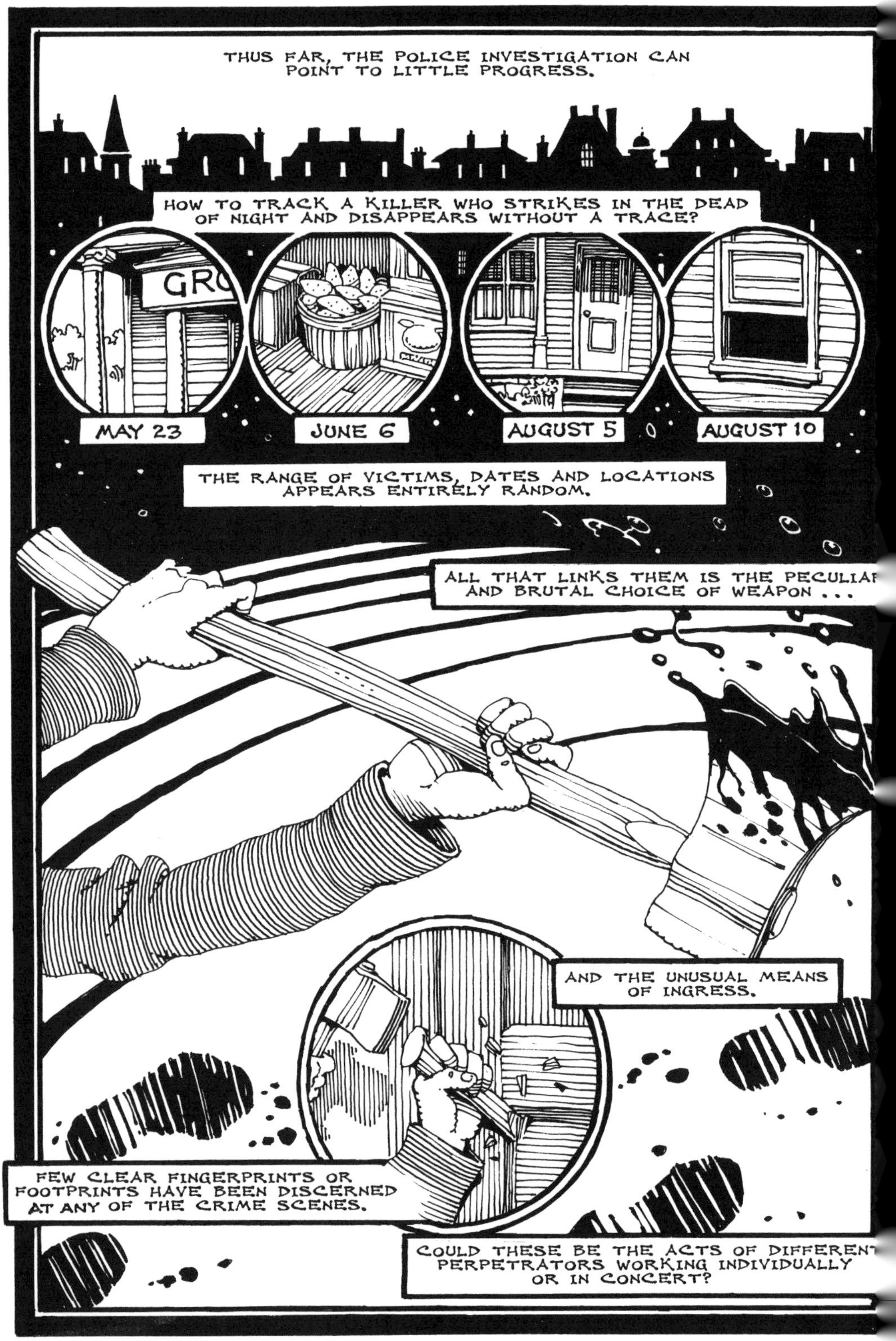
THUS FAR, THE POLICE INVESTIGATION CAN POINT TO LITTLE PROGRESS.
HOW TO TRACK A KILLER WHO STRIKES IN THE DEAD OF NIGHT AND DISAPPEARS WITHOUT A TRACE?
GRO
MAY 23
JUNE 6
AUGUST 5
AUGUST 10
THE RANGE OF VICTIMS, DATES AND LOCATIONS APPEARS ENTIRELY RANDOM.
ALL THAT LINKS THEM IS THE PECULIAR AND BRUTAL CHOICE OF WEAPON . . .
AND THE UNUSUAL MEANS OF INGRESS.
FEW CLEAR FINGERPRINTS OR FOOTPRINTS HAVE BEEN DISCERNED AT ANY OF THE CRIME SCENES.
COULD THESE BE THE ACTS OF DIFFERENT PERPETRATORS WORKING INDIVIDUALLY OR IN CONCERT?

MORE THAN ONE OBSERVER HAS RECALLED THE EXPLOITS OF THAT LONDON KILLER OF 30 YEARS AGO -- "JACK THE RIPPER."

SOME THEORIZED THAT HE WAS GUIDED BY THE PHASES OF THE MOON.

HE PREYED EXCLUSIVELY UPON STREET PROSTITUTES, BUT OTHERWISE NO PATTERN OR MOTIVE COULD BE FOUND IN HIS WORK.

AFTER A FINAL OUTRAGE HE VANISHED FOREVER.

ONE INVESTIGATOR HAS MADE REFERENCE TO ROBERT LOUIS STEVENSON'S WELL-KNOWN TALE OF "DR. JECKYL AND MR. HYDE"...

THE STRANGE CASE OF DR. JECKYL AND MR HYDE

R.L. STEVENSON

AND POSTULATES A MURDERER OF THE "DUAL PERSONALITY" TYPE:

AN INDIVIDUAL OF ORDINARY HABIT AND APPEARANCE, WHO LEADS AN OUTWARDLY NORMAL LIFE ...

PERHAPS EVEN RESPECTED BY HIS FELLOW CITIZENS.

BUT UPON ACTIVATION OF A CERTAIN UNCONSCIOUS IMPULSE ...

HIS DARKEST SELF WILL EMERGE ...

AN URGE THAT CANNOT BE SATISFIED BUT WITH BLOOD!

AS SUMMER PASSES INTO FALL AND WINTER, WITH NO FURTHER ATTACKS, THE HYSTERIA BEGINS TO FADE.

THE WORLD WAR ENDS WITH THE ARMISTICE OF NOVEMBER 11.

THE CITY'S SOLDIERS ARRIVE HOME TO VICTORY PARADES AND WIDESPREAD CELEBRATION.

AS THE YEAR 1919 PROGRESSES, THE SAVAGE EVENTS OF THE PREVIOUS YEAR ARE FORGOTTEN . . .

ALMOST!

132

PART IV

JAZZ IT!

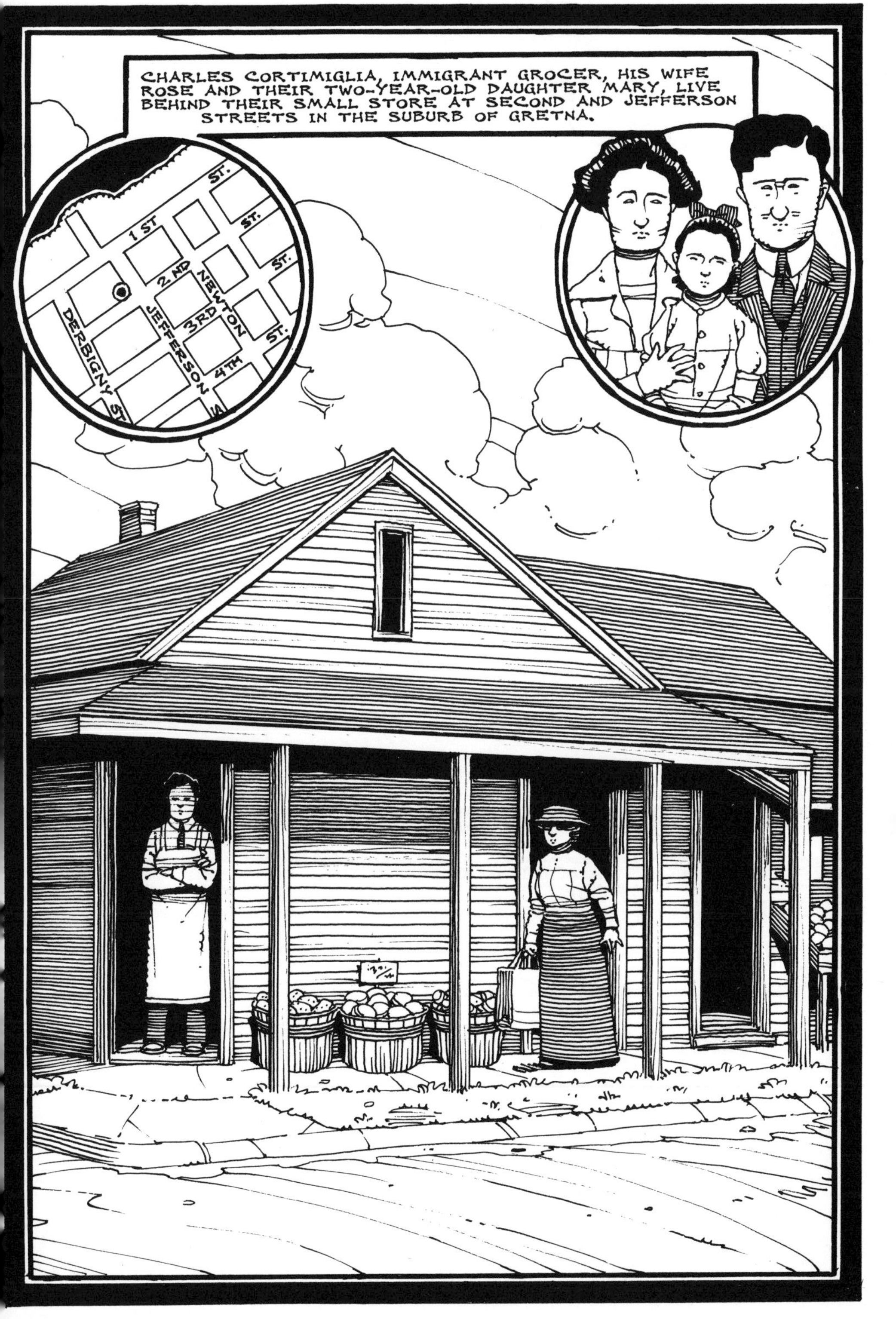
CHARLES CORTIMIGLIA, IMMIGRANT GROCER, HIS WIFE ROSE AND THEIR TWO-YEAR-OLD DAUGHTER MARY, LIVE BEHIND THEIR SMALL STORE AT SECOND AND JEFFERSON STREETS IN THE SUBURB OF GRETNA.
1 ST
ST.
ST.
2 ND
NEWTON
ST.
3RD
JEFFERSON
DERBIGNY ST
4TH
ST.

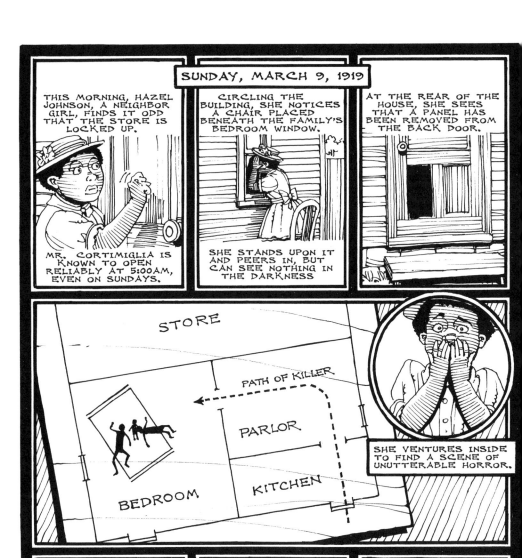

SUNDAY, MARCH 9, 1919

THIS MORNING, HAZEL JOHNSON, A NEIGHBOR GIRL, FINDS IT ODD THAT THE STORE IS LOCKED UP.

MR. CORTIMIGLIA IS KNOWN TO OPEN RELIABLY AT 5:00AM, EVEN ON SUNDAYS.

CIRCLING THE BUILDING, SHE NOTICES A CHAIR PLACED BENEATH THE FAMILY'S BEDROOM WINDOW.

SHE STANDS UPON IT AND PEERS IN, BUT CAN SEE NOTHING IN THE DARKNESS

AT THE REAR OF THE HOUSE, SHE SEES THAT A PANEL HAS BEEN REMOVED FROM THE BACK DOOR.

STORE

PATH OF KILLER

PARLOR

KITCHEN

BEDROOM

SHE VENTURES INSIDE TO FIND A SCENE OF UNUTTERABLE HORROR.

ROSE CORTIMIGLIA, WITH DEEP GASHES TO HER HEAD, HOLDS THE DEAD FORM OF HER DAUGHTER.

MARY...
MARY...

HER HUSBAND CHARLES LIES BESIDE THEM, ALSO WITH SEVERAL TERRIBLE WOUNDS TO THE SKULL.

A FIERCE STRUGGLE APPEARS TO HAVE TAKEN PLACE IN THE ROOM.

THE MANY RELIGIOUS IMAGES ON THE WALL GAZE DOWN UPON THE GRUESOME TABLEAU.

136

THE COUPLE, STILL CLINGING TO LIFE, ARE FERRIED ACROSS THE RIVER TO CHARITY HOSPITAL.

MRS. CORTIMIGLIA HAS SUSTAINED FIVE SEVERE CUTS TO THE HEAD, BUT WILL MOST LIKELY SURVIVE.

HER HUSBAND, HIS SKULL CRUSHED BY HEAVY BLOWS FROM THE BLUNT END OF AN AXE, IS NOT EXPECTED TO LIVE.

POLICE CONDUCT A THOROUGH SEARCH OF THE STORE AND RESIDENCE ...

UNCOVERING MANY SIMILARITIES TO THE PREVIOUS MURDERS.

THE CHISELED DOOR PANEL IS THE FIRST OBVIOUS ECHO ...

THERE IS ALSO THE ITALIAN ORIGIN OF VICTIMS AND THE GROCERY AS CRIME SCENE.

THE BLOOD-SMEARED WEAPON IS FOUND STASHED BENEATH THE KITCHEN DOORSTEP.

IT IS ASSUMED TO BELONG TO MR. CORTIMIGLIA SINCE NO OTHER AXE IS FOUND ON THE PROPERTY.

FURNITURE IN THE BEDROOM HAS BEEN MOVED, A TRUNK AND DRESSER OPENED AND RIFLED.

DETECTIVES INSIST, HOWEVER, THAT ROBBERY IS NOT THE MOTIVE. THESE ARE FALSE CLUES, A DISTRACTION.

RECOVERING CONSCIOUSNESS IN HER HOSPITAL ROOM, ROSE REMEMBERS WAKING IN THE NIGHT TO SEE HER HUSBAND STRUGGLING WITH AN AXE-WIELDING INTRUDER.

AFTER DISABLING HIM, THE ATTACKER GOES AFTER HER AND HER DAUGHTER.

IN ADDITION, IT SEEMS THAT SHE CAN IDENTIFY THE MAN: SHE NAMES FRANK, THE 17-YEAR-OLD SON OF THEIR NEIGHBOR IORLANDO JORDANO.

THE JORDANOS OPERATE A COMPETING GROCERY ON THE SAME BLOCK.

ASKING AROUND THE NEIGHBORHOOD, POLICE FIND THAT "BAD BLOOD" EXISTS BETWEEN THE TWO FAMILIES ...

DATING FROM THE TIME SOME YEARS AGO, WHEN THE CORTIMIGLIAS MANAGED THE JORDANOS' STORE.

THE JORDANOS ASSUMED MANAGEMENT THEMSELVES, PUTTING THE CORTIMIGLIAS OUT OF WORK.

THE AGGRIEVED COUPLE CONSTRUCTED A BRAND NEW STORE JUST A FEW DOORS AWAY ...

AND HAVE SINCE CONDUCTED A VERY SUCCESSFUL ENTERPRISE.

THIS SEEMS THE PERFECT RECIPE FOR A DRAMA OF NEIGHBORHOOD RESENTMENT.

THE JORDANOS VIGOROUSLY PROTEST THEIR INNOCENCE. THEIR RELATIONS WITH THE CORTIMIGLIAS, THEY INSIST, HAVE BEEN CORDIAL.

THE SON, AT OVER SIX FEET AND MORE THAN 200 POUNDS, COULD NEVER HAVE FIT THROUGH A DOOR PANEL.

IN A FEW DAYS, CHARLES CORTIMIGLIA SURPRISES EVERYBODY BY REGAINING CONSCIOUSNESS.

HE VERIFIES THAT THE ATTACKER WAS NOT HIS NEIGHBOR BUT AN UNKNOWN INDIVIDUAL.

FRANK JORDANO SAYS THAT HE HAD A DREAM OF AN UNNAMED EVIL STRIKING THE NEIGHBORHOOD.

THE TWO ARE PLACED UNDER ARREST FOR THE MURDER OF MARY CORTIMIGLIA

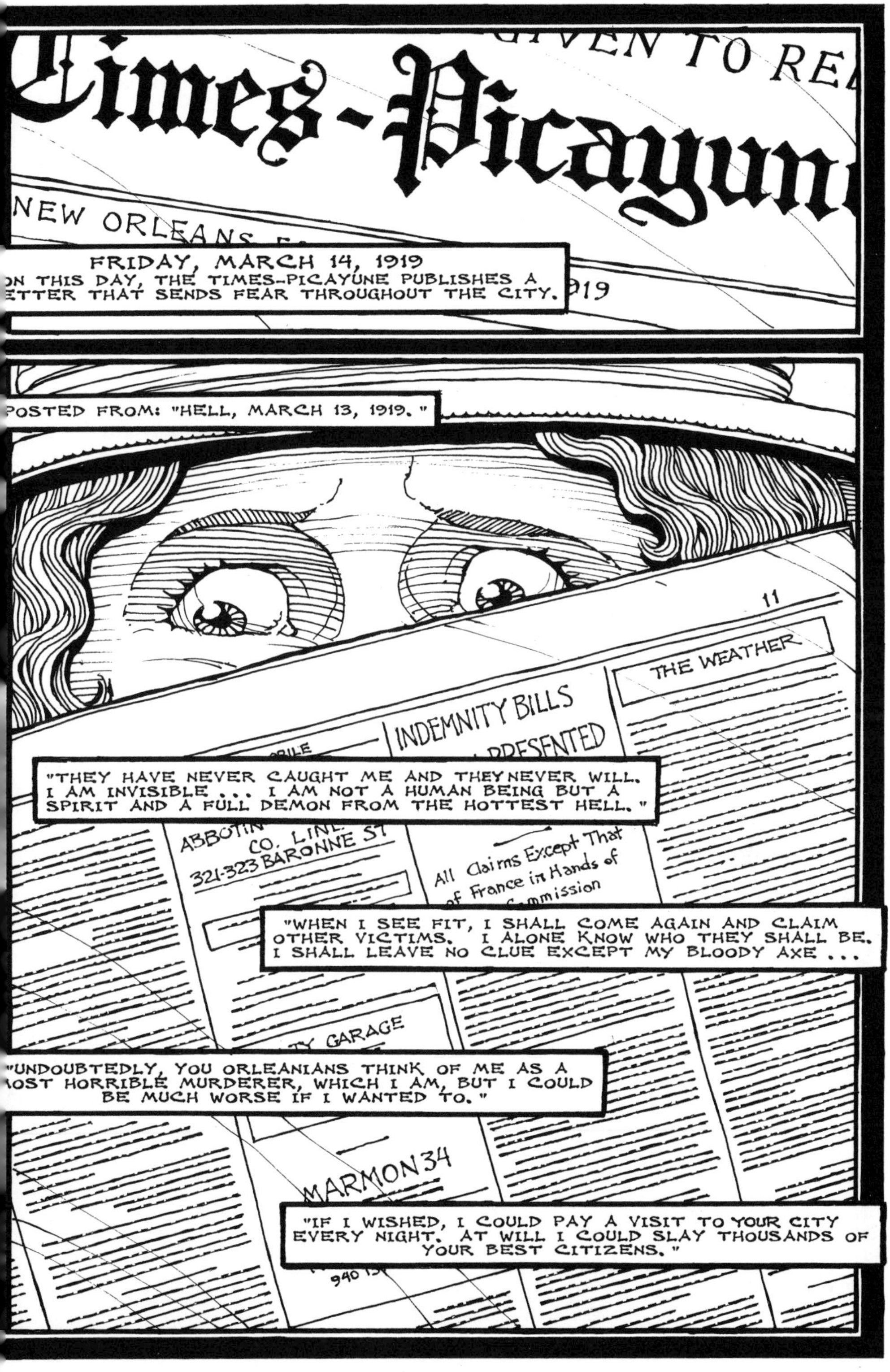
Times-Picayune
NEW ORLEANS
FRIDAY, MARCH 14, 1919
ON THIS DAY, THE TIMES-PICAYUNE PUBLISHES A LETTER THAT SENDS FEAR THROUGHOUT THE CITY.
POSTED FROM: "HELL, MARCH 13, 1919."
THE WEATHER
INDEMNITY BILLS
PRESENTED
"THEY HAVE NEVER CAUGHT ME AND THEY NEVER WILL. I AM INVISIBLE . . . I AM NOT A HUMAN BEING BUT A SPIRIT AND A FULL DEMON FROM THE HOTTEST HELL."
CO. LINE
321-323 BARONNE ST
All Claims Except That of France in Hands of Commission
"WHEN I SEE FIT, I SHALL COME AGAIN AND CLAIM OTHER VICTIMS. I ALONE KNOW WHO THEY SHALL BE. I SHALL LEAVE NO CLUE EXCEPT MY BLOODY AXE . . .
GARAGE
"UNDOUBTEDLY, YOU ORLEANIANS THINK OF ME AS A MOST HORRIBLE MURDERER, WHICH I AM, BUT I COULD BE MUCH WORSE IF I WANTED TO."
MARMON 34
"IF I WISHED, I COULD PAY A VISIT TO YOUR CITY EVERY NIGHT. AT WILL I COULD SLAY THOUSANDS OF YOUR BEST CITIZENS."

THE WRITER GOES ON TO ISSUE A DIRE WARNING:

"NOW, TO BE EXACT, AT 12:15 (EARTHLY TIME) ON NEXT TUESDAY NIGHT, I AM GOING TO VISIT NEW ORLEANS AGAIN, IN MY INFINITE MERCY, I AM GOING TO MAKE A PROPOSITION TO YOU PEOPLE. HERE IT IS:"

"I AM VERY FOND OF JAZZ MUSIC, AND I SWEAR BY ALL THE DEVILS IN THE NETHER REGIONS THAT EVERY PERSON SHALL BE SPARED IN WHOSE HOME A JAZZ BAND IS IN FULL SWING AT THE TIME I HAVE MENTIONED."

"ONE THING IS CERTAIN AND THAT IS THAT SOME OF THOSE PEOPLE WHO DO NOT JAZZ IT ON TUESDAY NIGHT (IF THERE BE ANY) WILL GET THE AXE."

FORD CARS

THE WRITER SIGNS HIMSELF: "THE AXEMAN."

THE QUESTION OF WHETHER THIS MESSAGE IS FROM THE KILLER OF SOME MALIGN PRANKSTER SEEMS NOT TO MATTER.

ITS JEERING TONE PUTS MANY IN MIND OF THE NOTORIOUS MISSIVES FROM "JACK THE RIPPER," WHO ALSO COINED HIS OWN APPELLATION AND ADDRESSED ONE LETTER "FROM HELL."

THE FOLLOWING WEDNESDAY, OCTOBER 19, IS ST. JOSEPH'S DAY, A TIME OF FEASTING AND CELEBRATION WITHIN THE ITALIAN COMMUNITY.

ACCORDINGLY, ON THE TUESDAY NIGHT BEFORE, THE CITY'S CAFES AND DANCE HALLS ARE PACKED WITH DESPERATE REVELERS.

"AXE-MAN" PARTIES IN PRIVATE HOMES GIVE A SENSE OF SAFETY IN NUMBERS.

GRAMOPHONES BLARE AND PIANO ROLLS TINKLE THROUGHOUT THE NIGHT.

ALONG THE RIVERFRONT AND IN THE POOREST QUARTERS, THE PEOPLE IMPROVISE THEIR OWN DISTINCTIVE MUSIC.

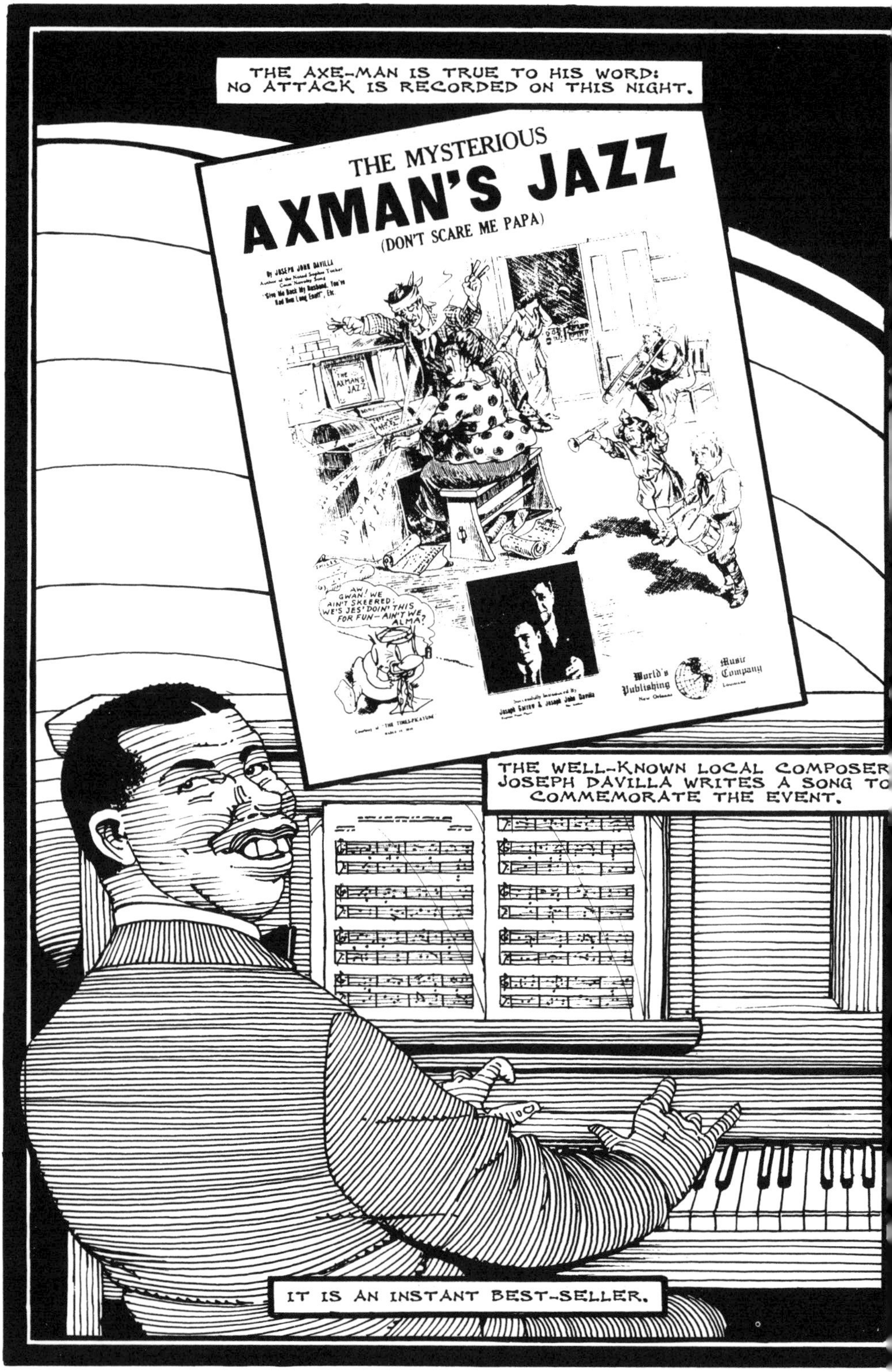
THE AXE-MAN IS TRUE TO HIS WORD: NO ATTACK IS RECORDED ON THIS NIGHT.
THE MYSTERIOUS
AXMAN'S JAZZ
(DON'T SCARE ME PAPA)
By JOSEPH JOHN DAVILLA
THE AXMAN'S JAZZ
AW! GWAN! WE AIN'T SKEERED; WE'S JES' DOIN' THIS FOR FUN—AIN'T WE, ALMA?
World's Publishing Music Company
New Orleans
THE WELL-KNOWN LOCAL COMPOSER JOSEPH DAVILLA WRITES A SONG TO COMMEMORATE THE EVENT.
IT IS AN INSTANT BEST-SELLER.

PART V

THE FINAL OUTRAGE

THE TRIAL OF IORLANDO AND FRANK JORDANO FOR THE ASSAULT ON THE CORTIMIGLIAS AND THE MURDER OF THEIR DAUGHTER OPENS AT THE COURTHOUSE IN GRETNA.

DESPITE PERSUASIVE FACTS POINTING TO THEIR INNOCENCE, AND THE REFUSAL OF CHARLES CORTIMIGLIA TO IDENTIFY THEM...

THE ARE CONVICTED SOLELY UPON THE TESTIMONY OF ROSE.

THE JUDGE SENTENCES FRANK JORDANO TO DEATH AND HIS FATHER TO LIFE IMPRISONMENT

HAS THE AXE-MAN BEEN PUT AWAY?

FEW PEOPLE ACTUALLY BELIEVE THIS.

IN THE HEAT OF THE SUMMER, HE SHOWS HIMSELF AGAIN.

SUNDAY, AUGUST 10, 1919
ON THIS MORNING, STEPHEN BOCA, A GROCER AND ITALIAN IMMIGRANT, STUMBLES FROM HIS HOME BEHIND HIS STORE ON ELSIAN FIELDS AVENUE ...

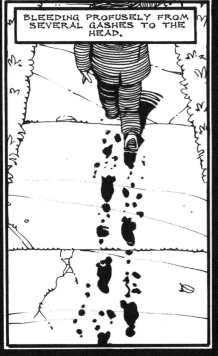

BLEEDING PROFUSELY FROM SEVERAL GASHES TO THE HEAD.

HE MAKES IT ONE HALF BLOCK, TO THE HOME OF A FRIEND, FRANK GENUSA, WHO TREATS HIS WOUNDS AND CALLS FOR HELP.

BOCA RECOVERS AT CHARITY HOSPITAL, BUT CAN RECALL LITTLE OF THE ATTACK, WHICH CAME IN THE MIDDLE OF THE NIGHT.

AT HIS HOME, POLICE FIND THE WELL-KNOWN SIGNS OF THE AXE-MAN A PANEL CHISELED FROM THE REAR DOOR...

AND AN AXE DISCARDED IN THE KITCHEN.

TUESDAY, SEPTEMBER 2, 1919
A DRUGGIST NAMED WILLIAM CARSON HEARS SUSPICIOUS SOUNDS OUTSIDE HIS REAR DOOR.

HE FIRES SEVERAL SHOTS, AND THE WOULD-BE INTRUDER DASHES AWAY...

LEAVING BEHIND AN AXE!

WEDNESDAY, SEPTEMBER 3, 1919
A YOUNG WOMAN NAMED SARA LAUMANN IS ASSAULTED IN HER BED BY A MAN WITH AN AXE.

SHE SUSTAINS SEVERAL WOUNDS TO HER HEAD AND RECOVERS AT CHARITY HOSPITAL.

THE MAN CAME AT HER IN THE DARK, SHE SAYS, AND SHE CAN OFFER NO DESCRIPTION.

THE ATTACKER'S WEAPON IS FOUND IN THE YARD...

BUT OTHERWISE THIS CRIME DIFFERS MARKEDLY FROM THE PREVIOUS WORK OF THE AXE-MAN.

MISS LAUMANN IS A 19-YEAR-OLD SINGLE WOMAN, NEITHER AN IMMIGRANT NOR A GROCER.

ENTRY TO THE HOME WAS APPARENTLY GAINED THROUGH A WINDOW.

IS THIS THE ACT OF A DIFFERENT VILLAIN?

OR IS THE SPECTRAL MURDERER WIDENING HIS FIELD OF VICTIMS?

ONCE AGAIN, FEAR TAKES UP RESIDENCE IN NEW ORLEANS. WHO WILL BE NEXT?

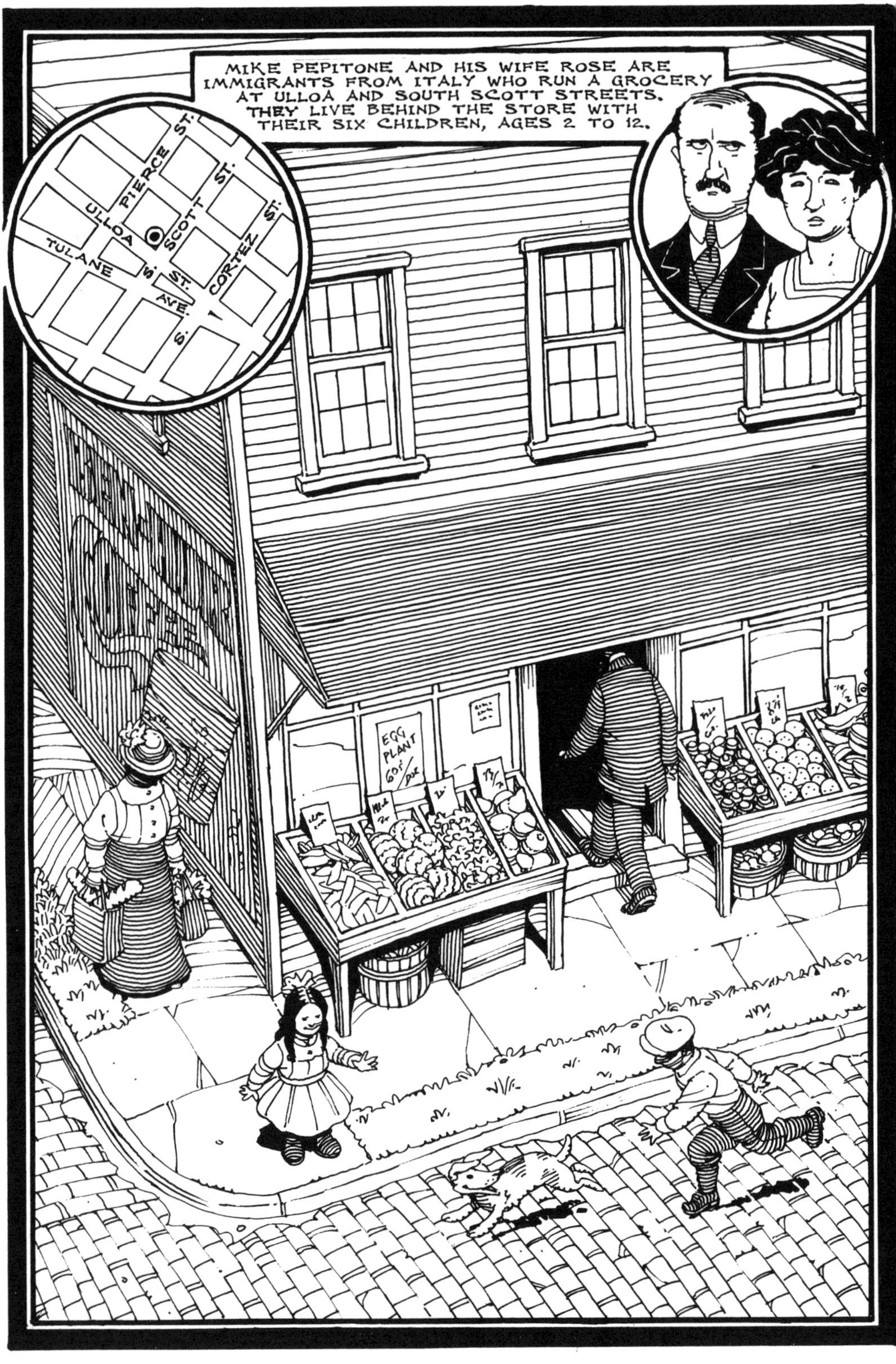
MIKE PEPITONE AND HIS WIFE ROSE ARE IMMIGRANTS FROM ITALY WHO RUN A GROCERY AT ULLOA AND SOUTH SCOTT STREETS. THEY LIVE BEHIND THE STORE WITH THEIR SIX CHILDREN, AGES 2 TO 12.
PIERCE ST.
SCOTT ST.
ULLOA
TULANE AVE.
S. SCOTT ST.
S. CORTEZ ST.
EGG PLANT 60¢ DOZ

MONDAY, OCTOBER 27, 1919
BEN CORCORAN, A SHERIFF'S DEPUTY, HAPPENS TO WALK PAST THE STORE IN THE EARLY MORNING HOURS, WHEN HE IS ACCOSTED BY THE PEPITONES' HYSTERICAL 11-YEAR-OLD DAUGHTER.

INSIDE, HE ENCOUNTERS A SCENE OF CARNAGE.

MIKE PEPITONE, AGE 36, LIES UPON HIS BED, HIS SKULL RENT BY SEVERAL BLUNT WOUNDS.

THE IMAGE OF THE VIRGIN ABOVE THE BED IS DEFACED BY SPATTERS OF BLOOD.

HOLDING ON BARELY TO LIFE, HE IS RUSHED TO CHARITY HOSPITAL, WHERE HE DIES HOURS LATER.

THE VICTIM'S WIFE IS UNHARMED ...

AS ARE THE SIX CHILDREN, WHO SLEEP IN THE ADJOINING ROOM.

ACCORDING TO ROSE, THE COUPLE RETIRED AT MIDNIGHT.

AT ABOUT 1:50AM, SHE WAS AWAKENED BY THE SCREAMS OF HER HUSBAND.

SHE LOOKED UP TO SEE A PAIR OF SHADOWS RETREAT INTO THE CHILDRENS' ROOM.

YES --- SHE CLAIMS TO HAVE SEEN THE SHADOWS OF TWO LARGE MEN.

SHE HURRIED INTO THE NEXT ROOM ...

BUT THE ASSAILANTS HAD ESCAPED VIA THE REAR DOOR

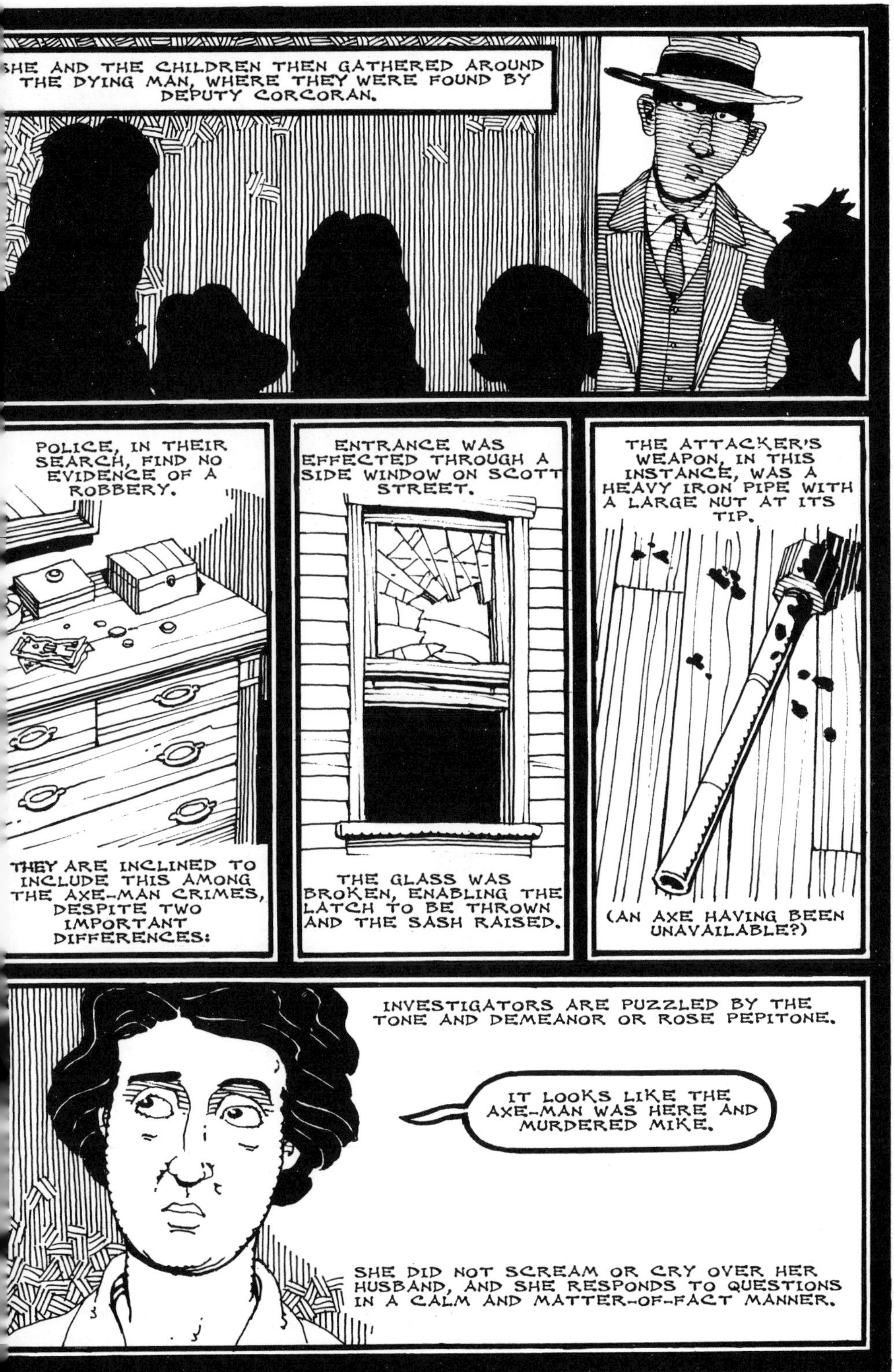
SHE AND THE CHILDREN THEN GATHERED AROUND THE DYING MAN, WHERE THEY WERE FOUND BY DEPUTY CORCORAN.
POLICE, IN THEIR SEARCH, FIND NO EVIDENCE OF A ROBBERY.
THEY ARE INCLINED TO INCLUDE THIS AMONG THE AXE-MAN CRIMES, DESPITE TWO IMPORTANT DIFFERENCES:
ENTRANCE WAS EFFECTED THROUGH A SIDE WINDOW ON SCOTT STREET.
THE GLASS WAS BROKEN, ENABLING THE LATCH TO BE THROWN AND THE SASH RAISED.
THE ATTACKER'S WEAPON, IN THIS INSTANCE, WAS A HEAVY IRON PIPE WITH A LARGE NUT AT ITS TIP.
(AN AXE HAVING BEEN UNAVAILABLE?)
INVESTIGATORS ARE PUZZLED BY THE TONE AND DEMEANOR OR ROSE PEPITONE.
IT LOOKS LIKE THE AXE-MAN WAS HERE AND MURDERED MIKE.
SHE DID NOT SCREAM OR CRY OVER HER HUSBAND, AND SHE RESPONDS TO QUESTIONS IN A CALM AND MATTER-OF-FACT MANNER.

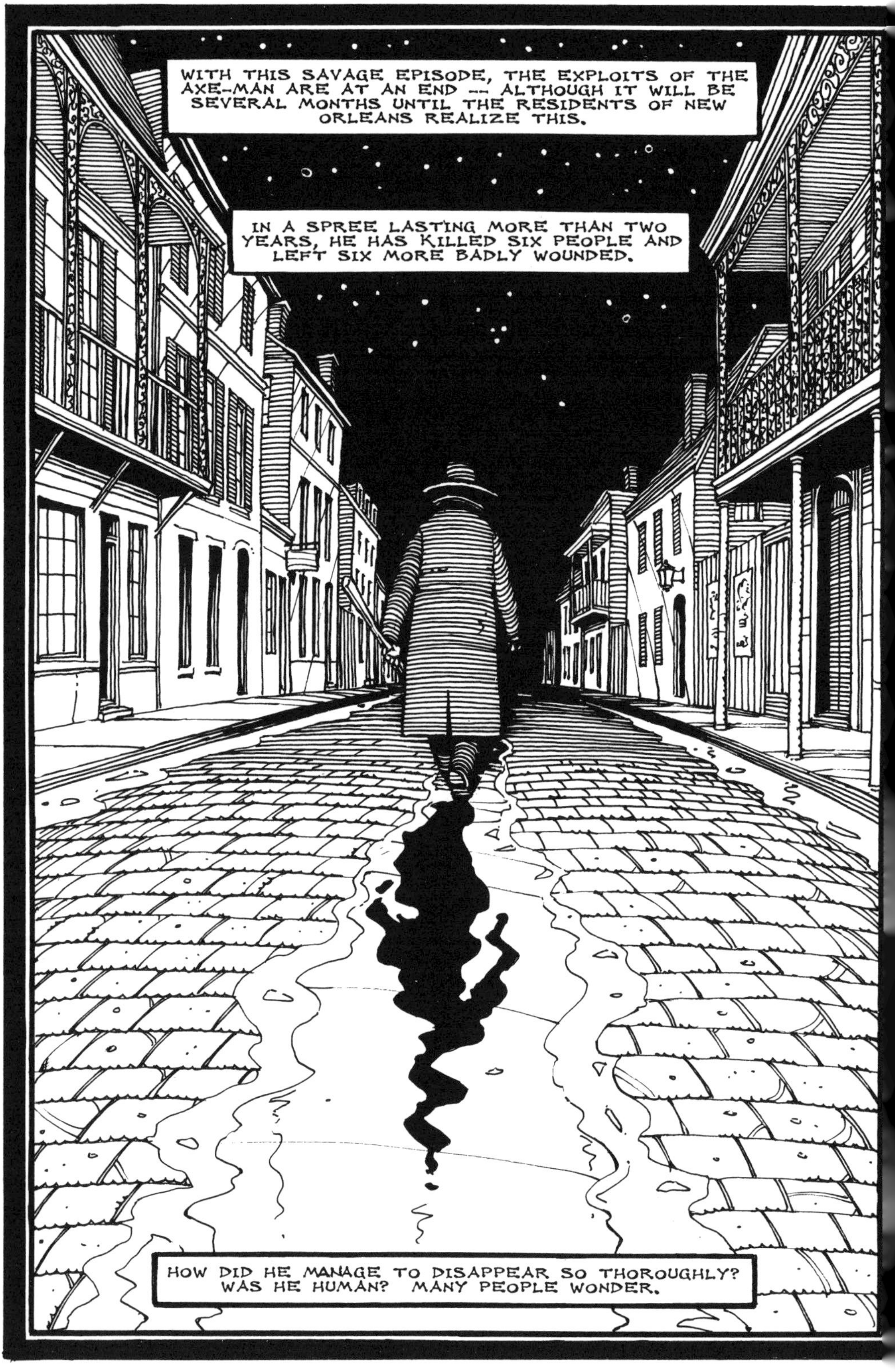
WITH THIS SAVAGE EPISODE, THE EXPLOITS OF THE AXE-MAN ARE AT AN END -- ALTHOUGH IT WILL BE SEVERAL MONTHS UNTIL THE RESIDENTS OF NEW ORLEANS REALIZE THIS.
IN A SPREE LASTING MORE THAN TWO YEARS, HE HAS KILLED SIX PEOPLE AND LEFT SIX MORE BADLY WOUNDED.
HOW DID HE MANAGE TO DISAPPEAR SO THOROUGHLY? WAS HE HUMAN? MANY PEOPLE WONDER.

PART VI

WHO WAS IT ?

THURSDAY, DECEMBER 2, 1920
MORE THAN A YEAR AFTER THE FINAL AXE-MAN ATROCITY, THERE OCCURS AN INTRIGUING CODA TO THE STORY.

A MAN NAMED JOSEPH MUMPHRE IS SHOT TO DEATH ON A BUSY STREET CORNER IN DOWNTOWN LOS ANGELES.

HIS ASSAILANT, A VEILED WOMAN IN BLACK, SURRENDERS HERSELF AT THE SCENE.

SHE GIVES HER NAME AS ESTHER ⌐LBANO BUT WILL SAY NOTHING MORE.

HOWEVER, SHE SOON REVEALS HERSELF TO BE ROSE PEPITONE, THE WIDOW OF THE AXE-MAN'S LAST VICTIM ...

AND SHE CLAIMS THAT MUMPHRE KILLED HER HUSBAND!

AN INVESTIGATION INTO THE BACKGROUND OF JOSEPH MUMPHRE LENDS CREDENCE TO THE WOMAN'S ACCUSATIONS.

IN NEW ORLEANS, HE WAS A PETTY CRIMINAL AND BLACKMAILER WHO OCCAISIONALLY WORKED AS AN ASSASSIN FOR THE MAFIA.

HE SERVED A TERM IN THE LOUISIANA STATE PRISON BEGINNING IN 1912 (JUST AFTER THE 1911 SERIES OF AXE MURDERS).

HE WAS RELEASED IN MAY OF 1918, JUST BEFORE THE FIRST AXE-MAN KILLING.

HE WAS INCARCERATED FOR BURGLARY FROM AUGUST 1918 TO MARCH 1919, COINCIDING WITH THE HIATUS IN THE MURDERS.

AND HE RELOCATED TO LOS ANGELES SHORTLY AFTER THE FINAL KILLING.

NO OTHER EVIDENCE OR MOTIVE CAN BE TRACED TO HIM.

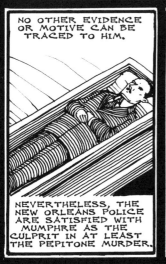

NEVERTHELESS, THE NEW ORLEANS POLICE ARE SATISFIED WITH MUMPHRE AS THE CULPRIT IN AT LEAST THE PEPITONE MURDER.

THEIR FILES SHOW THAT ONE PIETRO PEPITONE, FATHER OF MIKE, YEARS AGO KILLED A BLACK HAND EXTORTIONIST NAMED PAUL DE CRISTINA.

COULD THE MURDER OF THE SON HAVE BEEN REVENGE FOR THAT ACT?

ROSE PEPITONE IS PUT ON TRIAL FOR KILLING MUMPHRE.

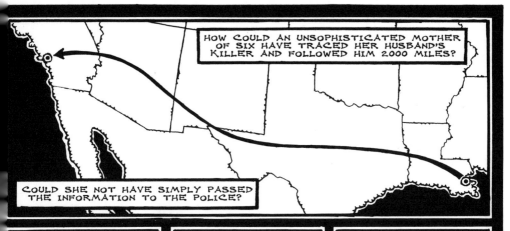

HOW COULD AN UNSOPHISTICATED MOTHER OF SIX HAVE TRACED HER HUSBAND'S KILLER AND FOLLOWED HIM 2000 MILES?

COULD SHE NOT HAVE SIMPLY PASSED THE INFORMATION TO THE POLICE?

SOME THEORIZE THAT SHE WAS CARRYING ON A LOVE AFFAIR WITH MUMPHRE.

THE TWO PLOTTED THE MURDER TOGETHER AND AFTERWARD, HE ABANDONED HER.

MRS. PEPITONE IS CONVICTED AND SENTENCED TO TEN YEARS IMPRISONMENT.

SHE IS RELEASED AFTER THREE YEARS...

AND PROMPTLY DISAPPEARS.

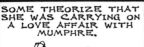

MONDAY, DECEMBER 6, 1920
ROSE CORTIMIGLIA RECANTS HER TESTIMONY AGAINST FRANK AND IORLANDO JORDANO.

SHE SAYS THAT ST. JOSEPH APPEARED TO HER IN A DREAM AND CONVINCED HER TO TELL THE TRUTH.

SHE ACCUSED THEM, SHE SAYS, OUT OF SPITE AND JEALOUSY, STEMMING FROM THE FAMILIES' LONG-STANDING FEUD.

FATHER AND SON ARE GIVEN FULL PARDONS AND SET FREE.

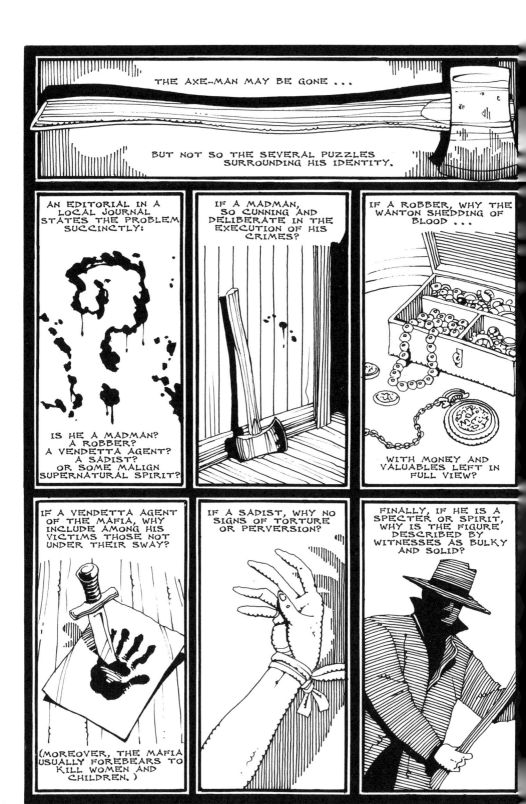

THE AXE-MAN MAY BE GONE ...

BUT NOT SO THE SEVERAL PUZZLES SURROUNDING HIS IDENTITY.

AN EDITORIAL IN A LOCAL JOURNAL STATES THE PROBLEM SUCCINCTLY:

IS HE A MADMAN? A ROBBER? A VENDETTA AGENT? A SADIST? OR SOME MALIGN SUPERNATURAL SPIRIT?

IF A MADMAN, SO CUNNING AND DELIBERATE IN THE EXECUTION OF HIS CRIMES?

IF A ROBBER, WHY THE WANTON SHEDDING OF BLOOD ...

WITH MONEY AND VALUABLES LEFT IN FULL VIEW?

IF A VENDETTA AGENT OF THE MAFIA, WHY INCLUDE AMONG HIS VICTIMS THOSE NOT UNDER THEIR SWAY?

(MOREOVER, THE MAFIA USUALLY FOREBEARS TO KILL WOMEN AND CHILDREN.)

IF A SADIST, WHY NO SIGNS OF TORTURE OR PERVERSION?

FINALLY, IF HE IS A SPECTER OR SPIRIT, WHY IS THE FIGURE DESCRIBED BY WITNESSES AS BULKY AND SOLID?

160

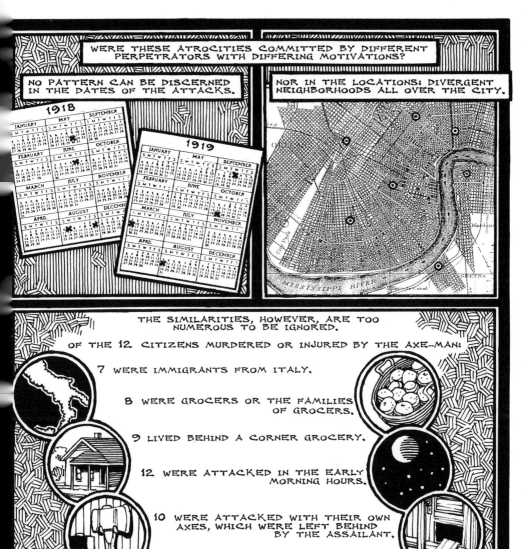

WERE THESE ATROCITIES COMMITTED BY DIFFERENT PERPETRATORS WITH DIFFERING MOTIVATIONS?

NO PATTERN CAN BE DISCERNED IN THE DATES OF THE ATTACKS.

1918

1919

NOR IN THE LOCATIONS: DIVERGENT NEIGHBORHOODS ALL OVER THE CITY.

THE SIMILARITIES, HOWEVER, ARE TOO NUMEROUS TO BE IGNORED.

OF THE 12 CITIZENS MURDERED OR INJURED BY THE AXE-MAN:

7 WERE IMMIGRANTS FROM ITALY.

8 WERE GROCERS OR THE FAMILIES OF GROCERS.

9 LIVED BEHIND A CORNER GROCERY.

12 WERE ATTACKED IN THE EARLY MORNING HOURS.

10 WERE ATTACKED WITH THEIR OWN AXES, WHICH WERE LEFT BEHIND BY THE ASSAILANT.

THE HOMES OF 8 WERE ENTERED THROUGH A CHISELED-OUT PANEL OF A REAR DOOR.

LINGERING QUESTIONS:

HOW COULD THE KILLER HAVE FOUND HIS WEAPON AND VICTIMS IN THE DARK OF NIGHT UNLESS HE WAS FAMILIAR WITH THE PREMISES?

HOW COULD HE HAVE COMPLETED THE LABORIOUS PROCESS OF CHIPPING AWAY A DOOR PANEL WITHOUT WAKING THE HOUSEHOLD?

HOW COULD A GROWN MAN FIT THROUGH THE SMALL OPENING LEFT BY THE PANEL?
(WAS THE OPENING SIMPLY USED TO REACH THROUGH AND UNLATCH THE DOOR? UNLIKELY SINCE THE DOORS WERE FOUND SECURELY LOCKED BY THOSE FIRST ON THE SCENE.)

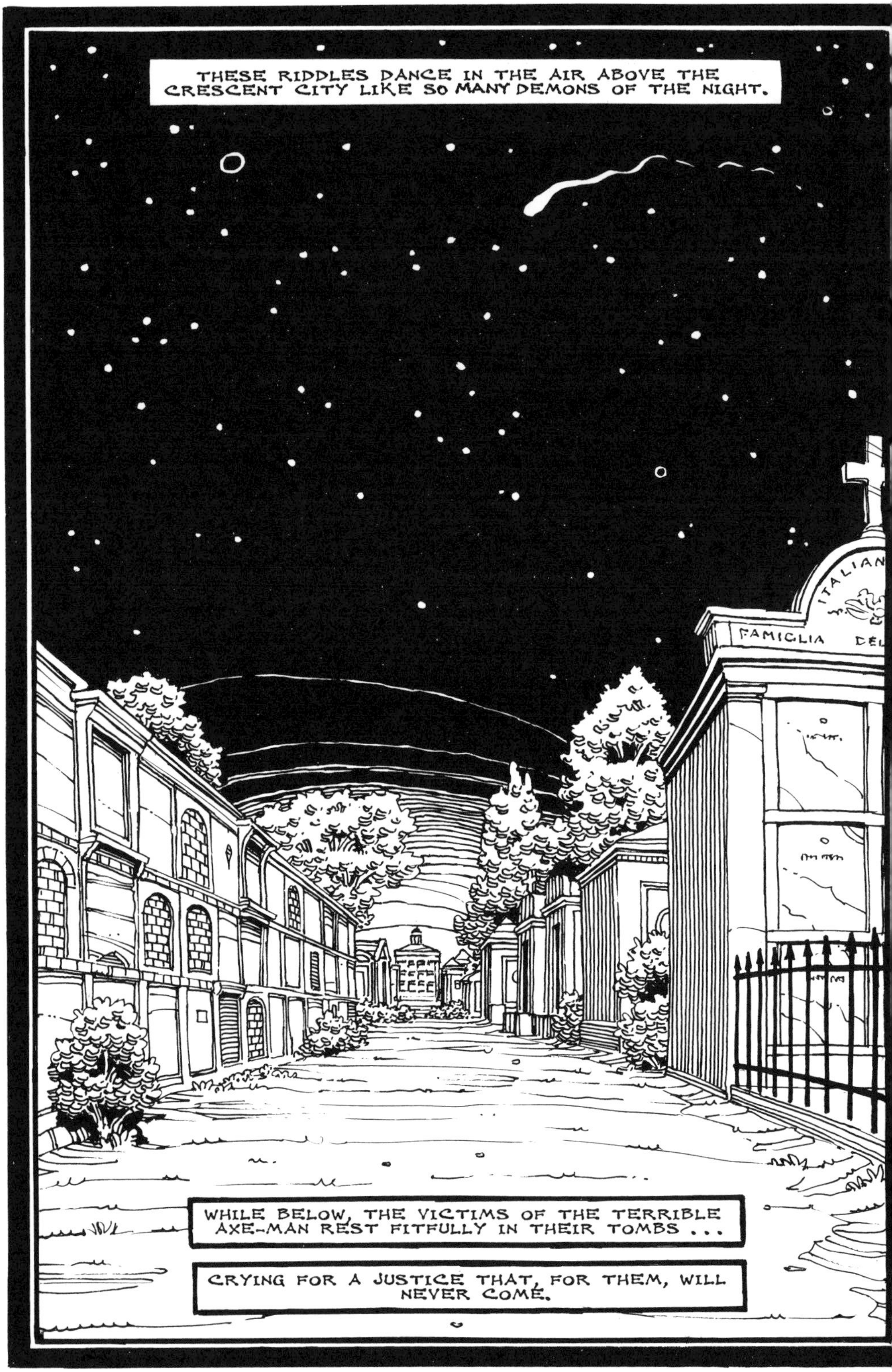

THESE RIDDLES DANCE IN THE AIR ABOVE THE CRESCENT CITY LIKE SO MANY DEMONS OF THE NIGHT.
ITALIAN
FAMIGLIA DEL
WHILE BELOW, THE VICTIMS OF THE TERRIBLE AXE-MAN REST FITFULLY IN THEIR TOMBS . . .
CRYING FOR A JUSTICE THAT, FOR THEM, WILL NEVER COME.

MADISON SQUARE
TRAGEDY

The Murder of STANFORD WHITE

25
June
1906

WRITTEN AND ILLUSTRATED BY
RICK GEARY

MADISON SQUARE TRAGEDY
BIBLIOGRAPHY

Crimes of Passion, no author credited. (London, Verdict Press, 1975)

Langford, Gerald, *The Murder of Stanford White.* (New York, Indianapolis, The Bobbs-Merrill Co., Inc., 1962)

Lowe, David Garrard, *Stanford White's New York.* (New York, Watson-Guptill Publications, 1999)

Mooney, Michael Macdonald, *Evelyn Nesbit and Stanford White: Love and Death in the Gilded Age.* (New York, William Morrow and Co., Inc, 1976)

Thaw, Harry K. *The Traitor.* (Philadelphia, Dorrance & Company, 1926)

Uruburu, Paula, *American Eve: Evelyn Nesbit, Stanford White, the Birth of the "It" Girl, and the Crime of the Century.* (New York, Riverhead Books, 2008)

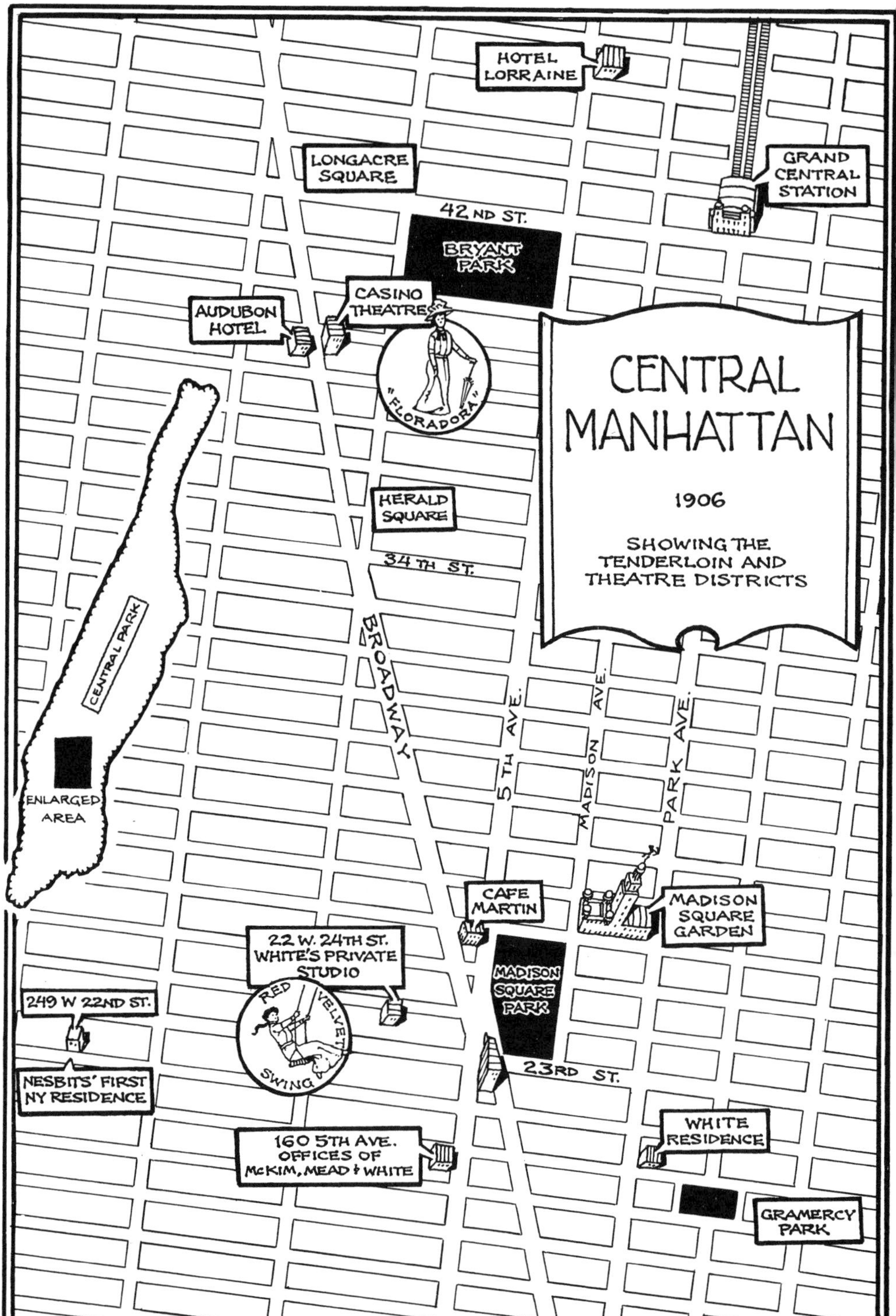
CENTRAL MANHATTAN
1906
SHOWING THE TENDERLOIN AND THEATRE DISTRICTS
HOTEL LORRAINE
GRAND CENTRAL STATION
LONGACRE SQUARE
42ND ST.
BRYANT PARK
CASINO THEATRE
AUDUBON HOTEL
"FLORADORA"
HERALD SQUARE
34TH ST.
BROADWAY
5TH AVE.
MADISON AVE.
PARK AVE.
CENTRAL PARK
ENLARGED AREA
CAFE MARTIN
MADISON SQUARE GARDEN
MADISON SQUARE PARK
22 W. 24TH ST. WHITE'S PRIVATE STUDIO
RED VELVET SWING
249 W 22ND ST.
NESBITS' FIRST NY RESIDENCE
23RD ST.
WHITE RESIDENCE
160 5TH AVE. OFFICES OF McKIM, MEAD & WHITE
GRAMERCY PARK

PART I

THE CITY OF
THE NEW CENTURY

THE YEAR 1901.

AS THE GREAT ENGINE OF THE TWENTIETH CENTURY
ROARS TO LIFE, THE CITY OF NEW YORK PROVIDES
ITS PROPULSION.

BURSTING WITH OPTIMISM AND ENTERPRISE, THE CITY LOOKS TO THE FUTURE.

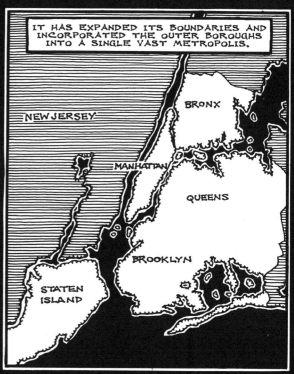

IT HAS EXPANDED ITS BOUNDARIES AND INCORPORATED THE OUTER BOROUGHS INTO A SINGLE VAST METROPOLIS.

NEW JERSEY

BRONX

MANHATTAN

QUEENS

BROOKLYN

STATEN ISLAND

WAVES OF IMMIGRANTS HAVE INCREASED THE POPULATION TO FOUR MILLION SOULS.

A NEW ERA OF SOCIAL MOBILITY... ARTISTIC INNOVATION... ENGINEERING MARVELS.

SKY-SCRAPERS STRETCH TO THE HEAVENS.

A SYSTEM OF UNDERGROUND TRAINS, NOW UNDER CONSTRUCTION, WILL LINK ALL CORNERS OF THE CITY.

THE AUTOMOBILE, UNTIL RECENTLY A PLAYTHING FOR THE WEALTHY, IS NOW SEEN WITH INCREASING FREQUENCY ALONG THE AVENUES.

FLYING MACHINES FILL THE SKY.

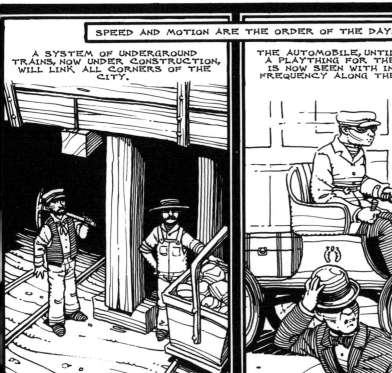

AND THE MOVING PICTURE CAMERA RECORDS IT ALL.

PRESIDENT THEODORE ROOSEVELT, THE FIRST CHIEF EXECUTIVE BORN IN THE CITY, TYPIFIES THE SPIRIT OF THE AGE.

THE NEW CULTURE OF CITY LIFE BRINGS HERETOFORE UNKNOWN PLEASURES AND DANGERS.

THE STORIES OF O. HENRY TELL OF ORDINARY PEOPLE MEETING THE COMPLICATED CHALLENGES OF THE URBAN ENVIRONMENT.

THE TRANSFORMATION OF SOCIETY IS GIVEN CHARACTER AND STYLE BY THE ILLUSTRATOR CHARLES DANA GIBSON.

THE "GIBSON GIRL" EXEMPLIFIES A NEW FREEDOM FOR WOMEN.

THE PRESIDENT'S FORTHRIGHT DAUGHTER, ALICE, SCANDALIZES THE NATION BY SMOKING IN PUBLIC.

IN NEW YORK, THE THEATRE EXPERIENCES AN IMMENSE BURST OF POPULARITY.

MUSICAL SHOWS DRAW GREAT CROWDS NIGHTLY.

THE THEATRE DISTRICT EXTENDS UP BROADWAY, FROM MADISON SQUARE AT 23RD STREET TO 42ND STREET AND LONGACRE SQUARE...

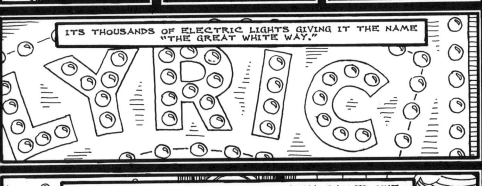

ITS THOUSANDS OF ELECTRIC LIGHTS GIVING IT THE NAME "THE GREAT WHITE WAY."

SURROUNDING IT IS THE BUSTLING AREA CALLED THE "TENDERLOIN," THE CENTER FOR PLEASURE AND VICE TO EVERY TASTE.

MERE BLOCKS AWAY IS FIFTH AVENUE, THE HOME OF UPSCALE MERCHANTS LIKE TIFFANY AND COMPANY...

AND, FARTHER NORTH, THE MANSIONS OF THE WEALTHY AND SUPER-WEALTHY: THE ASTORS, THE WHITNEYS, THE VANDERBILTS.

THE CITY'S LEADING ARCHITECTURAL FIRM IS McKIM, MEAD AND WHITE, WHO OPERATE FROM THEIR OFFICE AT 160 FIFTH AVE.

THEY ARE CHIEF AMONG MANY TO HAVE TRANSFORMED THE CITY OVER THE PAST TWO DECADES...

FROM A SEA OF DULL BROWNSTONE TO GLEAMING AVENUES OF MARBLE AND TERRA-COTTA THAT REFLECT THE GLORIES OF A EUROPEAN GOLDEN AGE.

172

THE MOST VISIBLE OF THE FIRM'S PARTNERS IS STANFORD WHITE.

AN AVID THEATREGOER, CLUBMAN, PATRON OF THE FINEST RESTAURANTS.

HIS SIX-FOOT FRAME, BRIGHT RED HAIR, AND BRISTLING MOUSTACHE MAKE HIM A STANDOUT IN ANY CROWD.

ON TUESDAY MORNING, JUNE 26, 1906, THE CITY IS STUNNED BY THE NEWS THAT WHITE HAS BEEN MURDERED.

New York American

RD WHITE ON ROOF GARDEN!

SHOOTS ARCHITECT IN BACK AS HE SITS TALKING TO WOMAN

TRAGIC OPENING NIGHT

NEWSPAPERS BLARE THE SHOCKING HEADLINES.

THE TRAGEDY OCCURRED THE NIGHT BEFORE, AT THE ROOFTOP THEATRE OF THE ARCHITECT'S BEST-KNOWN STRUCTURE: MADISON SQUARE GARDEN ON 26TH STREET.

THE CITY IS ENTRANCED AS THE STORY UNFOLDS.

173

THERE IS NO MYSTERY AS TO THE PERPETRATOR, WHO SURRENDERED AT THE SCENE: THE "MAD" MILLIONAIRE HARRY K. THAW OF PITTSBURGH.

HE DID IT, HE CLAIMS, TO AVENGE THE HONOR OF HIS WIFE, THE FORMER MODEL AND SHOW-GIRL EVELYN NESBIT.

IN THE DAYS TO COME, THAW LIVES A PRIVILEDGED EXISTENCE AT THE CITY JAIL...

AS HIS WIFE'S EVERY MOVEMENT IS MOBBED BY THE CURIOUS PRESS AND PUBLIC...

AND THE SCANDALOUS PRIVATE LIFE IF STANFORD WHITE IS REVEALED FOR ALL TO SEE.

TELL OF FORD WHITE'S DE...

"HUNTER" O SECRE

BUT LET US REVIEW THE LIVES OF THESE THREE AND TRACE THE PATHS THAT LED THEM TO THE FATAL NIGHT.

PART II

"STANNY"

AT THE DAWN OF THE NEW CENTURY, STANFORD WHITE, AT AGE 47, HAD REACHED THE PINNACLE OF HIS FAME AND INFLUENCE.

HE WAS BORN ON NOVEMBER 9, 1853, IN NEW YORK CITY...

THE YOUNGER OF TWO SONS BORN TO RICHARD GRANT WHITE AND ALEXINA MEASE WHITE.

THE FAMILY HOME ON EAST 10TH STREET.

THE FATHER WAS A NOTED ESSAYIST, NOVELIST, EDITOR, MUSIC AND DRAMA CRITIC -- BUT THE FAMILY WAS NOT WEALTHY.

HE FOUND STEADIER WORK AT THE NEW YORK CUSTOM HOUSE.

LITTLE "STANNY" WAS FULL OF ENERGY, EVER IN MOTION.

HE GREW UP IN A MILIEU OF GENTEEL BOHEMIANISM, AMID THE SOCIETY OF ARTISTS, WRITERS AND INTELLECTUALS.

176

FROM CHILDHOOD, HE SHOWED A TALENT FOR DRAWING, AND, BY AGE 17, HIS AMBITION WAS TO BE A PAINTER.

HIS PARENTS, HOWEVER, COULD NOT AFFORD COLLEGE OR ART SCHOOL.

INSTEAD, THROUGH HIS FATHER'S CONNECTIONS, HE ENTERED AN APPRENTICESHIP IN THE IN THE OFFICE OF AMERICA'S PRE-EMINENT ARCHITECT, HENRY H. RICHARDSON.

FROM HIS HEADQUARTERS ON HANOVER STREET IN LOWER MANHATTAN RICHARDSON HAD TRANSFORMED AMERICA WITH HIS PECULIARLY PERSONAL ROMANESQUE STYLE.

HE BECAME A MENTOR TO WHITE, WHO WORKED FOR HIM ON BOSTON'S TRINITY CHURCH...

AND THE NEW YORK STATE CAPITOL IN ALBANY.

THROUGH HIS WORK WITH RICHARDSON, WHITE MET THE TWO MEN WHO WOULD BECOME HIS CLOSEST FRIENDS: THE ARCHITECT CHARLES FOLLEN McKIM...

AND THE SCULPTOR AUGUSTUS ST. GAUDENS.

THE THREE YOUNG MEN TOGETHER MADE A GRAND TOUR OF EUROPE IN 1878~79...

WHITE SKETCHING AT EVERY OPPORTUNITY.

HE WAS PROFOUNDLY INSPIRED BY THE ROMANESQUE CHURCHES OF SOUTHERN FRANCE...

AND THE RENAISSANCE STYLES OF ROME AND VENICE, WHICH HE DREAMED OF TRANSPLANTING TO AMERICA.

BACK FROM EUROPE, HE JOINED THE FIRM FOUNDED BY McKIM AND WILLIAM RUTHERFORD MEAD.

McKIM, MEAD AND WHITE WAS BORN. THREE VERY DIFFERENT PERSONALITIES, THOUGH ALWAYS IN TUNE.

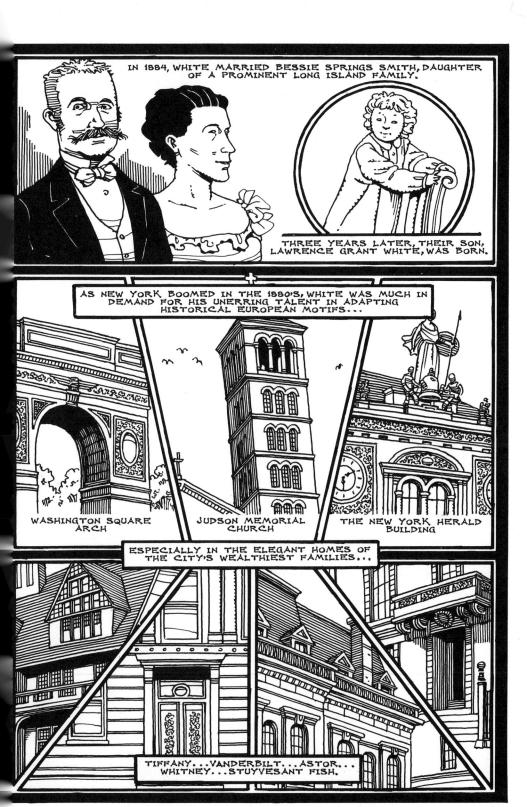

IN 1884, WHITE MARRIED BESSIE SPRINGS SMITH, DAUGHTER OF A PROMINENT LONG ISLAND FAMILY.

THREE YEARS LATER, THEIR SON, LAWRENCE GRANT WHITE, WAS BORN.

AS NEW YORK BOOMED IN THE 1880'S, WHITE WAS MUCH IN DEMAND FOR HIS UNERRING TALENT IN ADAPTING HISTORICAL EUROPEAN MOTIFS...

WASHINGTON SQUARE ARCH

JUDSON MEMORIAL CHURCH

THE NEW YORK HERALD BUILDING

ESPECIALLY IN THE ELEGANT HOMES OF THE CITY'S WEALTHIEST FAMILIES...

TIFFANY...VANDERBILT...ASTOR... WHITNEY...STUYVESANT FISH.

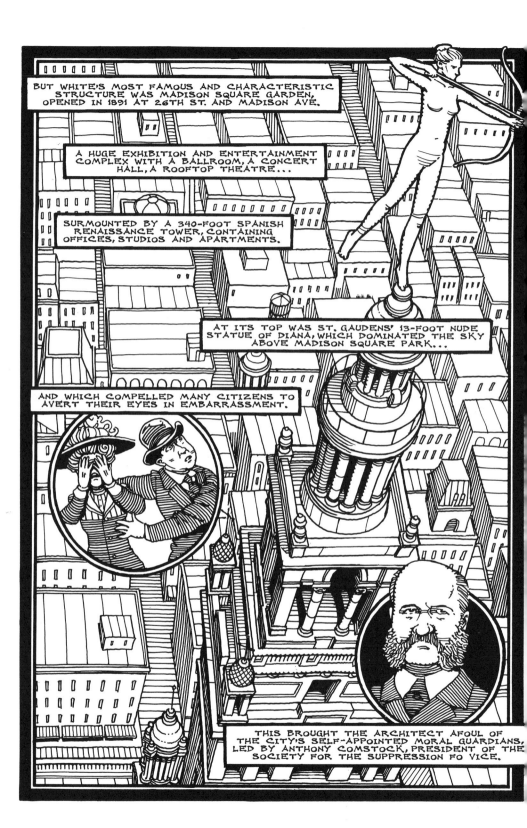

BUT WHITE'S MOST FAMOUS AND CHARACTERISTIC STRUCTURE WAS MADISON SQUARE GARDEN, OPENED IN 1891 AT 26TH ST. AND MADISON AVE.

A HUGE EXHIBITION AND ENTERTAINMENT COMPLEX WITH A BALLROOM, A CONCERT HALL, A ROOFTOP THEATRE...

SURMOUNTED BY A 340-FOOT SPANISH RENAISSANCE TOWER, CONTAINING OFFICES, STUDIOS AND APARTMENTS.

AT ITS TOP WAS ST. GAUDENS' 13-FOOT NUDE STATUE OF DIANA, WHICH DOMINATED THE SKY ABOVE MADISON SQUARE PARK...

AND WHICH COMPELLED MANY CITIZENS TO AVERT THEIR EYES IN EMBARRASSMENT.

THIS BROUGHT THE ARCHITECT AFOUL OF THE CITY'S SELF-APPOINTED MORAL GUARDIANS, LED BY ANTHONY COMSTOCK, PRESIDENT OF THE SOCIETY FOR THE SUPPRESSION FO VICE.

WHITE WAS ALSO A WELL-KNOWN PRESENCE IN THE SOCIAL LIFE OF THE CITY — THE QUINTESSENTIAL "MAN ABOUT TOWN."

GREGARIOUS AND EXUBERANT, FILLED WITH RESTLESS ENERGY, HE CULTIVATED A WIDE CIRCLE OF FRIENDSHIPS AMONG THE CULTURAL AND FINANCIAL ELITE.

HE ALSO HAD AN UNFORTUNATE TASTE FOR YOUNGER WOMEN.

AMONG HIS FRIENDS, HIS FLIRTATIONS WERE NOTORIOUS.

WHILE HIS TOLERANT WIFE BESSIE SPENT HER DAYS AT THE FAMILY'S COUNTRY ESTATE ON LONG ISLAND...

OR AT THEIR CITY RESIDENCE ON GRAMERCY PARK...

"STANNY" MAINTAINED AN APARTMENT IN THE TOWER OF MADISON SQUARE GARDEN...

WHERE HE OFTEN THREW LAVISH PARTIES...

AS WELL AS A PRIVATE STUDIO ON 24TH ST., WHERE HE ENTERTAINED HIS "CONQUESTS"...

EQUIPPED, IT WAS SAID, WITH A RED VELVET SWING.

DESPITE HIS PENCHANT FOR HIGH LIVING, WHITE, UNBEKNOWNST TO MANY, WAS IN DEEP FINANCIAL TROUBLE.

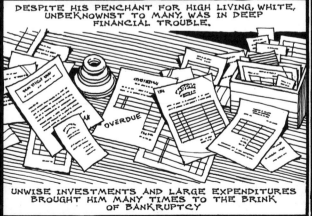

UNWISE INVESTMENTS AND LARGE EXPENDITURES BROUGHT HIM MANY TIMES TO THE BRINK OF BANKRUPTCY

AND WOULD EVENTUALLY CAUSE HIS EXPULSION AS A PARTNER IN HIS OWN FIRM.

IN THE AUTUMN OF 1901, WHITE'S LOVE OF MUSICAL THEATRE — AND THE FEMALE PERFORMERS THEREIN — BROUGHT HIM NIGHT AFTER NIGHT TO THE POPULAR REVUE "FLORADORA"...

THEN IN THE MIDST OF A LONG RUN AT THE CASINO THEATRE ON BROADWAY AT 39TH STREET.

MUSICAL SENSATION "FLORADORA" 14th WEEK

IN ONE OF THE SHOW'S NUMBERS, A YOUNG "SPANISH DANCER" HAD ALREADY ATTRACTED THE EYE OF MANY A MALE THEATREGOER.

HER NAME, HE DISCOVERED, WAS EVELYN NESBIT...

AND HE SET THE WHEELS IN MOTION TO ARRANGE A MEETING.

PART III

EVELYN

AS THE NEW CENTURY BEGAN, EVELYN NESBIT, AGE 16, WAS
NEWLY ARRIVED IN THE CITY AND ON THE BRINK OF HER
NOTORIOUS CAREER.

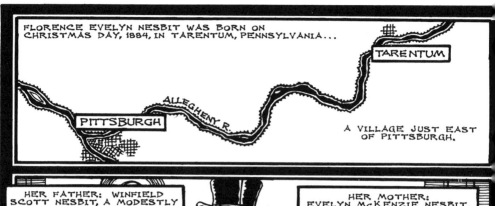

FLORENCE EVELYN NESBIT WAS BORN ON CHRISTMAS DAY, 1884, IN TARENTUM, PENNSYLVANIA...

TARENTUM

PITTSBURGH

ALLEGHENY R.

A VILLAGE JUST EAST OF PITTSBURGH.

HER FATHER: WINFIELD SCOTT NESBIT, A MODESTLY SUCCESSFUL ATTORNEY.

HER MOTHER: EVELYN McKENZIE NESBIT.

HER BROTHER, HOWARD, WAS BORN TWO YEARS LATER.

LITTLE FLORENCE WAS HIGH-SPIRITED AND SELF-ASSURED.

HER FATHER ENCOURAGED HER TO READ, SUPPORTED HER INTEREST IN MUSIC AND DANCE.

IN 1895, THE FAMILY RELOCATED TO PITTSBURGH, WHERE MR. NESBIT, AT AGE 40, SUDDENLY DIED.

WIDOW AND CHILDREN WERE PLUNGED INTO POVERTY.

THEY LIVED AND WORKED IN A SERIES OF SHABBY BOARDING HOUSES.

AT TIMES, THE CHILDREN WERE SENT, TOGETHER OR SEPARATELY, TO LIVE WITH VARIOUS RELATIVES...

WHILE MRS. NESBIT SEARCHED FOR EMPLOYMENT AS A SEAMSTRESS OR DRESS DESIGNER.

ALL TOO OFTEN, THE BROTHER AND SISTER FOUND THEIR MOTHER SOBBING HYSTERICALLY.

OH, WHAT WILL BECOME OF US?!

THESE YEARS OF DEPRIVATION WILL HAVE A LASTING EFFECT UPON THE GIRL.

FEELINGS OF ABANDONMENT AND REJECTION WILL NEVER ENTIRELY GO AWAY.

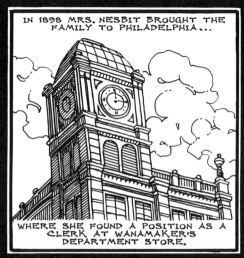

IN 1898 MRS. NESBIT BROUGHT THE FAMILY TO PHILADELPHIA...

WHERE SHE FOUND A POSITION AS A CLERK AT WANAMAKER'S DEPARTMENT STORE.

EVENTUALLY, BOTH CHILDREN WERE GIVEN JOBS AT THE STORE.

FLORENCE WAS A STOCK GIRL AND SOMETIMES WORKED THE COUNTER.

IT WAS NOT LONG BEFORE HER NATURAL ADVANTAGES BECAME EVIDENT.

AT AGE 14, FLORENCE WAS DEVELOPING INTO A BEAUTIFUL YOUNG LADY.

ONE DAY, SHE WAS NOTICED ON THE SIDEWALK BY A LOCAL ILLUSTRATOR.

AND A CAREER AS ARTISTS' MODEL OPENED UP TO HER.

THE YOUNG LADY BECAME MUCH IN DEMAND BY PHILADELPHIA'S PAINTERS AND ILLUSTRATORS...

AND, IN TIME, BY THE CITY'S PHOTOGRAPHERS.

HER INNOCENT VISAGE MADE HER NATURAL FOR ANGELS AND ALLEGORICAL SUBJECTS.

SHE WAS KNOWN AS "LITTLE MISS NESBIT."

THE HOURS SPENT HOLDING A SINGLE POSITION GAVE HER THE COMPOSURE AND INSCRUTABILITY THAT FORMED HER UNIQUE LOOK.

THE NEW AND STEADY INCOME ALLOWED MRS. NESBIT TO LEAVE WANAMAKER'S...

AND TAKE OVER THE MANAGEMENT OF HER DAUGHTER'S CAREER.

IN 1900, THE FAMILY MOVED TO NEW YORK CITY.

THEY LIVED AT FIRST IN A SINGLE ROOM AT 249 WEST 22ND ST.

FLORENCE EVELYN WAS IMMEDIATELY TAKEN UP BY THE CITY'S FINEST PAINTERS AND PHOTOGRAPHERS. (SHE PREFERRED PHOTOGRAPHERS SINCE THEY PAID BETTER AND DID NOT REQUIRE HOURS OF SITTING MOTIONLESS.)

VANITY FAIR

HARPER'S BAZ

THE LADIES HOME JOURNAL

THE COSMOPOLITA

AT THE START OF 1901 SHE HAD JUST TURNED 16, AND SOON HER FACE WAS EVERYWHERE.

Lutze BEER

The Little Bird

THE PUBLIC WONDERED ABOUT HER. PHOTOGRAPHERS CALLED HER THE LITTLE SPHINX. SHE WAS BOTH CHILD AND WOMAN.

POST CARD

CHARLES DANA GIBSON DEPICTED HER AS "THE ETERNAL QUESTION."

TO THE EXTENT THAT SHE WAS AMBITIOUS AT ALL, EVELYN, AS SHE NOW CALLED HERSELF, WANTED TO BE ON THE STAGE.

IN MAY OF 1901, SHE WAS HIRED TO JOIN THE CAST OF "FLORADORA."

AS THE "SPANISH DANCER" SHE EXCITED THE INTEREST OF THOSE MEN WHO CAME NIGHT AFTER NIGHT TO APPRAISE THE FEMALE PERFORMERS.

AT FIRST, MRS. NESBIT OBJECTED, BUT THE GIRL'S APPEAL WAS OBVIOUS.

SOMEHOW, HER AGE WAS OVERLOOKED.

THE OTHER GIRLS OF THE CHORUS WERE EVELYN'S FIRST REAL FRIENDS.

MOST OF THEM HOPED TO "SNAG" WEALTHY HUSBANDS.

FLOWERS ARRIVED BACKSTAGE NIGHTLY...

AND THE "STAGE DOOR JOHNNIES" AWAITED OUTSIDE.

AMONG HER MANY ADMIRERS WAS THE MILLIONAIRE BANKER JAMES GARLAND.

ALTHOUGH MARRIED AND IN HIS 60'S, HE ATTENDED EVELYN WITH PARTICULAR VIGOR.

HE TREATED HER AND HER MOTHER TO WEEKEND YACHTING EXCURSIONS ALONG THE HUDSON RIVER.

EVELYN KEPT AN ACTIVE SCHEDULE, POSING DURING THE DAY AND DANCING ONSTAGE AT NIGHT.

ONE DAY IN SEPTEMBER OF 1901, SHE WAS INVITED TO LUNCH BY ONE OF HER CHUMS IN THE CHORUS, TO MEET SOME "SOCIETY FRIENDS."

THEIR DESTINATION, HOWEVER, WAS NOT ONE OF THE CITY'S FINER RESTAURANTS...

F.A.O. SCHWARZ.

22

BUT A NONDESCRIPT BUILDING AT 22 WEST 24TH STREET. ON THE GROUND FLOOR WAS THE TOY EMPORIUM OF F. A. O. SCHWARZ.

THEY ENTERED THROUGH A SIDE DOOR AND CLIMBED A FLIGHT OF STAIRS.

WAITING AT THE TOP WAS THE TOWERING RED-HAIRED ARCHITECT STANFORD WHITE.

HIS PRIVATE STUDIO WAS LINED WITH RED VELVET, FILLED WITH FINE PAINTINGS AND ANTIQUE FURNITURE.

A SECOND GENTLEMAN JOINED THEM FOR THE ELABORATE LUNCH, WHICH WAS DELIVERED FROM DELMONICO'S

EVELYN TASTED HER FIRST GLASS OF CHAMPAGNE.

AFTERWARD, WHITE USHERED THE LADIES TO AN UPSTAIRS ROOM, WHERE A RED VELVET SWING HUNG FROM THE CEILING.

THEY TOOK TURNS BEING PUSHED BY THE ARCHITECT...

ALL OF IT QUITE CAREFREE AND INNOCENT.

AFTER THAT DAY, WHITE BECAME A KIND OF BENEVOLENT FATHER FIGURE TO EVELYN AND HER FAMILY.

HE CULTIVATED AND CHARMED MRS. NESBIT AND CONVINCED HER THAT HE HAD NOTHING BUT THE MOST PROTECTIVE OF INTENTIONS.

HE SECURED, FOR THE FAMILY, ROOMS AT THE AUDUBON HOTEL ACROSS BROADWAY FROM THE CASINO THEATRE...

AND LATER MOVED THEM INTO A PERSONALLY DESIGNED SUITE AT THE WELLINGTON HOTEL, ON 7TH AVENUE.

HE PAID FOR A PRIVATE SCHOOL FOR YOUNG HOWARD...

AND HAD EVELYN'S TEETH, TWO OF WHICH WERE SLIGHTLY DISCOLORED, REPAIRED BY HIS PERSONAL DENTIST.

AFTER SEVERAL MORE LUNCHES, EVELYN FOUND HERSELF MUCH ATTRACTED TO THE CHARISMATIC OLDER MAN.

TO HER, HE WAS UNFAILINGLY KIND GENEROUS AND ATTENTIVE.

HE BROUGHT HER TO ELEGANT PARTIES AT HIS MADISON SQUARE GARDEN APARTMENT, WHERE SHE MINGLED WITH THE ELITE OF MUSIC, ART, FINANCE, AND POLITICS.

WHITE WOULD SOMETIMES ESCORT HER TO THE VERY TOP OF THE TOWER...

WHERE SHE COULD REACH UP AND TOUCH THE FOOT OF DIANA...

THE CITY SPREAD BELOW HER.

BUT IT WAS NOT LONG BEFORE "STANNY'S" TRUE INTENTIONS REVEALED THEMSELVES.

IN NOVEMBER, HE ARRANGED FOR MRS. NESBIT TO VISIT RELATIVES IN PITTSBURGH...

AND ONE NIGHT INVITED EVELYN, AFTER THE PERFORMANCE OF "FLORADORA," TO HIS 24TH STREET ROOMS.

SHE THOUGHT IT ODD, AT FIRST, THAT NO ONE ELSE WAS THERE.

BUT SHE FELT PERFECTLY SAFE WITH THE OLDER MAN.

THEY ENJOYED A FINE MEAL AND DRANK MUCH CHAMPAGNE.

192

AFTER DINNER, AS EVELYN WILL DESCRIBE IT YEARS LATER, HE GUIDED HER UP A NARROW BACK STAIRWAY...

TO A SMALL ROOM CROWDED WITH PAINTINGS AND STATUARY.

BEHIND A TAPESTRY WAS AN EXOTIC BEDROOM, LINED WITH MIRRORS AND ILLUMINATED SUBTLY BY INDIRECT COLORED LIGHTS.

ANOTHER GLASS OF CHAMPAGNE— WAS IT DRUGGED?

AND EVELYN PASSED OUT.

SHE WILL REMEMBER NOTHING UNTIL WAKING UP SOMETIME LATER IN WHITE'S BED. SHE WAS NAKED, AND THE ARCHITECT WAS LYING NAKED BESIDE HER!

SHE KNEW AT ONCE WHAT HAD HAPPENED. SHE COULD FEEL IT. SHE HAD BEEN VIOLATED!

SHE SCREAMED AND CRIED, WHILE THE FLUSTERED OLDER MAN TRIED TO COMFORT HER.

HE WARNED HER TO TELL NO ONE.

EVELYN RETURNED TO HER HOTEL IN A STATE OF INSENSIBILITY...

AND REMAINED IN A STUPOR FOR SEVERAL DAYS.

BUT WHITE CONTINUED HIS ATTENTIONS, AND EVELYN REMAINED DRAWN TO HIM.

TO HER HE WAS "A FORCE OF NATURE." TO HIM SHE WAS "THE PERFECT PRIZE."

HIS PET NAME FOR HER WAS "KITTENS."

THEY CARRIED ON A DISCREET LOVE AFFAIR WHILE OUTWARDLY HE PLAYED THE ROLE OF PROTECTOR AND BENEFACTOR.

SHE WAS INTRODUCED TO A LIFE OF LUXURY AND PLEASURE.

HE COMPLETELY TOOK OVER HER EDUCATION, CULTURAL, SOCIAL– AND SEXUAL.

BUT INEVITABLY THEIR ASSIOCIATION BEGAN TO LOSE ITS INTENSITY.

BY THE DAWN OF 1902, EVELYN HAD ACCEPTED THE REALITY THAT WHITE TRULY LOVED HIS WIFE AND WOULD NEVER LEAVE HIS FAMILY...

WHILE HIS EYE CONTINUED TO BE DRAWN TO NEWER AND YOUNGER "PRIZES."

IN APRIL, "FLORADORA" ENDED ITS RUN, AND EVELYN ACCEPTED A FEATURED ROLE IN A NEW MUSICAL REVUE, "THE WILD ROSE."

ONE YOUNG MAN WHO PRESSED HIS ATTENTIONS WAS 20-YEAR-OLD JACK BARRYMORE, YOUNGEST OF THE FAMED ACTING SIBLINGS...

ETHEL

LIONEL

SHE ALSO BEGAN TO ACCEPT LUNCHEON AND DINNER INVITATIONS FROM THE WOULD-BE SUITORS WHO CONTINUED TO SWARM THE STAGE DOOR.

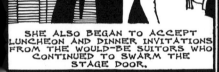

AT THAT TIME PURSUING A CAREER AS A NEWSPAPER CARTOONIST.

THEY BEGAN AN INTENSE BUT CHASTE LOVE AFFAIR THAT WAS GOSSIPED ABOUT IN THE NEWSPAPERS.

IN TIME, THEY TALKED OF MARRIAGE.

BUT MRS. NESBIT THOUGHT BARRYMORE A WASTREL AND DISAPPROVED OF THE ROMANCE.

SHE ENLISTED STANFORD WHITE TO QUASH IT.

AT A MEETING IN THE NESBITS' HOTEL SUITE, THE ARCHITECT QUIZZED THE YOUNG MAN AS TO HIS INTENTIONS.

WHAT WILL YOU LIVE ON?

WE'LL LIVE ON LOVE.

IN SHORT ORDER, ARRANGEMENTS WERE MADE TO WITHDRAW EVELYN FROM HER MODELING AND THEATRICAL CAREERS...

AND ENROLL HER AT AN ALL-GIRL PRIVATE BOARDING SCHOOL: THE DEMILLE SCHOOL IN POMPTON LAKES, NEW JERSEY.

EVELYN RESISTED BEING YANKED FROM HER GLAMOROUS LIFE IN NEW YORK, BUT AT AGE 17 THERE WAS LITTLE SHE COULD DO.

AND SOON SHE FELL OBEDIENTLY INTO THE ACADEMIC ROUTINE...

INTERRUPTED OCCASIONALLY BY VISITS FROM JOURNALISTS...

AND FROM STANFORD WHITE, STILL KEEPING A FATHERLY EYE UPON HER.

IT WAS AT THIS TIME THAT ONE OF HER NEW YORK ADMIRERS RENEWED HIS PURSUIT.

DURING THE RUNS OF "FLORADORA" AND "THE WILD ROSE," HE HAD FLOODED HER WITH FLOWERS AND LETTERS.

WHEN THEY HAD FIRST MET SHE COULD SEE THE "MADNESS" IN HIS EYES.

PART IV

HARRY

IN 1901, WHEN HE FIRST LAID EYES ON EVELYN NESBIT,
HARRY K. THAW, AGE 30, HAD THE MEANS TO INDULGE HIS
EVERY DESIRE.

HE WAS BORN FEBRUARY 12, 1871, IN PITTSBURGH, THIRD OF FIVE CHILDREN BORN TO WILLIAM K. THAW, WHO MADE THE FAMILY'S FORTUNE IN STEEL, COKE AND RAILROADS...

AND MARY COPLEY THAW.

HIS BROTHERS: JOSIAH AND EDWARD
HIS SISTERS: MARGARET AND ALICE.

HARRY GREW UP SPOILED AND PETTED BY HIS ADORING MOTHER.

BUT HE WAS A "NERVOUS" CHILD...

PRONE TO TANTRUMS AND EPISODES OF "EXCITEMENT"...

TO SUCH A DEGREE THAT SHE FEARED HE MIGHT HAVE INHERITED THE STRAINS OF INSANITY THAT RAN THROUGH BOTH SIDES OF THE FAMILY.

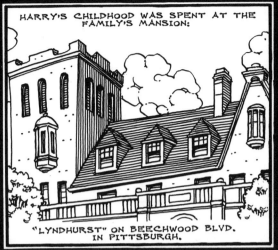

HARRY'S CHILDHOOD WAS SPENT AT THE FAMILY'S MANSION:

"LYNDHURST" ON BEECHWOOD BLVD. IN PITTSBURGH.

AS A YOUTH HE MADE SEVERAL TOURS OF EUROPE WITH HIS MOTHER AND SIBLINGS.

HE ATTENDED WOOSTER PREP SCHOOL AND THEN THE UNIVERSITY OF PITTSBURGH...

BUT HE DISPLAYED MORE INTEREST IN POKER, LIQUOR, AND WOMEN THAN IN ACADEMIC PURSUITS.

AFTER A BRIEF TERM AT HARVARD, HE WAS EXPELLED FOR "IMMORAL PRACTICES."

IN TRUTH, ALL HE WANTED TO BE WAS A RICH IDLER...

THUS DISPLEASING THE ELDER THAW, WHO, UPON HIS PASSING, LEFT HARRY WITH A MONTHLY ALLOWANCE OF A MERE $2500.

HIS MOTHER SOON RAISED THE AMOUNT TO $80,000.

HARRY WORKED TO ESTABLISH AN UNSAVORY REPUTATION FOR HIMSELF IN THE UNITED STATES AND THE CAPITALS OF EUROPE.  HE THREW LAVISH PARTIES AND DINNERS.	HE ONCE DROVE AN AUTOMOBILE THROUGH A FIFTH AVENUE STORE WINDOW. 	HE CHASED A CAB DRIVER, WHOM HE THOUGHT HAD CHEATED HIM, WITH A SHOTGUN. 
HE RODE A HORSE INTO A NEW YORK MEN'S CLUB WHICH HAD DENIED HIM MEMBERSHIP. 	DARKER RUMORS ABOUNDED:  POSING AS "MR. REID," A THEATRICAL COACH, HE WOULD RENT CHEAP ROOMS TO WHICH HE WOULD LURE YOUNG ASPIRING ACTRESSES.	HE WOULD THEN BIND AND WHIP THEM. 
AT LEAST ONE HE FORCED INTO A BATHTUB AND POURED SCALDING WATER OVER HER...  ALL OF THIS IN THE GUISE OF A GALLANT PROTECTOR OF FEMALE VIRTUE.	EARLY ON, HE ALLIED HIMSELF WITH ANTHONY COMSTOCK, IN THE ONGOING CRUSADE AGAINST VICE...	AND NURTURED AN ESPECIAL HATRED FOR THAT SATANIC DEFILER OF WOMEN... STANFORD WHITE.

BY 1898, HARRY HAD ESTABLISHED HIMSELF MORE OR LESS PERMANENTLY IN NEW YORK CITY...

IN ROOMS AT THE KNICKERBOCKER HOTEL, ACCOMPANIED BY HIS LONG-SUFFERING MANSERVANT BEDFORD.

HE ATTENDED THE THEATRE REGULARLY, THE BETTER TO FIND YOUNG LADIES IN NEED OF RESCUE.

SOMETIME IN THE FALL OF 1901, HE FIRST WONDERED ABOUT THE BEAUTIFUL SPANISH DANCER IN THE CAST OF "FLORADORA."

HE WATCHED HER FOR A SOLID MONTH FROM HIS BOX AT THE CASINO THEATRE, AND DID THE SAME WHEN SHE APPEARED IN "THE WILD ROSE."

BY THEN, HE HAD HEARD THE GOSSIP ABOUT EVELYN NESBIT'S "SPECIAL" RELATIONSHIP WITH STANFORD WHITE.

HE BEGAN TO ENTREAT HER WITH FLOWERS, GIFTS, EVEN CASH...

AND WITH LETTERS MYSTERIOUSLY SIGNED "MR. MUNROE."

FINALLY, ACCOMPANIED BY A FRIEND, SHE MET HIM FOR LUNCH AT RECTOR'S RESTAURANT ON BROADWAY AT 44TH STREET.

THERE, BETWEEN HIS EXCITED MONOLOGUES, HE DROPPED TO HIS KNEES, KISSED HER SKIRT, AND CONFESSED HIS TRUE IDENTITY.

I AM NOT MR. MUNROE, I AM HARRY K. THAW OF PITTSBURGH.

YOU'VE HEARD OF ME?

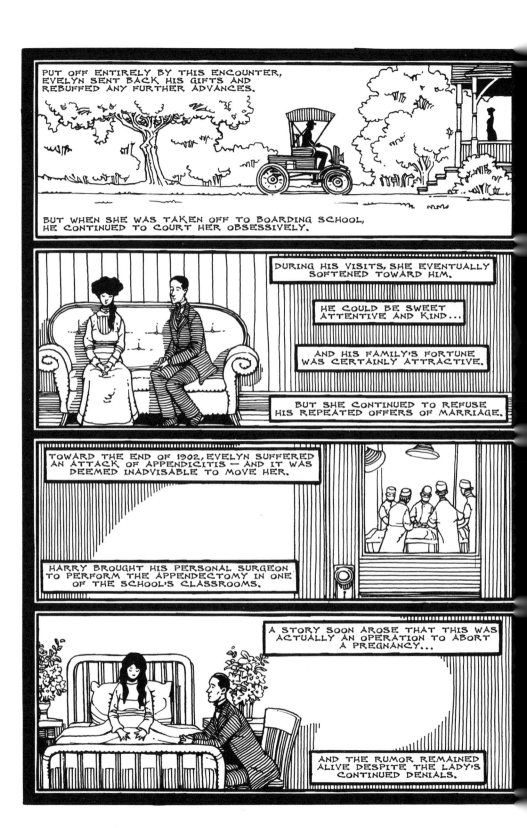

PUT OFF ENTIRELY BY THIS ENCOUNTER, EVELYN SENT BACK HIS GIFTS AND REBUFFED ANY FURTHER ADVANCES.

BUT WHEN SHE WAS TAKEN OFF TO BOARDING SCHOOL, HE CONTINUED TO COURT HER OBSESSIVELY.

DURING HIS VISITS, SHE EVENTUALLY SOFTENED TOWARD HIM.

HE COULD BE SWEET ATTENTIVE AND KIND...

AND HIS FAMILY'S FORTUNE WAS CERTAINLY ATTRACTIVE.

BUT SHE CONTINUED TO REFUSE HIS REPEATED OFFERS OF MARRIAGE.

TOWARD THE END OF 1902, EVELYN SUFFERED AN ATTACK OF APPENDICITIS — AND IT WAS DEEMED INADVISABLE TO MOVE HER.

HARRY BROUGHT HIS PERSONAL SURGEON TO PERFORM THE APPENDECTOMY IN ONE OF THE SCHOOL'S CLASSROOMS.

A STORY SOON AROSE THAT THIS WAS ACTUALLY AN OPERATION TO ABORT A PREGNANCY...

AND THE RUMOR REMAINED ALIVE DESPITE THE LADY'S CONTINUED DENIALS.

EARLY IN THE NEW YEAR, HARRY, WHO HAD MANAGED TO WIN OVER MRS. NESBIT, SUGGESTED AN OCEAN VOYAGE AND A TOUR OF EUROPE TO AID IN EVELYN'S RECOVERY.

IN MAY OF 1903, SHE AND HER MOTHER DEPARTED FOR ENGLAND. HARRY FOLLOWED ON A SEPARATE SHIP.

IN LONDON AND PARIS, THEY STAYED IN SEPARATE HOTELS.

HARRY WAS ON HIS BEST BEHAVIOR.

ALL THE WHILE, HE PRESSED EVELYN TO MARRY HIM, AND SHE KEPT REFUSING.

I CANNOT MARRY YOU!

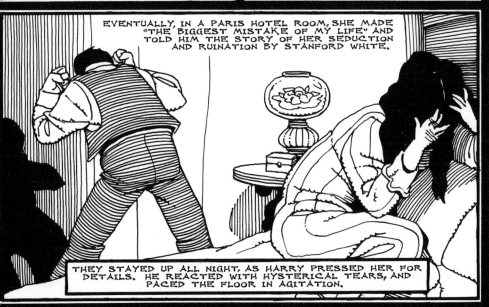

EVENTUALLY, IN A PARIS HOTEL ROOM, SHE MADE "THE BIGGEST MISTAKE OF MY LIFE" AND TOLD HIM THE STORY OF HER SEDUCTION AND RUINATION BY STANFORD WHITE.

THEY STAYED UP ALL NIGHT, AS HARRY PRESSED HER FOR DETAILS. HE REACTED WITH HYSTERICAL TEARS, AND PACED THE FLOOR IN AGITATION.

BEFORE LONG, A GROWING TENSION BETWEEN HARRY AND MRS. NESBIT RESULTED IN HER RETURN TO LONDON...

AND, EVENTUALLY, TO AMERICA.

TO MAINTAIN APPEARANCES, HE HIRED A LADY AS CHAPERONE.

AND HE AND EVELYN CONTINUED THEIR TOUR OF THE CONTINENT: GERMANY, THE NETHERLANDS, AUSTRIA.

IN AUSTRIA, HE RENTED AN ENTIRE CASTLE HIGH IN THE MOUNTAINS: SCHLOSS-KATZENSTEIN.

THEY OCCUPIED SEPARATE ROOMS.

HERE, ONE TERRIFYING NIGHT, HE BURST INTO HER ROOM, NAKED AND IN A FURY.

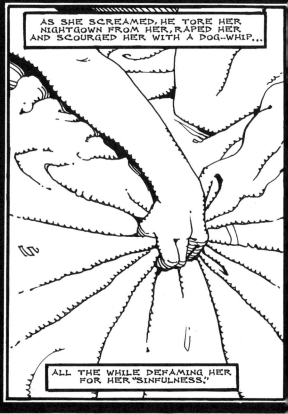

AS SHE SCREAMED, HE TORE HER NIGHTGOWN FROM HER, RAPED HER AND SCOURGED HER WITH A DOG-WHIP...

ALL THE WHILE DEFAMING HER FOR HER "SINFULNESS."

FOR THE REMAINDER OF THEIR THREE WEEKS AT THE CASTLE, EVELYN REFUSED TO LEAVE HER ROOM.

AFTER THAT, THEY CONTINUED THEIR JOURNEY: TO SWITZERLAND AND BACK TO PARIS...

HARRY BEHAVING AS IF NOTHING HAD HAPPENED, EVELYN ALTERNATELY SILENT AND SOBBING.

ONCE, WHILE HE WAS OUT, SHE DISCOVERED HIS NEEDLES!

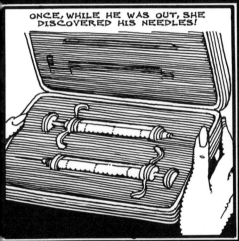

IN OCTOBER, EVELYN RETURNED ALONE TO NEW YORK.

HARRY CAME SOME WEEKS LATER.

SHE SECLUDED HERSELF AT DIFFERENT HOTELS...

AND QUIETLY TRIED TO RESUME HER MODELING AND STAGE CAREERS.

DURING THIS TIME, SHE RESISTED SEEKING OUT "STANNY."

BUT AFTER A CHANCE ENCOUNTER ON THE STREET, HE TELEPHONED HER.

BY THIS TIME, EVELYN'S MOTHER HAD ALLIED HERSELF WITH THE ARCHITECT TO WREST HER DAUGHTER FROM THE INFLUENCE OF HARRY THAW.

WHITE HAD CONTINUED HIS FINANCIAL SUPPORT OF MRS. NESBIT AND HOWARD, NOW AGE 15.

WHITE AND OTHERS FILLED EVELYN IN ON HARRY'S DECADENT HISTORY...

INCLUDING HIS ADDICTIONS TO BOTH COCAINE AND MORPHINE.

ONE DAY IN NOVEMBER, WHITE BROUGHT EVELYN TO THE OFFICE OF AN ATTORNEY, A MISSHAPEN MAN NAMED ABE HUMMEL.

FROM HER, THE LAWYER TOOK A DETAILED DEPOSITION, LAYING OUT THAW'S MANIA AND CRUELTY DURING THEIR EUROPEAN EXCURSION.

WHEN HARRY RETURNED TO THE CITY, HE RENEWED HIS COURTSHIP WITH EVEN GREATER ZEAL...

AND EVELYN, WHO HAD LITTLE KNOWLEDGE OF WHAT WOULD CONSTITUTE A "NORMAL" LOVE AFFAIR, SLOWLY RESPONDED TO HIS SINCERE AND ERNEST ENTREATIES.

IN THE SPRING OF 1904, THEY MADE ANOTHER TOUR OF EUROPE, THIS TIME WITH NO OUTRAGEOUS EPISODES.

SHE AT LAST GAVE IN TO HIS REPEATED PROPOSALS, AND THEY WERE MARRIED ON APRIL 5, 1905...

THE BRIDE: AGE 20.

THE GROOM: 34.

IN A SMALL CEREMONY AT THE HOME OF REV. McEWAN, OF THE THIRD PRESBYTERIAN CHURCH IN PITTSBURGH.

THE BRIDE'S MOTHER, WHO HAD BY THEN WASHED HER HANDS OF HER WAYWARD DAUGHTER AND REMARRIED, ATTENDED WITH HER HUSBAND, CHARLES HOLMAN.

THE NEWLYWEDS DEPARTED FOR A HONEYMOON TRIP TO ARIZONA AND CALIFORNIA.

THERE WAS NO LOVE LOST BETWEEN THE BRIDE AND THE FORMIDABLE MOTHER THAW...

WHO HAD OPPOSED THE MATCH FROM THE BEGINNING.

LIKEWISE HARRY'S SISTERS: ALICE, WHO HAD MARRIED AN IMPOVERISHED NOBLEMAN, THE EARL OF YARMOUTH

AND MARGARET, WHO WAS WED TO GEORGE CARNEGIE, NEPHEW OF THE STEEL MAGNATE.

AFTER THE EXCITEMENT OF BROADWAY AND EUROPE, EVELYN FOUND LIFE AT "LYNDHURST" EXCRUCIATINGLY MONOTONOUS FILLED WITH CHURCH WORK AND DOMESTIC CHATTER.

PITTSBURGH SOCIETY WOULD NOT RECEIVE HER.

TO THE FAMILY'S EMBARRASSMENT, A SERIES OF SENSUOUS PHOTOGRAPHS SHE HAD POSED FOR YEARS EARLIER MADE THEIR WAY INTO A LOCAL NEWSPAPER.

HARRY, INITIALLY ATTENTIVE SPENT MORE AND MORE TIME AWAY FROM HOME.

MARRIAGE DID NOT SOFTEN HARRY'S RAGE AND RESENTMENT TOWARD STANFORD WHITE.

HE CONTINUED TO PESTER EVELYN FOR DETAILS OF HER RELATIONSHIP WITH THE ARCHITECT.

SHE SURRENDERED THE LETTERS THAT HER SEDUCER HAD WRITTEN TO HER.

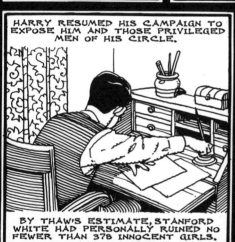

HARRY RESUMED HIS CAMPAIGN TO EXPOSE HIM AND THOSE PRIVILEGED MEN OF HIS CIRCLE.

BY THAW'S ESTIMATE, STANFORD WHITE HAD PERSONALLY RUINED NO FEWER THAN 378 INNOCENT GIRLS.

HE HIRED DETECTIVES TO FOLLOW THE MAN'S EVERY MOVEMENT...

AS WELL AS THOSE OF EVELYN.

HE CLAIMED THAT WHITE, IN TURN, HAD HIRED CRIMINALS FROM THE NOTORIOUS MONK EASTMAN GANG TO FOLLOW AND ELIMINATE HIM.

HE PURCHASED A PISTOL AND PRACTICED WITH IT ON THE GROUNDS OF "LYNDHURST."

HARRY SENT EVELYN TO HIS PERSONAL DENTIST, TO HAVE THE WORK THAT WHITE HAD PAID FOR REVERSED.

HE NEXT CAME UP WITH THE IDEA THAT HIS WIFE SHOULD NEVER AGAIN UTTER THE ARCHITECT'S NAME.

SHE WILL ONLY REFER TO HIM AS "THE BEAST" OR SIMPLY AS "THE B," WHICH CAN ALSO STAND FOR "THE BOUNDER" OR "THE BLACKGUARD."

EARLY IN 1906, HARRY DECIDED THAT ANOTHER TOUR OF EUROPE WAS IN ORDER.

IN JUNE, PREPARATORY TO THEIR DEPARTURE, THEY CAME TO NEW YORK.

MOTHER THAW WHO WOULD ACCOMPANY THEM IN EUROPE, HAD SET SAIL ON AN EARLIER VESSEL.

THEY TOOK A SUITE AT THE HOTEL LORRAINE, FIFTH AVENUE AT 49TH STREET.

HARRY SPENT HIS DAYS WITH HIS MALE CRONIES, WHILE EVELYN SHOPPED ALONG FIFTH AVENUE...

FOLLOWED AT A DISCREET DISTANCE BY HER HUSBAND'S DETECTIVES.

PART V

THE FATAL NIGHT

MONDAY, JUNE 25, 1906,
IS OPPRESSIVELY HOT AND MUGGY.

NEW YORKERS, SEEKING RELIEF, HAVE NO INKLING OF THE
DRAMA THAT WILL PLAY OUT THIS EVENING AT MADISON
SQUARE GARDEN.

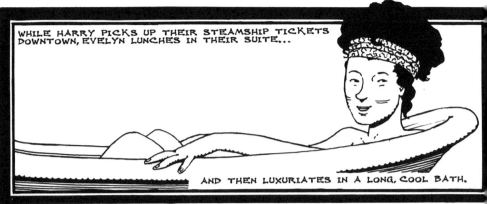

WHILE HARRY PICKS UP THEIR STEAMSHIP TICKETS DOWNTOWN, EVELYN LUNCHES IN THEIR SUITE...

AND THEN LUXURIATES IN A LONG, COOL BATH.

132

IN THE EVENING, HARRY BECOMES IMPATIENT WITH HIS WIFE'S PREPARATIONS AND GOES OUT ALONE.

AT ABOUT 7:00PM, EVELYN MEETS HER HUSBAND IN THE BAR AT SHERRY'S RESTAURANT, NEAR THEIR HOTEL AT FIFTH AVENUE AND 44TH STREET.

JOINING THEM IS A JOURNALIST FRIEND OF HARRY'S, TRUXTON BEALE.

SHE FINDS IT ODD THAT HARRY WEARS A HEAVY OVERCOAT, WHICH HE DECLINES TO REMOVE IN THE STIFLING HEAT.

THEY DECIDE UPON DINNER AT CAFE MARTIN, ON 26TH STREET BETWEEN BROADWAY AND FIFTH AVENUE...

A POPULAR GATHERING SPOT FOR THE THEATRE CROWD.

THEY ARRIVE THROUGH THE 26TH ST. ENTRANCE AND ARE SHOWN TO A TABLE IN THE MAIN DOWNSTAIRS DINING ROOM.

HERE, THEY ARE MET BY THEIR OTHER COMPANION FOR THE EVENING: TOMMY McCALEB, AND OLD FAMILY FRIEND OF THE THAWS.

EVELYN, FACING THE RESTAURANT'S FIFTH AVENUE ENTRANCE, SUDDENLY BECOMES NERVOUS AND APPREHENSIVE...

FOR ENTERING THE ESTABLISHMENT IS NONE OTHER THAN STANFORD WHITE.

IN THE AFTERNOON, HE WATCHES THE FINAL RUN-THROUGH OF THE MUSICAL REVUE "MAMZELLE CHAMPAGNE"...

WHICH WILL PREMIERE TONIGHT AT MADISON SQUARE GARDEN'S ROOFTOP THEATRE.

HE ASKS THE STAGE MANAGER IF AN INTRODUCTION MIGHT BE ARRANGED TO A PARTICULAR CHORUS GIRL WHO HAS ATTRACTED HIS EYE.

LATER IN THE DAY, WHITE MEETS HIS SON, LAWRENCE, AN ARCHITECTURE STUDENT ON A VISIT HOME, WITH A FRIEND, FROM HARVARD.

THEY DECIDE UPON DINNER AT CAFÉ MARTIN BEFORE ATTENDING THE THEATRE.

ENTERING FROM THE FIFTH AVENUE SIDE, THE PARTY PASSES THROUGH THE MAIN DINING ROOM BEFORE GOING UPSTAIRS TO THE SMALLER EUROPEAN-STYLE CAFÉ.

IF WHITE NOTICES EVELYN AND HARRY, HE GIVES NO INDICATION OF IT.

HARRY, HIS BACK TO THE RESTAURANT, HAS APPARENTLY NOT NOTICED WHITE'S ENTRANCE.

EVELYN CONTEMPLATES NOT TELLING HIM, BUT THINKS BETTER OF IT AND PASSES HIM A NOTE:

The B was here but left —

HARRY IS GREATLY ANGERED AT HAVING MISSED HIS NEMESIS.

THE PARTY QUICKLY FINISHES DINNER AND LEAVES THE RESTAURANT.

THEY THEN WALK THE TWO BLOCKS TO MADISON SQUARE GARDEN, WHERE THEY HAVE TICKETS FOR THE OPENING NIGHT OF "MAMZELLE CHAMPAGNE."

EVELYN THINKS THIS CHOICE OF ENTERTAINMENT ODD, SINCE HER HUSBAND USUALLY AVOIDS ANY LOCATION ASSOCIATED WITH "THE B."

THE PARTY ENTERS THE OPEN-AIR THEATRE AT ABOUT 9:00PM, THE SHOW ALREADY IN PROGRESS...

AND ARE SHOWN TO WHAT HARRY CALLS "ROTTEN SEATS" SOME DISTANCE FROM THE STAGE.

THE THEATRE IS SET UP AS AN INFORMAL NIGHT-CLUB IN WHICH PATRONS MAY CIRCULATE AMONG THE TABLES.

HARRY SEEMS MORE THAN USUALLY AGITATED.

HE GETS UP FROM THE TABLE, PACES ABOUT THE ROOM, AND SITS DOWN AGAIN...

AND THEN STARTS THE PROCESS ANEW...

ALL THE TIME WEARING HIS STRAW BOATER AND HEAVY OVERCOAT.

FOR A TIME, HE SITS WITH THE FINANCIER JAMES CLINCH SMITH, BROTHER-IN-LAW, IRONICALLY, OF STANFORD WHITE.

AT ABOUT 11:00PM, WHITE ENTERS THE THEATRE AND PROCEEDS ALONE TO HIS FRONT ROW TABLE. (LAWRENCE AND HIS FRIEND HAVE GONE TO A DIFFERENT SHOW.)

THERE IS A SMALL COMMOTION IN THE AUDIENCE, AS PEOPLE ACKNOWLEDGE HIS PRESENCE.

EVELYN IS STRUCK WITH FEAR, BUT HARRY, BACK AT THE TABLE, DOES NOT SEEM TO HAVE NOTICED THE ARCHITECT'S ARRIVAL.

EVELYN SUGGESTS THAT THEY LEAVE. EVERYONE IS AGREEABLE, AND THE PARTY WALKS TOWARD THE ELEVATORS.

SHE IS ALMOST INSIDE WHEN SHE LOOKS BACK... WHERE IS HARRY?

THE SOLOIST ONSTAGE, BACKED BY A CHORUS OF LOVELY LADIES, SINGS "I COULD LOVE A MILLION GIRLS."

SUDDENLY, HARRY IS STANDING AT WHITE'S TABLE.

THE ARCHITECT MAKES A MOVE TO RISE, AND, FROM TWO FEET AWAY, THAW FIRES TWICE, DIRECTLY INTO THE MAN'S FACE.

A THIRD SHOT ENTERS HIS SHOULDER.

HIS FACE A MASK OF BLOOD, WHITE COLLAPSES TO THE FLOOR, TAKING THE TABLE WITH HIM.

218

AT FIRST, THE THEATRE IS STUNNED INTO SILENCE. A MOMENT LATER, ALL IS CHAOS.

THE STAGE MANAGER ORDERS THE PLAYERS TO CONTINUE THEIR NUMBER, BUT ALL OF THEM FLEE THE STAGE.

HARRY MAKES NO ATTEMPT TO ESCAPE. HOLDING THE REVOLVER ALOFT, HE EMPTIES THE REMAINING BULLETS.

I DID IT BECAUSE HE RUINED MY WIFE! HE HAD IT COMING TO HIM!

A NEW YORK CITY FIREMAN, PAUL BRUDI, HAPPENS TO BE PRESENT. HE TAKES THE ASSAILANT INTO CUSTODY.

EVELYN AND HER HUSBAND MEET IN THE ELEVATOR.

OH, HARRY, WHAT HAVE YOU DONE?

IT'S ALL RIGHT DEAR. I HAVE PROBABLY SAVED YOUR LIFE.

THE FIRST POLICEMAN ON THE SCENE IS OFFICER ANTHONY DEBES OF THE TENDERLOIN PRECINCT.

YOU'RE UNDER ARREST.

HERE'S A BILL, OFFICER. GET MR. ANDREW CARNEGIE ON THE PHONE, AND TELL HIM I'M IN TROUBLE.

I AM HARRY THAW OF PITTSBURGH!

THE PRISONER IS WALKED TO THE PRECINCT STATION...

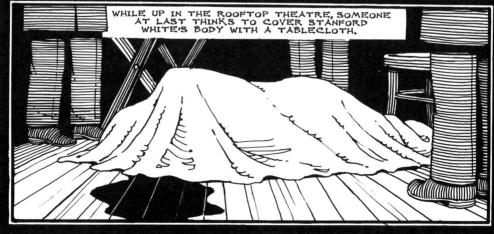
WHILE UP IN THE ROOFTOP THEATRE, SOMEONE AT LAST THINKS TO COVER STANFORD WHITE'S BODY WITH A TABLECLOTH.

PART VI

TRIALS AND
TRIBULATIONS

CRIMINAL COURT
BUILDING

THE WHEELS OF THE JUSTICE SYSTEM GRIND TO A
RESOLUTION UNSATISFACTORY TO EVERYONE CONCERNED.

THE MURDER IS A WINDFALL FOR NEW YORK'S NEWSPAPERS, WHICH KEEP IT IN THE HEADLINES DAILY.

"THE ROOFTOP MURDER," A MOVING PICTURE FROM EDISON'S STUDIO, IS IN THE NICKELODEONS WITHIN A WEEK OF THE TRAGEDY.

THURSDAY, JUNE 28
THE BODY OF STANFORD WHITE IS TRANSPORTED TO ST. JAMES, LONG ISLAND, FOR A FUNERAL SERVICE AT THE TOWN'S EPISCOPAL CHURCH...

AND IS LAID TO REST IN THE ADJOINING GRAVEYARD.

IN THE MEANTIME, HARRY THAW OCCUPIES A CELL AT THE CITY PRISON IN DOWNTOWN MANHATTAN — KNOWN AS "THE TOMBS."

BUT HE DOES NOT EXACTLY LANGUISH.

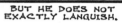

HE ENTERTAINS VISITORS, ENJOYS MEALS FROM DELMONICO'S, GIVES INTERVIEWS TO ANY AND ALL JOURNALISTS.

HE DISPLAYS NO REMORSE FOR HIS ACT. IN FACT...

I BELIEVE THE COMMUNITY OWES ME A DEBT OF THANKS.

IN THE OUTSIDE WORLD, AS WHITE'S SCANDALOUS EXPLOITS ARE EXPOSED TO THE READING PUBLIC, SYMPATHY FALLS DECIDEDLY ON THE KILLER'S SIDE.

IT SEEMS THAT THE "UNWRITTEN LAW" CONTINUES TO HOLD A POWERFUL SWAY.

THE THAW FAMILY'S LAWYERS, INEXPERIENCED IN THE CRIMINAL REALM, BRING IN AN OUTSIDE ATTORNEY...

LEWIS DELAFIELD, WHO PREPARES A DEFENSE OF INSANITY.

BUT HARRY ACCUSES HIM OF COLLUDING WITH THE STATE TO "RAILROAD" HIM INTO AN ASYLUM.

SO DELAFIELD IS FIRED, AND IN TIME A NEW MAN IS BROUGHT IN TO LEAD THE DEFENSE TEAM...

DELPHIN DELMAS OF SAN FRANCISCO, KNOWN AS "THE NAPOLEON OF THE WESTERN BAR," A SPECIALIST IN MURDER CASES. NO CLIENT OF HIS HAS EVER BEEN CONVICTED.

DELMAS THROWS OUT ANY REFERENCE TO INSANITY AND PLANS A DEFENSE BASED UPON AN INNOVATIVE INTERPRETATION OF THE "UNWRITTEN LAW."

IN IT, HARRY, UPON SPYING THE DEPRAVED ARCHITECT THAT NIGHT, WAS DRIVEN HELPLESSLY TO A "TEMPORARY BRAINSTORM."

THE DISTRICT ATTORNEY, WILLIAM T. JEROME, IS HAVING NONE OF THIS NONSENSE.

HE IS A YOUNG, AGGRESSIVE, INCORRUPTIBLE REFORMER IN THE MOLD OF PRESIDENT THEODORE ROOSEVELT.

(HE ALSO HAPPENS TO HAVE BEEN A CLOSE FRIEND OF STANFORD WHITE'S.)

HE PLANS TO PRESENT A STRAIGHTFORWARD PROSECUTION OF MURDER IN THE FIRST DEGREE.

AS THE TRIAL NEARS, EVELYN DUTIFULLY VISITS HER HUSBAND IN HIS CELL ALMOST EVERY DAY...

ENDURING THE SUFFOCATING CRUSH OF JOURNALISTS AND THE CURIOUS PUBLIC.

SPECULATION IS ACTIVE AS TO WHAT FINANCIAL AGREEMENT SHE HAS STRUCK WITH THE THAW FAMILY FOR HER CONTINUED SUPPORT OF HARRY'S DEFENSE.

SHE HAS REHEARSED HER TESTIMONY FOR COUNTLESS HOURS WITH ATTORNEY DELMAS.

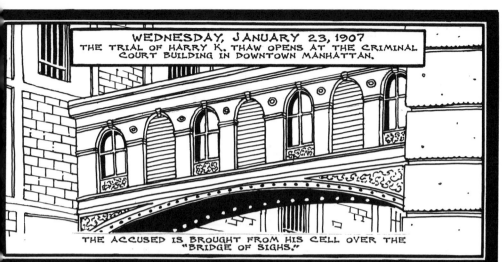

WEDNESDAY, JANUARY 23, 1907
THE TRIAL OF HARRY K. THAW OPENS AT THE CRIMINAL
COURT BUILDING IN DOWNTOWN MANHATTAN.

THE ACCUSED IS BROUGHT FROM HIS CELL OVER THE
"BRIDGE OF SIGHS."

JUSTICE JAMES FITZGERALD, OF THE
NEW YORK SUPREME COURT, PRESIDES.

IN A DECISION THAT IS ALMOST
UNPRECEDENTED, HE HAS
ANNOUNCED THAT THE JURY WILL
BE "INCARCERATED"
(SEQUESTERED) FOR THE
DURATION OF THE TRIAL.

CONSEQUENTLY, THE JURY-
SELECTION PROCESS IS SLOW
AND DIFFICULT.

AFTER EIGHT DAYS, A PANEL OF TWELVE GOOD MEN IS AT
LAST SEATED...

A BROAD SELECTION OF SALESMEN, CLERKS, MANAGERS, AND AGENTS.

MONDAY, FEBRUARY 4
THE STATE DISPOSES OF ITS CASE
BEFORE THE NOON RECESS.

FOUR WITNESSES FROM THE ROOF
GARDEN DESCRIBE HAVING SEEN
HARRY THAW SHOOT STANFORD
WHITE.

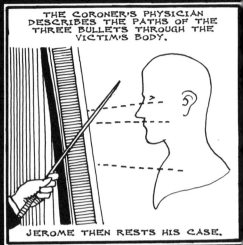

THE CORONER'S PHYSICIAN
DESCRIBES THE PATHS OF THE
THREE BULLETS THROUGH THE
VICTIM'S BODY.

JEROME THEN RESTS HIS CASE.

IN THE AFTERNOON, THE OPENING STATEMENT FOR
THE DEFENSE IS DELIVERED NOT BY THE FAMED
ORATOR DELMAS BUT BY ONE OF THE THAW
FAMILY LAWYERS, THE AGED JOHN GLEASON.

IT LEAVES MANY
OBSERVERS
PUZZLED.

WE WILL PROVE THAT
HARRY THAW WAS INSANE WHEN
HE KILLED STANFORD WHITE.
WE WILL PROVE THAT HE WAS NOT
ACCOUNTABLE FOR HIS ACTIONS,
THAT HE BELIEVED HIMSELF TO BE
AN AGENT OF PROVIDENCE.

A ROSTER OF DOCTORS AND
ALIENISTS IS THEN CALLED...

WHO ATTEST TO THE DEFENDANT'S
"NEUROTIC TEMPERAMENT."

OTHER WITNESSES DESCRIBE
HARRY'S "IRRATIONAL" APPEARANCE
ON THE NIGHT OF THE MURDER.

THURSDAY, FEBRUARY 7
THE DAY AWAITED BY EVERYONE ARRIVES, AS MRS. EVELYN NESBIT THAW TAKES THE STAND.

WATCHING IN THE COURTROOM ARE HER MOTHER AND BROTHER, NOW THOROUGHLY ESTRANGED FROM HER...

WHO HAVE COME IN SUPPORT OF THE GOOD NAME AND MEMORY OF STANFORD WHITE.

MR. DELMAS GUIDES THE WITNESS THROUGH HER EARLY FRIENDSHIP WITH HARRY THAW, HIS SEVERAL PROPOSALS...

AND FINALLY THE NIGHT IN PARIS WHEN SHE REVEALED TO HIM HER SEDUCTION AND VIOLATION BY WHITE.

SHE REPEATS THE SORDID TALE: HER FIRST MEETING WITH THE ARCHITECT...

THE NOTORIOUS RED VELVET SWING...

AND, FINALLY, THE TERRIBLE NIGHT IN THE MIRRORED BEDROOM.

SHE LEAVES THE IMPRESSION THAT HER ENTIRE RELATIONSHIP WITH THE OLDER MAN WAS AGAINST HER WILL.

WHAT WAS THE EFFECT OF THIS STATEMENT OF YOURS UPON MR. THAW?

HE BECAME VERY EXCITED.

WILL YOU KINDLY DESCRIBE IT?

HE WOULD GET UP AND WALK UP AND DOWN THE ROOM A MINUTE, AND THEN SIT DOWN AND SAY "OH GOD! OH GOD!" AND BITE HIS NAILS AND KEEP SOBBING.

THE COURTROOM LISTENS IN STUNNED SILENCE...

WHILE HARRY THAW WRITHES IN HIS CHAIR, AS IF HEARING IT ALL FOR THE FIRST TIME.

TUESDAY, FEBRUARY 19
AFTER MANY DELAYS, MR. JEROME BEGINS THE CROSS-EXAMINATION.

BUT HE IS SEVERELY LIMITED IN ITS SCOPE DUE TO MR. DELMAS'S INGENIOUS TACTIC ON DIRECT:

THE DEFENSE COUNSEL INSTRUCTED EVELYN TO TESTIFY NOT AS TO THE TRUTH OF HER STORY...

BUT ONLY AS TO WHAT SHE HAD TOLD THE DEFENDANT.

THE DISTRICT ATTORNEY LEAPS FROM SUBJECT TO SUBJECT, HIS QUESTIONS DESIGNED TO HIGHLIGHT THE WITNESS' ADVENTUROUS CAREER.

UP UNTIL THE TIME YOU WENT INTO THE "FLORADORA" COMPANY IN 1901, HAD YOU EVER POSED IN THE NUDE?

NEVER!

DID YOU NOT HAVE A PLASTER CAST MADE OF YOURSELF IN THE NUDE IN THE SPRING OF 1901?

I DID NOT!

EVELYN, LOOKING FRAIL AND DELICATE, MANAGES TO HOLD HER OWN WITH DIGNITY AND SELF-POSSESSION.

ONCE, SHE COMES TO TEARS UNDER A SERIES OF QUESTIONS ABOUT STANFORD WHITE.

AFTER YOU HAD BEEN WRONGED BY STANFORD WHITE, DID YOU CONTINUE TO HAVE INTIMATE RELATIONS WITH HIM?

FOR A SHORT TIME, YES.

DID YOU EVER TELL ANY HUMAN BEING?

NO.

YOU ALWAYS RESISTED AND NEVER SUBMITTED WILLINGLY?

I ALWAYS RESISTED.

AFTER FOUR FULL DAYS, SHE IS DISMISSED FROM THE STAND.

DELMAS WRAPS UP HIS CASE BY CALLING MOTHER THAW.

SHE TESTIFIES AS TO HER SON'S EXTREME ANXIETY UPON THE MERE MENTION OF STANFORD WHITE.

AT THIS POINT, IN A DESIRE TO SETTLE THE QUESTION OF THE DEFENDANT'S MENTAL CONDITION, BOTH SIDES AGREE TO THE APPOINTMENT OF A "LUNACY COMMISSION."

> I AM PERFECTLY SANE, AND EVERYBODY WHO KNOWS ME KNOWS THAT I AM SANE.

AFTER SEVEN DAYS, THE THREE-MAN COMMISSION UNANIMOUSLY DECLARES HARRY THAW PERFECTLY SANE.

MONDAY, APRIL 8
DELPHIN DELMAS GIVES HIS DRAMATIC SUMMATION.

> IF THAW IS INSANE, IT IS WITH A SPECIES OF INSANITY THAT IS KNOWN FROM THE CANADIAN BORDER TO THE GULF... I SUGGEST THAT YOU LABEL IT "DEMENTIA AMERICANA." IT IS THAT SPECIES OF INSANITY THAT INSPIRES EVERY AMERICAN TO BELIEVE THAT HIS HOME IS SACRED... THAT WHOEVER VIOLATES THE SANCTITY OF HIS HOME OR THE PURITY OF HIS WIFE AND DAUGHTER HAS FORFEITED THE PROTECTION OF THE LAWS OF THIS STATE OR ANY OTHER STATE.

THE NEXT DAY WILLIAM T. JEROME SUMS UP THE STATE'S CASE.

> THIS IS A MERE COMMON SORDID VULGAR EVERYDAY TENDERLOIN HOMICIDE AND YOU KNOW IT! THIS IS A CASE WHERE A WOMAN LAY LIKE A TIGRESS BETWEEN TWO MEN EGGING THEM ON... WILL YOU ACQUIT A COLD-BLOODED DELIBERATE COWARDLY MURDERER BECAUSE HIS LYING WIFE HAS A PRETTY GIRL'S FACE?

WEDNESDAY, APRIL 10
AFTER JUSTICE FITZGERALD'S CHARGE, THE JURY RETIRES.

FRIDAY, APRIL 12
THEY RETURN TO TELL THE JUDGE THAT THEY ARE HOPELESSLY DEADLOCKED.

OF THE 12 MEN, SEVEN HAVE FOUND THAW GUILTY OF MURDER IN THE FIRST DEGREE, WHILE FIVE BELIEVE HIM NOT GUILTY BY REASON OF INSANITY.

IN A DAZE, EVELYN KISSES HER HUSBAND.

HARRY, ANGRY AND FRUSTRATED, IS DENIED BAIL AND RETURNED TO HIS CELL.

DELMAS WILL SOON BE OUT AS HEAD OF THE DEFENSE.

OVER THE NINE MONTHS DURING WHICH THE DEFENDANT AWAITS A SECOND TRIAL, HIS WIFE VISITS HIM REGULARLY.

STILL SUPPORTED BY THE THAW FAMILY, SHE KNOWS THAT SHE WILL BE CALLED UPON ONCE AGAIN TO PLAY THE ROLE OF LOYAL SPOUSE.

MONDAY, JANUARY 6, 1908 THE SECOND TRIAL OF HARRY THAW OPENS.

IT WILL PROVE TO BE A FASTER, MORE COMPACT VERSION OF THE FIRST ONE.

PRESIDING THIS TIME: JUSTICE VICTOR J. DOWLING OF THE NEW YORK SUPREME COURT.

THE NEW LEADER OF THE DEFENSE TEAM IS MARTIN W. LITTLETON...

ASSISTED BY RUSSELL PEABODY AND DANIEL O'REILLY.

WILLIAM JEROME, EAGER FOR A SECOND CHANCE, AGAIN TAKES UP THE PROSECUTION.

A JURY IS CHOSEN IN A MERE FOUR DAYS.

THE DISTRICT ATTORNEY ONCE MORE PRESENTS A STRAIGHTFORWARD CASE OF MURDER IN THE FIRST DEGREE.

WHILE THE DEFENSE, HAVING ABANDONED THE "UNWRITTEN LAW," INTRODUCES MEMBERS OF THE THAW FAMILY...

WHO AFFIRM THE STRAINS ON INSANITY IN THEIR LINEAGE.

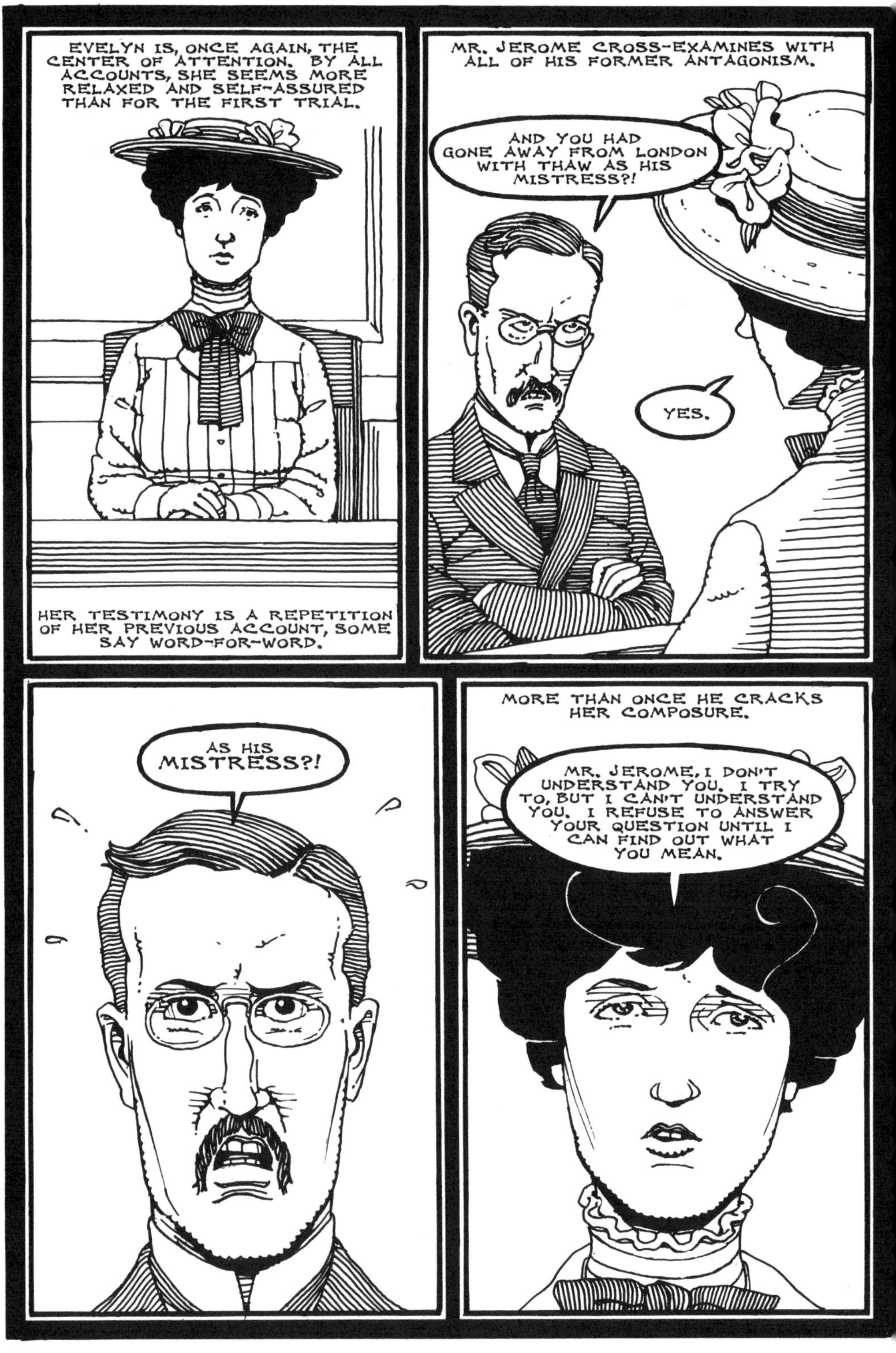
EVELYN IS, ONCE AGAIN, THE CENTER OF ATTENTION. BY ALL ACCOUNTS, SHE SEEMS MORE RELAXED AND SELF-ASSURED THAN FOR THE FIRST TRIAL.
HER TESTIMONY IS A REPETITION OF HER PREVIOUS ACCOUNT, SOME SAY WORD-FOR-WORD.
MR. JEROME CROSS-EXAMINES WITH ALL OF HIS FORMER ANTAGONISM.
AND YOU HAD GONE AWAY FROM LONDON WITH THAW AS HIS MISTRESS?!
YES.
AS HIS MISTRESS?!
MORE THAN ONCE HE CRACKS HER COMPOSURE.
MR. JEROME, I DON'T UNDERSTAND YOU. I TRY TO, BUT I CAN'T UNDERSTAND YOU. I REFUSE TO ANSWER YOUR QUESTION UNTIL I CAN FIND OUT WHAT YOU MEAN.

FRIDAY, JANUARY 31
THE CASE GOES TO THE JURY.

SATURDAY, FEBRUARY 1
THE VERDICT IS DELIVERED.

WE THE JURY FIND THE DEFENDANT NOT GUILTY AS CHARGED IN THE INDICTMENT, ON THE GROUND OF THE DEFENDANT'S INSANITY.

JUSTICE DOWLING PRONOUNCES THE SENTENCE: HARRY THAW WILL BE TRANSPORTED FORTHWITH TO THE MATTEAWAN ASYLUM FOR THE CRIMINALLY INSANE...

IN THE UPSTATE TOWN OF FISHKILL.

FISHKILL

NEW YORK

HARRY MAKES THE TRIP IN A PRIVATE RAILROAD CAR FILLED WITH FRIENDS AND JOURNALISTS.

I'LL BE OUT IN A FEW WEEKS.

HARRY IS AFFORDED HIS OWN ROOM AT MATTEAWAN, FURNISHED TO HIS COMFORT.

EVELYN TAKES A ROOM IN FISHKILL, THE BETTER TO VISIT HER HUSBAND REGULARLY...

WHILE A NEW SET OF LAWYERS BEGINS A LONG SERIES OF APPEALS AND WRITS OF HABEAS CORPUS.

ALL OF WHICH WILL BE DENIED.

IT IS A SLOW AND LABORIOUS PROCESS, BECAUSE VERY FEW OF THE PEOPLE INVOLVED, EVEN HIS MOTHER AND HIS WIFE...

WANT TO SEE HARRY SET LOOSE.

AS THE MONTHS DRAG ON, STRAINS UPON THE MARRIAGE BECOME EVIDENT.

NEVERTHELESS, EARLY IN 1910 EVELYN ANNOUNCES THAT SHE IS PREGNANT...

THE RESULT OF ONE OF HER CONJUGAL VISITS.

HARRY VEHEMENTLY DENIES THAT HE IS THE FATHER...

AND, FURTHER, ACCUSES HIS WIFE OF TRYING TO EXTORT MONEY FROM THE THAW FAMILY.

THURSDAY, OCTOBER 25, 1910

WHILE TOURING EUROPE TO ESCAPE THE AMERICAN PRESS, SHE GIVES BIRTH TO A BOY:

RUSSELL WILLIAM THAW.

UPON HER RETURN, SHE AND HER SON RESIDE IN NEW YORK, WHILE SHE TRIES TO REVIVE HER THEATRICAL CAREER.

STAGE DOOR

234

SUNDAY, AUGUST 17, 1913
IMPATIENT WITH THE LEGAL MACHINERY, HARRY THAW ESCAPES FROM MATTEAWAN.

AS A DUMFOUNDED GUARD WATCHES, THE PRISONER SIMPLY STROLLS THROUGH THE FRONT GATE...

AND INTO A WAITING AUTOMOBILE.

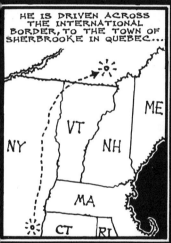

HE IS DRIVEN ACROSS THE INTERNATIONAL BORDER, TO THE TOWN OF SHERBROOKE IN QUEBEC...

ME

VT

NH

NY

MA

CT   RI

WHERE HE IS FETED AS A CELEBRITY.

NEVERTHELESS, HE MUST WAIT IN A CELL WHILE AN EXTRADITION HEARING DETERMINES HIS FATE.

DISTRICT ATTORNEY JEROME IS ONCE AGAIN PRESENT FOR THE PROSECUTION.

EVENTUALLY, THAW IS DEPORTED FROM CANADA TO NEW HAMPSHIRE...

AND, FINALLY, IN DECEMBER OF 1914, TO NEW YORK FOR YET A THIRD TRIAL...

THIS ONE FOR HIS VERY SANITY.

FRIDAY, JULY 16, 1915
AFTER A PROCEEDING THAT IS MORE OR LESS A COPY OF THE FIRST TWO, HARRY THAW, AGE 44, IS DECLARED SANE AND ACQUITTED OF ALL CHARGES.

IN PITTSBURGH, A CHEERING CROWD WELCOMES HIM HOME.

HE AND EVELYN ARE AT LAST DIVORCED.

HAVING RECEIVED BUT A PITTANCE IN SETTLEMENT FROM THE THAW FAMILY, EVELYN, AT AGE 30, IS PLUNGED ONCE AGAIN AGAIN INTO A HAND-TO-MOUTH EXISTENCE...

THIS TIME AS A SINGLE MOTHER.

FOR SEVERAL YEARS, SHE MANAGES TO LIVE UPON HER NOTORIETY.

THE STORY OF MY LIFE

EVELYN THAW

EVELYN THAW

SHE RELEASES A MEMOIR IN 1914.

SHE APPEARS IN A NUMBER OF MOVING PICTURES, AS VERSIONS OF HERSELF.

SHE TOURS THE COUNTRY AS PART OF A VAUDEVILLE DANCING ACT.

HER PARTNER, JACK CLIFFORD, BECOMES HER SECOND HUSBAND IN 1916.

BUT THE UNION IS A TROUBLED ONE, AND THEY SEPARATE IN 1918...

FINALLY DIVORCING IN 1933.

FOR THE REMAINDER OF HIS LIFE, HARRY THAW CANNOT MANAGE TO STAY OUT OF THE HEADLINES.

IN 1917, HE IS INDICTED FOR THE KIDNAPPING AND WHIPPING OF A 19-YEAR-OLD YOUTH, FREDERICK GUMP, AT A NEW YORK HOTEL.

AS A RESULT, HE IS COMMITTED TO THE MENTAL WARD OF THE PENNSYLVANIA STATE HOSPITAL IN PHILADELPHIA, FOR WHAT TURNS OUT TO BE SEVEN YEARS.

IN 1926, HE PRODUCES A DISJOINTED MEMOIR, IN WHICH HE DECLARES HIMSELF A BENEFACTOR OF THE HUMAN RACE.

THE TRAITOR

HARRY K. THAW

(THE TITLE REFERS TO HIS FIRST TRIAL LAWYER, DELAFIELD, WHO TRIED TO PAINT HIM AS INSANE.)

IN 1929, HE IS SUED BY A WOMAN, MARCIA ESTARDUS, WHO CLAIMS THAT HE BEAT HER IN HER NEW YORK APARTMENT.

IN 1937, HE IS SUED BY A HOTEL HEADWAITER, FOR INJURIES SUSTAINED FROM A FURIOUS PHYSICAL ASSAULT BY THE MILLIONAIRE.

HARRY THAW DIES AT AGE 76, ON FEBRUARY 22, 1947, SUFFERING A HEART ATTACK WHILE ON A VISIT TO MIAMI, FLORIDA.

AFTER THREE TRIALS, A SETTLEMENT IS PAID TO THE PLAINTIFF.

238

WHILE TRYING TO SCRAPE TOGETHER A LIVING, SHE ENDURES PERIODS OF ALCOHOL AND MORPHINE ABUSE.

PRODIGAL DAYS

EVELYN NESBIT

IN 1934, SHE BRINGS OUT A SECOND MEMOIR.

ON THE STRENGTH OF HER NAME, SHE MANAGES A SERIES OF NIGHTCLUBS AND SPEAKEASIES.

SHE TOURS IN A CABARET ACT SINGING NUMBERS LIKE:

"I'M JUST A BROAD-MINDED BROAD FROM BROADWAY..." ♪ ♫

IN 1955, SHE SERVES AS TECHNICAL ADVISOR FOR THE MOTION PICTURE "THE GIRL IN THE RED VELVET SWING," BASED IN PART UPON HER MEMOIRS.

SHE IS PORTRAYED BY THE RISING STARLET JOAN COLLINS.

EVELYN'S LAST YEARS ARE SPENT IN LOS ANGELES...

WHERE SHE PURSUES A LONG-HIDDEN TALENT AS PAINTER, SCULPTOR, AND CERAMIC ARTIST.

SHE DIES ON JANUARY 17, 1967, AT THE AGE OF 82.

239

MONUMENTS TO THE THREE PLAYERS IN THIS DRAMA CAN BE VISITED TODAY.

STANFORD WHITE'S STANDS IN THE GRAVEYARD OF THE ST. JAMES EPISCOPAL CHURCH, SUFFOLK COUNTY, LONG ISLAND.

THAT OF HENRY (HARRY) KENDALL THAW IS PART OF HIS FAMILY'S PLOT AT ALLEGHENY CEMETERY IN PITTSBURGH, PENNSYLVANIA.

HENRY KENDALL THAW

FEBRUARY 12 - 1871

FEBRUARY 22 - 1947

AND NOW ABIDETH FAITH, HOPE CHARITY, THESE THREE, BUT THE GREATEST OF THESE IS CHARITY.

MOTHER
EVELYN FLORENCE NESBIT
1884 ✝ 1967

THE MARKER FOR EVELYN FLORENCE NESBIT CAN BE FOUND AT THE HOLY CROSS CEMETERY IN CULVER CITY, CALIFORNIA.

240